HOLLAND AT WAR AGAINST HITLER

D0321891

The International School
of Amsterdam

A.J. Ernststraat 875
P.O. Box 7983
1008 AD Amsterdam
The Netherlands

HOLLAND AT WAR
AGAINST HITLER

Anglo-Dutch relations
1940–1945

Edited by
M. R. D. FOOT

With a Foreword by
HRH Prince Bernhard

FRANK CASS

WAANDERS UITGEVERS

First published 1990 in Great Britain by
FRANK CASS AND COMPANY LIMITED
Gainsborough House, 11 Gainsborough Road,
London E11 1RS, England

and in the United States of America by
FRANK CASS
c/o International Specialized Book Services, Inc.,
5602 N.E. Hassalo Street, Portland, Oregon 97213

Copyright © 1990 Frank Cass & Co. Ltd.

British Library Cataloguing in Publication Data

Holland at war against Hitler: Anglo-Dutch relations 1940–
    1945: proceedings of a conference held at University
    College London on 3, 4 and 5 April 1989.
    1. Netherlands. Foreign relations with Great Britain,
    history
    I. Foot, M.R.D. (Michael Richard Daniell) 1919–
    327.49204

ISBN 0-7146-3399-2

Library of Congress Cataloging-in-Publication Data

Holland at war against Hitler : Anglo-Dutch relations, 1940–1945 /
    edited by M.R.D. Foot.
        p.   cm.
    "Proceedings of a conference held at University College London on
3, 4 and 5 April 1989."
    ISBN 0-7146-3399-2
    1. World War, 1939–1945—Netherlands—Congresses.   2. World War,
1939–1945—Great Britain—Congresses.   3. Netherlands—Foreign
relations—Great Britain—Congresses.   4. Great Britain—Foreign
relations—Netherlands—Congresses.   I. Foot, M.R.D. (Michael
Richard Daniell), 1919–
D802.N4H64   1990
940.53'492—dc20   90-1614
                                                                   CIP

*All rights reserved. No part of this publication may be repro-
duced, stored in a retrieval system, or transmitted in any form,
or by any means, electronic, mechanical, photocopying,
recording, or otherwise, without the prior permission of Frank
Cass and Company Limited.*

Printed and bound in Great Britain by
BPCC Wheatons Ltd, Exeter

CONTENTS

CONTENTS

ILLUSTRATIONS

MAPS

ACKNOWLEDGEMENTS

The pair of maps on page 159 is taken from Chester Wilmot, *Struggle for Europe* (Collins, 1952); the map on page 160 from Hilary St George Saunders, *The Red Beret* (Michael Joseph, n.d.); and that on page 161 from Major-General R.E. Urquhart, *Arnhem* (Cassell, 1958).

The poem on page 240 comes from R. Gustafson ed., *Penguin Book of Canadian Verse* (1958).

Of the photographs, 1 (also reproduced on the back of the jacket) is by permission of Topham Picture Library; 2 and 5 are from Henri van der Zee, *The Hunger Winter* (1982) by permission of Jill Norman; 3 and 4 by permission of the Imperial War Museum; and 6 from Rijksvoorlichtingsdienst, by permission of ANEFO b.v. The jacket photograph is reproduced by kind permission of the Rijksinstituut voor Oorlogs Documentatie.

CONFERENCE PATRONS AND ADVISERS

Patrons

His Royal Highness Prince Bernhard of the Netherlands
His Royal Highness The Prince Philip, Duke of Edinburgh
His Excellency Dr P. J. H. Jonkman, Dutch Ambassador, London
His Excellency (Sir) Michael R. H. Jenkins, British Ambassador,
     The Hague
Jhr Mr J. L. R. Huydecoper van Nigtevecht, past Dutch
     Ambassador, London
Sir John Barnes, past British Ambassador, The Hague

Advisory Board

Sir Michael Howard, Regius Professor of Modern History, Oxford
Charles Wilson, Emeritus Professor of Modern History, Cambridge
Jonathan Israel, Professor of Dutch History, University College
     London
Donald Cameron Watt, Professor of Contemporary History,
     London School of Economics
Christopher Thorne, Professor of International Relations, Sussex
     University
Brian Bond, Professor of War Studies, King's College London
Drs Harry A. Paape, Director, Dutch State Institute for War
     Documentation
Dr C. M. Schulten, Head, Section Military History Dutch Army
Dr Paul Hayes, University Lecturer in International Relations,
     Oxford
Dr Christopher Andrew, Fellow of Corpus Christi College,
     Cambridge
Mrs Anna E. C. Harvey *née* Simoni, author of *Publish and be Free*
Gordon Marsden, Editor of *History Today*
General Sir John Hackett, former Principal of King's College
     London
General G. L. J. J. Huyser, former Chief of Dutch Defence Staff
(Sir) Charles Tidbury, Chairman, William & Mary Trust, London

G. Baron Kraijenhoff, Chairman, Willem III & Mary Stichting, Holland
Mr Louis Baron d'Aulnis de Bourouill, longest serving agent BI

Executive Committee

Chairman: Professor M. R. D. Foot
Secretary: Herman Friedhoff
Treasurer: Colonel Jaap Smit
Derek White, replacing Hilary Evans
Sir Roger Cary, Bt
Barry Price
A. D. H. Simonsz
Michael Butler

Soestdijk Palace, November 1989

As I had been much involved with Anglo-Dutch relations in the years
1940-1945, I was interested to hear that a conference on this subject
in London would form part of the William and Mary Tercentenary. From
interest and from curiosity, I attended the first day, and was so struck
by the liveliness of the gathering and by some of the personalities
present, that I jettisoned some other plans and stayed nearly to the
end.

We were able to watch scholars who had soaked themselves in their
subjects confronted by witnesses who had actually been present at the
time. As usual, scholars and witnesses did not always agree; nor did
all the prejudices participants brought to the conference vanish. Yet
quite a few misunderstandings were cleared up, and the reports gathered
here set out the current state of knowledge on five years that were
critical for both countries and for Europe.

I am glad to commend this volume not only to my own contemporaries,
now fading from the scene, but to younger citizens of both nations and
indeed of the whole world who want to understand the roots from which
freedom grows.

Prince of the Netherlands

EDITOR'S NOTE

The papers that follow are printed almost as they were delivered, at a conference attended by a mixture of scholars, teachers, diplomats, journalists, students and retired warriors; of ages as diverse as their experiences; many of whom already knew each other. It seemed a pity to spoil an atmosphere of lively discussion by imposing on it too uniformly stolid a style. The merely mechanical passages, bearing on how the conference was to run, and the grace-notes introducing and thanking set speakers, have been left out; as have a few passages of slight importance and a few repetitions.

Not much that was startlingly new emerged, but at least we were able to set out what the French call the *état des questions*, the stage that research has so far reached: which may help it to go farther. Much did appear that was familiar enough to the Dutch, but original and interesting to the English.

I must at the outset record a word of special gratitude, not only to our august patrons, several of whom honoured us by attending in person, and to our advisory committee, whose members gave invaluable help, but also to the other members of the executive committee, and to my wife, for having sustained the chairman's morale through the moments when it seemed there was no hope of getting the conference organized in time, or at all.

M.R.D.F.
London
8 January 1990

INTRODUCTION

M. R. D. Foot

The conference on Anglo-Dutch relations from 1940 to 1945, held at University College London on 3, 4 and 5 April 1989, covered a part – not the least interesting nor the simplest part – of the diplomatic and military history of the world war against Nazi Germany and imperial Japan. The historical context of Anglo-Dutch relations, close since the fall of the Roman Empire, bears setting out at the start.

There is no need to do more than glance at the prevalence of Dutch descent in East Anglia – borne out by hair colour, skin colour, skull shape, voice timbre – or at the spreading of Christian belief among the Frisians in the seventh and eighth centuries by three English saints, Wilfred, Willibrord and Boniface. As the woollen industry grew in the Middle Ages, so did English dependence on Flanders and Brabant; as the Dutch learned to wrestle with the sea, Dutch engineers came over to England and supervised the draining of the Fens. Both countries came out against Rome at the Reformation; England, definitively, under Queen Elizabeth I, and Holland under the inspiration of William of Orange. The Dutch and the English made common cause against Philip II of Spain, after his marriage to Elizabeth's elder sister, Queen Mary I of England, turned out – mercifully for the Protestant interest – childless. Yet because the Protestantism of each country had a liberal tinge, in each a sizeable body of Roman Catholics remained.

Dutchmen and Englishmen then became rivals on the high seas, each seeking to exclude the other from new-formed colonies; this rivalry led to three short Anglo-Dutch wars in the mid-seventeenth century, and changed the name of New Amsterdam to New York. The two nations joined forces again at the end of that century, in the struggle against King Louis XIV of France that gave another William of Orange a strategic reason for asserting his wife's claim to become Mary II, and his own to be William III, of England. The conference formed a part of the celebration of the tercentenary of their accession.

Thereafter each country remained – when unconquered – under constitutional rather than despotic government; each cherished traditions of freedom of thought and respect for privacy as well as culture. The great war against Louis XIV exhausted the Dutch more than it did the English; during the eighteenth century, the English expanded farther and faster. In the next great war, against revolutionary and Napoleonic France, the Dutch were overwhelmed. Yet it remained, as it had long been, a fixed principle of English foreign policy that the Low Countries should remain outside the control of any continental power that sought to rival England: even when from 1810 to 1814 the lands that today form the kingdom of the Netherlands were divided among eleven *départements* of the French Empire. At the congress of Vienna, Lord Castlereagh insisted on the creation of a strong Dutch kingdom, which comprised the whole of present-day Holland, Belgium and Luxembourg. A Dutch contingent fought in Wellington's army at Waterloo, where the Prince of Orange who commanded it was wounded.

Roman Catholic Belgium broke away from the new kingdom in 1830, and after some fighting in 1831–32 – Dutch troops against Belgian and French – was declared a perpetually neutral state in 1839. Its neutrality was guaranteed, in a treaty negotiated by Lord Palmerston, by Austria, England, France, Prussia and Russia, the great powers of the day. Its territory included the western half of Luxembourg; of which the eastern half formed a truncated grand duchy that had the King of Holland as grand duke. After a sharp Franco-Prussian quarrel in 1867, this grand duchy was placed under a less stringent guarantee by the same five great powers. From the mid-nineteenth century, the kingdom of the Netherlands pursued a policy of strict neutrality also; it fell outside the rival great power blocs.

In the Franco-Prussian war of 1870–71, all the Low Countries managed to maintain neutrality. While it was still going on, Bismarck's Prussia became the core of a new German Empire. The English and German industrial revolutions turned England and Germany into world powers, while the Netherlands, comparatively speaking, marked time. In 1890 the grand duchy of Luxembourg ceased to belong to the kingdom, for King William III of the Netherlands died leaving only a daughter, Wilhelmina, then aged ten, to whom the ancient Salic law forbade succession to the grand duchy. That passed to her father's cousin Adolphus of Nassau; Wilhelmina was crowned Queen of the Netherlands when she came of age in 1898.

By this time the Anglo-German antagonism was starting to become sharp. To Germans England seemed a barrier athwart the path of German overseas expansion. Germany, admitted by the English to be Europe's strongest power on land, seemed to them after the German navy laws of 1898 and 1900 to be building a battle fleet that could only be meant to fight the Royal Navy. In an age in which monarchs counted for more than they do today, the personal antagonism between King Edward VII of England and Kaiser Wilhelm II of Germany, who were uncle and nephew, was not an influence for peace. In 1914, four years after Edward VII's death, another great war began, with a German conquest of Belgium that flouted Palmerston's guarantee, and thus brought England into the war as Germany's enemy.

All through the war the Netherlands maintained a rigid neutrality, though both warring sides' officials and agents were busy on Dutch territory. Anglo-Dutch relations, like Germano-Dutch relations, got cooler as the war went on. Each of the combatants became exasperated that the Dutch would not join in against their opponents; and as far as the English were concerned, Dutch obstinacy was compounded right at the end of the war. The German Kaiser, having lost the confidence of his general staff, abdicated, and took a train into the Netherlands on the night of 9/10 November 1918; the Dutch refused to surrender him for trial, and let him settle at Doorn, where he died of old age in 1941.

Only the belligerents took part in the Paris Peace Congress of 1919–20; the Dutch did not sign the Treaty of Versailles, which was so much resented and misrepresented in the new German republic, though the Belgians did. The Netherlands were nevertheless admitted among the founder members of the League of Nations. Of the League it can be said, as was said of Prohibition in America, that it was 'an experiment noble in purpose', which turned out to encourage gangsters instead. Like all the other member states, great and small, the Dutch undertook the obligation to fight any member that attacked another. And like all the others, when it came to the crunch – Corfu 1923, Manchuria 1931, Ethiopia 1935 – the Dutch found it convenient not to fight after all.

From January 1933 onwards, the Dutch had a ringside seat at the Nazi circus. They could see only too clearly – even more clearly than the English could – the nature of the Nazi régime: the tremendous enthusiasm that it aroused at home, and the damage it might easily inflict abroad. A trickle of Jewish refugees, soon growing towards a flood, early made it clear that not everything under the new régime was sweetness and light. The Dutch could at least console themselves with the thought that they were by Nazi standards fairly pure racially; they did not stand at the top of any list of peoples to be enslaved. A small group of Dutchmen even embraced Nazi ideas, and formed a national socialist party which secured four seats in each of the two houses of parliament at the general election of May 1937.

As Nazi expansionism – *pace* A. J. P. Taylor, who was already too ill to be invited to this conference – became more and more clear, the Dutch government clung more and more firmly to its by now long-standing doctrine of neutrality. The Dutch were not invited to the Munich gathering in September 1938, which was attended only by England, France, Germany and Italy; neither Soviet Russia nor any of the lesser European powers were represented, save for the Czecho-slovaks, whose spokesmen were summoned in the small hours of the concluding night, held for a while under Gestapo guard, and informed that their country was to be dismembered.

England's attempt to appease Germany's appetite for territory failed: eleven months after Munich, Hitler's attack on Poland on 1 September 1939 brought on another world war. The Dutch govern-ment continued to observe a policy of rigid official neutrality, for it was by now alarmed at the spectacle of a fully mobilized next-door neigh-bour, and did not want to provoke Germany in any way. Less officially, English secret service men in The Hague were able to talk round Major-General van Oorschot, the head of Dutch intelligence, when his wireless interception service caught them communicating with a dissi-dent German general in the Rhineland. The Dutch deciphered without too much trouble the code that was being used, and provided a security officer, Dirk Klop, to accompany Payne Best and Stevens when they went to meet their agent at a frontier café near Venlo on 9 November 1939. Klop was shot dead in the scuffle that ensued, when Best and Stevens were kidnapped by a gang of SS thugs; their supposed general was Major Walter Schellenberg, also of the SS. Van Oorschot was dismissed, and the Dutch government felt it had had a lucky escape from being charged with unneutral conduct and invaded straight away.

Another unofficial intelligence contact, in Berlin, was to the advantage of the Dutch. Their Military Attaché, Colonel Sas, was befriended by Hans Oster, Admiral Canaris's deputy at the head-quarters of the Abwehr, the German armed forces' security service. Several times over Oster, who was already Hitler's enemy in his heart, confided to Sas in the strictest confidence the date on which the Germans intended to overrun the Low Countries: *Fall Gelb* (Case Yellow) was the codename. His information was always accurate at the moment he delivered it; but, well informed as he was, even he could not keep up with Hitler's rate of change of mind.

Grimm's story of the boy who cried 'Wolf' is painfully in point. Oster warned Sas, yet again, that *Fall Gelb* was imminent: on 9 May 1940. Sas informed both his own government and the Belgian Military Attaché in Berlin, who was a friend. The warning had been given too often; this time it failed to make much impact.

Repeated assurances of goodwill had been offered to the Dutch régime by the Nazis, at every level from Hitler upwards. Like other Nazi promises, these were worthless. As dawn broke on Friday, 10 May 1940, the full might of a *Blitzkrieg* fell, suddenly, on the Dutch, who were wholly unprepared for it, and suffered severely from shock. Queen Wilhelmina had received personal assurance from Hitler that he would respect the neutrality of the Netherlands; she felt a sense of personal outrage that he had done nothing of the kind, and moreover had sent a company of parachutists to kidnap her. In this they just failed; her son-in-law and her palace guards saw them off.

On the fourth day of fighting, 13 May, she sailed from the Hook of Holland on a British destroyer, hoping to carry on the war from Zeeland, but got taken to Harwich instead. She had brought with her a briefcase of essential papers, but not so much as a toothbrush in the way of personal belongings, and had to throw herself on the hospitality of her distant cousin King George VI.

Next day, Rotterdam encountered the fate that Barcelona and Warsaw had met already; the fate of Coventry next November and of Belgrade next spring; a fate repaid, at an awesome rate of interest, to the major cities of Germany from Cologne in 1942 to Dresden in 1945: savage attack from the air. That evening the Dutch armed forces, having reached the limit of what they were able to do to resist, laid down their arms.

Armistice is not the same as surrender: the Queen was still at war.

She had been for nearly six years a widow. Her only child, Princess Juliana, with her husband Prince Bernhard and their two small daughters, were also brought away to England by destroyer. The Prince at once returned to the Continent to fight, but was quickly persuaded to return. His wife and children went off to Canada in a Dutch cruiser; he stayed in England, learning to fly a light bomber and being available to help his mother-in-law.

The Queen also had her cabinet with her in exile. This bewildered body of elderly gentlemen, only one of whom had his wife with him, were not inspired to martial effort by their Prime Minister, de Geer, who was convinced that Germany's superior strength could not be resisted. He was allowed to retire, and find his way home through Spain and France. Dutch cabinets, notoriously, take weeks – months, even – to form. In the summer of 1940, every ordinary rule was broken. On 28 August, within 48 hours of de Geer's departure, Queen Wilhelmina sent for her minister of justice, Gerbrandy, and appointed him prime minister.

Gerbrandy had only recently entered politics; he had been a professor of law at Amsterdam university. He was a short, burly, energetic Frisian, a devout Calvinist and a hard worker; under his guidance, the Dutch in exile began to play some real part in the war. Yet how were these few leaders to establish any touch with their following? The Queen made many inspiring broadcasts; her subjects could soon only listen to them in peril of arrest, because Holland became one of the occupied countries in which wireless sets were banned. That did not stop people from owning, or even building, them secretly; but the inward traffic was limited, and the outward traffic – back to the Queen – hardly existed at all.

Though she and her cabinet were exiled from their country and separated from their parliament as well as their people, they were not destitute. Through the Dutch legation in London (soon raised to embassy status), they remained in touch with the Dutch colonial empire, in both the East and West Indies; through the London offices of Dutch shipping lines, and of KLM, they could control a valuable merchant fleet and some up-to-date air transport. Wilhelmina, as unpompous as a monarch could be, settled in a villa at Roehampton.

The Dutch East Indian Empire did not last. It was one of the early targets of Japanese expansion, in the winter of 1941–42; under the ill co-ordinated ABDA – American-British-Dutch-Australian – command, much of the Dutch Navy succumbed to superior Japanese fire power in the battle of the Java Sea in February. What was left of the Navy made itself useful under British Admiralty guidance; and Dutch pilots and aircrew in exile formed a valuable reinforcement for the Royal Air Force. A brigade of infantry, named after Princess Irene, was formed from successful escapers from the Netherlands, and took part in Operation 'Overlord', the Allied landing in north-west Europe that began in Normandy in June 1944 and ended on the Elbe in May 1945.

Sparse and secret contacts were maintained between the Dutch crown and the forces of internal resistance in Holland, through too many Dutch and British secret services. This is not the moment to plumb the intricacies of this subject, about which a little more will be found below. Notoriously, the German secret services had much the better of the game in 1942–43; and profound suspicions about the quality of Dutch resistance seemed to affect the Allied High Command when the land war got close to Dutch territory in the autumn of 1944.

Notoriously, again, Montgomery's attempt at a single thrust past the German right flank (Operation Market Garden) failed to carry the last, critical Rhine bridge at Arnhem in September 1944; and the rail strike which the Dutch resistance mounted to assist Market Garden had unintended but dreadful consequences during the unforgotten 'Hunger Winter' that followed. In the end, the German right flank was broken by the Rhine crossing at Wesel in March 1945, and the final advance on Berlin swept past instead of through the occupied northern half of the Netherlands.

For a moment, let us cast an eye on British politics. These were in abeyance for much of the war, conducted by Churchill through an all-party coalition. There had been no general election since 1935. Parliament had renewed its own tenure from year to year, in the belief that a general election was too risky a distraction from war with a neighbour. The neighbour once defeated, the wartime coalition broke up, and a general election took place in July 1945.

To the astonishment of the rest of the world, Churchill was defeated and had to resign. The nation voted, not so much against him as against his friends; we were all most grateful to him for having carried us through our darkest hour, but many of us nourished bitter memories of how badly his party had handled home as well as foreign affairs between the latest two great wars.

The new government had the barest of majorities of votes cast, but a substantial majority in the House of Commons; under the leadership of Attlee and the party label of Labour, it consisted of a coalition of moderate and more extreme socialists. It is remembered by the nation for having created the modern welfare state; historians recall it rather for having liberated the Indian sub-continent from British rule in 1947. Its sharply anti-imperialist tone produced, as we shall see, some sharp edges in Anglo-Dutch relations.

Yet its foreign minister, Bevin, highly skilled in negotiations after forty years' struggles as a trade union official, was determined to tie Britain in to Europe as tightly as he could, instead of leaving it as isolated as it had been in his boyhood. He was one of the principal architects both of the Marshall Plan and of NATO; so Dutch resentments about their vanishing East Indian Empire could be swallowed up in relief that both the prosperity and the security of their homeland were assured.

The original Benelux treaty that united the three states of the Netherlands, Belgium and Luxembourg into a single customs union derived from a convention signed in London by the three governments in exile on 5 September 1944, as a gesture to indicate that none of the three foresaw a safe independent existence without the other two, once the war was over. From 1 January 1948 the three countries' markets were linked behind a common customs barrier. Indeed, from this act of faith derived in turn the European Coal and Steel Community, the

European Economic Community, and one of the world's better hopes of prosperity rather than confusion.

By an interesting example of how history merges into politics, on the last day of the conference we were able to hear Dr Frits Bolkestein, then the Dutch Minister of Defence, on the principles of Dutch foreign and defence policy: a talk delivered, on the day of Mr Gorbachev's arrival in London for discussions with Mrs Thatcher, to remind them of the necessity for NATO to remain strong.

OPENING ADDRESSES

The Hon. Archibald Hamilton

It is a great honour to be invited to address so distinguished and learned a gathering at the start of your proceedings. The tercentenary of William and Mary reminds us of the long-standing and close relationship between our two countries, nowhere more evident today than in our close co-operation on defence within the NATO alliance. On the eve of the celebration of the 40th anniversary of NATO, I strongly support the idea embodied in this conference, of reviewing the momentous events of 1940–45, and the relationship between the United Kingdom and the Netherlands, with the benefit of contributions from some of the participants in those events. I am sure that those contributions will be specially valued, and may remind us of the debt we owe to the courage and dedication of many British and Dutch men and women who bore heavy burdens and took great risks during those dark and dangerous years in the uncertain hope that later generations should enjoy a lasting peace. I know that one of the principal aims of this conference is to pass on the knowledge of these contemporaries to those who can only read about such events: a very worthwhile way of reinforcing the lesson we need constantly to transmit to younger people who have no direct experience of wars. Peace is a hard-won benefit, and it is far better to deter war from ever starting, through strong defences, than to run the risk through short-sightedness and self-delusion of allowing any potential aggressor to believe he can achieve his aims by force of arms. In many ways, NATO grew out of the events of 1944–45, when the largest Allied fleet ever assembled projected across the Channel the army which liberated Western Europe.

It was not all fighting and destruction. One of the imaginative uses of military power at the time was the dropping by air of supplies to the inhabitants of the Netherlands after the last cruel winter of that war. The lessons of wartime co-operation have, I believe, been carried forward into the NATO alliance, and are at least partly responsible for

1

the effectiveness of our present co-operation. You will have the good fortune of hearing Dr Bolkestein, the Dutch Defence Minister, bring the story of our defence co-operation up to date. Regrettably, but perhaps fittingly, I shall be in Brussels visiting NATO at that time. I am sure he will allude to the success of the alliance as it enters its fifth decade. It is an indication of its success and its apparent permanence on the international scene, that it is sometimes quite easy to overlook the difficult circumstances of its creation, and to underestimate the achievement it represents. We should not forget that the strength and resolution of NATO have played an important part in encouraging the long-overdue changes now in train in the Soviet Union and eastern Europe. We welcome these changes – particularly the promised reduction in forces, which we look forward eagerly to seeing implemented. Our political opponents in parliament talk as if the cuts promised by Mr Gorbachev have already taken place; they are actually not scheduled to start taking place until this month. But in the light of the lessons of history, and knowing the dreadful price we must pay if we miscalculate, we cannot use these changes as an excuse for allowing our defences to become inadequate. For one thing, it is too early to know whether Mr Gorbachev's plans, by our standards relatively modest, will come about. We also have to take account of capability as well as intentions. Of course it is always easier to argue for effective defence when the threat is obvious. But we have a responsibility to meet the challenge of the effect on public perceptions of new Soviet attitudes.

We have a good story to tell. NATO has succeeded in keeping the peace in Europe for 40 years, and the current agenda on arms control are largely based on NATO initiatives. This may all seem a long way from what was going on in 1940–45, but I believe the common links and perceptions, forged then between the UK and the Netherlands, helped to cement one of the closest bilateral relationships in the alliance; which in turn underpins the solidarity and cohesion of all the allies. It seems to me, therefore, appropriate that this important period be examined, and the public's attention be drawn to this aspect of the long and close relationship between our countries. I will not trespass any further on your time, but I should like simply to wish you all a very successful and fruitful conference.

The Chairman*

This conference forms a part of the celebration of Anglo-Dutch friendship that accompanies the tercentenary of the Glorious Revolution of 1688 and the coronation of William III and Mary II of England in 1689. The committee that has organized it must begin by recognizing its debts of gratitude: to the William and Mary Tercentenary Trust, for invaluable support; to one – *one* – of the great Anglo-Dutch multinational firms, Unilever, for a most handsome cheque; to the authorities of University College, for providing both a lecture room and a common-room where we can eat and drink between sessions; to both the British and the Dutch governments for having put their hands in their pockets and helped us; to the Dutch Railways and to Holland International for a useful gesture of support; to Dr Jonkman, the Royal Netherlands Ambassador in London, whose approval has been sensed at every stage and whose Embassy provided the executive committee with a firm base from which to work.

We are also under an intellectual debt to the late Henri Michel, the doyen of resistance historians, who first drew attention to the distinction – obvious the moment you see it stated – between external resistance, carried out by those who fled their country, and internal resistance, the work of those who stayed behind under the jackboot of occupation. On our first day we shall consider external resistance, on our second, internal; on the third, a point where the two fused as the liberating armies fought across Dutch territory, and the results for the future development of Europe.

There is no need to press far the historical analogies between King William III of England and his successor as ruler of the Netherlands, Queen Wilhelmina, but they did exist. Both were devoted Protestants; and each fought valiantly against a man who sought to tyrannize over Europe. Louis XIV and Adolf Hitler were poles apart in manners and in ancestry, but did share some political aims: both were tyrants at home and bullies abroad.

In addition to our other support from exalted quarters, I am happy to pass on to the conference warm wishes for its success from one who

---

*The editor chaired every meeting except the fourth, at which he was a speaker; that meeting was chaired by Dr Christopher Andrew.

3

stood by Queen Wilhelmina in one of Holland's and of England's darkest hours: Queen Elizabeth the Queen Mother.

CHAPTER ONE

THE DUTCH GOVERNMENT IN EXILE

Louis de Jong

I would like to begin with a personal recollection.

On 16 May 1940, two days after the capitulation of the Dutch Army, I set foot on British soil as a penniless refugee. Six weeks later I got a job as an official of the Netherlands Government Information Service. On the initiative of the Minister of Justice, Professor Gerbrandy, who had been active in the field of broadcasting in pre-war Holland and who was well aware of the importance of the BBC and of broadcasting in general, the Netherlands government had decided to start, if possible, a broadcasting service of its own, *Radio Oranje* – Radio Orange. The BBC, keen to preserve the monopoly of its European Service, had declined this idea but its objections were put aside by the Ministry of Information. Radio Orange started with a staff of two and I was one of them. Now Gerbrandy's idea had been opposed by some members of the Dutch cabinet and by no one more strenuously than the Prime Minister, de Geer, and it was at his insistence that the cabinet had decided that Radio Orange would only be allowed to broadcast texts that had been approved by four ministers, including de Geer.

At the end of July the new service opened with a stirring address by Queen Wilhelmina, by whom the war with Nazi Germany was characterized as a struggle between good and evil. Some two weeks later the staff of Radio Orange circulated a text, written by one of the Dutch newspaper correspondents in London, which ended by saying that Hitler, although virtually master of the European Continent, would be defeated, just as had happened to Napoleon one-and-a-half centuries earlier. Usually the detailed comments of the four ministers did not go further than the desk of the Head of the Government Information Service, but in this case de Geer's comment was passed on

5

to the staff of Radio Orange and I read that he, the Prime Minister, was of opinion that the comparison with Napoleon should be deleted, because (and I now quote his comment to the best of my recollection), 'as the Minister of Defence has pointed out in recent meetings of the cabinet, Hitler can no longer be defeated'.

It was quite a shock and you may well understand how glad I was, indeed how glad all officials of the Government Information Service were, when, a few weeks later, it was announced that de Geer had resigned and that Gerbrandy was his successor.

We owe this momentous change to Queen Wilhelmina. So it is necessary to give you some information on her attitude and on her constitutional position.

Ascending to the throne in 1898, when she was 18, she had sworn always to act in accordance with the constitution. This constitution, adopted in the middle of the nineteenth century, was closely modelled on the unwritten (still unwritten) British constitution. It included the important stipulation that the King (or Queen) of the Netherlands was inviolate, the ministers being responsible for all governmental acts. In this situation, as had been pointed out by Walter Bagehot, three rights were retained by the King (or Queen): the right to encourage, the right to warn and the right to be informed, and it is clear that this third right is the most important of the three, because encouragements and warnings should be based on adequate information. In the second half of the nineteenth century, however, relations between King William III, Queen Wilhelmina's father, and the successive cabinets became so strained that but little information was passed on to the King. In the minutes of the cabinet's sessions, for instance, which, once a month, were sent to the King's private office, no reference was made to really important decisions or broad discussions and, Wilhelmina having become Queen, this situation was not changed.

There is but one of the many ministers who served during her reign who, in her personal memoirs, written and published after her abdication, is remembered with something close to affection: not Gerbrandy (and I will make clear to you later why not) but his predecessor during the First World War, Cort van der Linden. Gerbrandy's name, however, is mentioned and that is more than can be said of nearly all others who, as she used to say, had 'simply been thrown in the dustbin of history'. Why the praise for Cort van der Linden? He was praised because, having learned to value the Queen's insight, it had been his habit really to consult her whenever the country's neutrality seemed to be endangered. In the inter-war period, however, the Queen was not in a position in which she could really influence government policy. When the cabinet in the early thirties proved to be unable to prevent mass unemployment, she seriously considered abdication.

Much earlier than the cabinet, she was aware of the dangers presented by Nazi Germany. The German attack on 10 May 1940 was so unnerving to Prime Minister de Geer that when he had to make calls from the shelter where his cabinet, formed a few weeks before the outbreak of the Second World War, was in session, he was unable to dial the telephone. The Queen, however, acted with fortitude. Prince Bernhard was directed by her to bring Crown Princess Juliana and her two infant daughters to safety. She herself decided to leave The Hague as soon as it appeared likely that she might fall into the hands of Adolf Hitler. Not having consulted or even informed the cabinet, she left on her own responsibility and, when the cabinet joined her in London, the spirit of defeatism which came to permeate its discussions deeply disturbed her.

Early in July the cabinet decided to move the government's seat to the Netherlands East Indies, which meant that she too would have to go there. She refused, choosing an argument which was as non-political as irrefutable: her health, she said, made it impossible for her to move to a tropical climate, and the address with which she opened the broadcasts of Radio Orange was directed not only against Adolf Hitler but also against her own Prime Minister and all others who thought as he did. In August she informed de Geer that she had lost all confidence in him. His will to fight having evaporated he offered his resignation which she promptly accepted, confident that Gerbrandy would be willing to succeed de Geer, which indeed he did. In setting up his new cabinet, in which he retained his colleagues (they, after all, represented most of the country's political parties), Gerbrandy accepted political responsibility for the momentous change that had occurred, but it is quite clear that historical responsibility lies with no one else but Queen Wilhelmina.

Why was she able to act as she did? Because, of the three forces that had determined national policy – the Queen, the cabinet and parliament – only two had been left: the Queen and the cabinet. In pre-war years there had been several conflicts between the Queen and the cabinet, but whenever the cabinet had said that a line of action proposed by the Queen would be unacceptable to parliament and was therefore declined, the struggle was over and the Queen had lost. In London, however, there was no Dutch parliament and the Extraordinary Advisory Council (*Buitengewone Raad van Advies*) that was set up in 1942 was not given any real power. So government policy now was the outcome of those two forces which were inextricably bound to each other: the Queen and the cabinet. Whatever the cabinet proposed could only lead to action if the Queen put her signature to the decrees and decree-laws submitted to her, and whatever the Queen proposed could only be realized if the cabinet or individual cabinet ministers were willing to draft the decrees and decree-laws which she considered desirable.

Now, do not infer from what I have told you so far that the history of the Netherlands government in exile is but a record of a continuous struggle between Queen Wilhelmina and the Gerbrandy cabinet. There was a war to be waged and won, and one may say that in all matters pertaining to that war, there were no serious conflicts between the Queen and the cabinet. Such conflicts as did occur referred to the post-war period.

The Queen's papers, which I was able to study, make it abundantly clear that she fervently hoped that after liberation the Dutch constitution would be changed, decisively, in her favour. She considered herself to be the embodiment of the Dutch nation, and the events of that harrowing summer of 1940 had fortified her conviction that it would be in the best interests of that nation if the main lines of government policy were to be drawn by her and not by cabinet ministers, for most of whom the dustbin would be waiting: the constitution, therefore, would have to be changed according to the rules prescribed in it. These said that any change had to be approved twice by parliament with at least a two-thirds majority, first by the parliament that was in session, and second, general elections having been held, by the next parliament. After liberation a new cabinet would be set up and it was the Queen's right to determine by whom. She hoped that that cabinet would be willing to work out proposals for the constitutional changes she had in mind. These changes would have to be approved by the first post-war parliament. Which parliament? The one that was in session when the Netherlands were occupied had been elected in 1937. Both the Queen and the Gerbrandy cabinet were of opinion that it had lost its representative character. It would be some time before general elections could be held. Therefore there would have to be a temporary parliament, the members of which would have to be nominated by the government; and the Queen firmly believed that in that temporary parliament the Dutch resistance movement would act as a united and dominating force. That temporary parliament having agreed to change the constitution, these changes would become fully effective after they had been approved by the parliament that would result from the first general elections.

Before going further I would like to stress that during the war years

Queen Wilhelmina certainly was not the only one who believed that it would be in the nation's interest if, after liberation, she obtained a position which, perhaps, might best be compared to that of the present President of France. Before the war she had been esteemed but I do not think one can say that she was truly popular. Moreover, the monarchy as an institution was at that time rejected by perhaps one quarter of the electorate, mostly socialists and communists. In this respect the Nazi occupation effected important changes. The House of Orange became the symbol of the nation's will to regain independence and Queen Wilhelmina, frequently broadcasting to occupied Holland (virtually all her speeches were written by her personally), found exactly the right note of indignation and compassion. People were proud of her, and many of the mainly young people who escaped to Britain told her that her personal standing had soared to unprecedented heights. This may have made it easier for her not to pay attention to a warning on the part of the leaders of the pre-war political parties which reached London in 1942. Gerbrandy had been able to submit to them, through Switzerland, the question whether any change was desired in the constitutional position of the Crown and they had replied 'no'. They realized that the Queen, if she obtained more power, might well become the centre of deep dissensions and that as a result both the position of the House of Orange and the stability of the state might be endangered.

Now, how did Queen Wilhelmina set about fostering the constitutional changes dear to her?

First, she tried to obtain for her son-in-law, Prince Bernhard, the position of Commander-in-Chief of the Dutch armed forces. As far as these armed forces were concerned, which were small, this position would not be very important, but as Commander-in-Chief the Prince would be the head of the Military Administration (*Militair Gezag*) which, under the overall authority of General Eisenhower, would run the Netherlands during the first period after liberation. The Queen's proposal was accepted by the Gerbrandy cabinet, which I consider strange because the cabinet was well aware of the Queen's wish to obtain more power – a wish which was not shared by the cabinet. It may be (but I am unable to prove this) that Gerbrandy, acceding to the Queen's wish, knew that the government's proposal would be rejected by General Eisenhower, as indeed it was. This was the Queen's first disappointment.

Second, the Queen refused to sign any decree-law pertaining to the setting-up of the temporary parliament, not even the last draft which was submitted to her by all members of the cabinet. She said that she first wanted to consult the representatives of the resistance movement which, as I have already pointed out, she hoped would manifest itself in that temporary parliament as a united and dominating force. In September 1944, without the knowledge – let alone the approval – of the cabinet, she invited the resistance movement to send a delegation to her in London. This invitation merely led to acrimonious debates among the various resistance groups, showing that the Queen's view of the resistance movement was far too simplistic, and the upshot was that no delegation was sent. This was the second disappointment.

By that time little was left of the excellent relationship between the Queen and her Prime Minister which had marked his first two years in office. When, at the end of January 1945, Gerbrandy's cabinet fell apart as a result of various tensions, the description of which would take me too much time, the Queen desperately tried to find someone else whom she might charge with the task of setting up a new cabinet. There was no one and it was left to van Kleffens, the Minister of Foreign Affairs, who refused to succeed Gerbrandy, to point out to the Queen that Gerbrandy's excellent reputation in the councils of the Allied governments made it imperative to retain him as Prime Minister. Gerbrandy consented, although with a heavy heart. Do keep in mind that all these discussions manifested themselves in a period when, north of the big rivers (the Netherlands south of those rivers had already been liberated), the western, most densely populated part of the country, living in the grip of the so-called hunger winter, was in mortal danger.

Most of the members of the succeeding Gerbrandy cabinet were chosen by the Queen personally. They, however, in that last hectic phase of the war, had no time to consider any constitutional changes and it may be that, when liberation came, Queen Wilhelmina already realized that it would be unwise to add a constitutional problem to the daunting problems of reconstruction which would face the first post-war cabinet. Before charging two men, Schermerhorn and Drees, with the task of forming that cabinet, the Queen conducted a wide range of consultations but, as far as I know, in none of these did she broach the question of whether it would be possible to prepare the changes in the constitution she at heart desired. So no changes were made.

Sometimes it is one of the most difficult tasks imposed on all of us by life itself not to pursue dangerous illusions but to accept reality as it is. Overcoming her own imperious nature, Queen Wilhelmina did. It was a hard-won victory and one, I think, which has been greatly to the benefit of both the House of Orange and the Netherlands.

Now I feel I have to make an apology to the Dutch part of my audience to-day. As far as they have read the various volumes of my work *The Kingdom of the Netherlands in the Second World War* (I would like to add that I intend to write a succinct version which will also be published in English), I have told them nothing that is really new. I thought, however, that my British listeners would be interested in the theme on which I concentrated, particularly because so far it has not been dealt with in any publication in English. I have, however, some time in hand and I would like to use it to make some remarks on a few topics which do belong to the theme of this important conference but which, according to the programme, will not be introduced and discussed in detail.

First, I want to stress the importance of the contribution to the war effort of the Dutch merchant navy.

When the German attack came, most of our sea-going vessels were on the high seas. They were immediately put at the disposal of the London Ministry of Transport, later of the Combined Shipping Board in Washington. Apart from some 200 coasters, over 20 sea-going tugs and nearly 40 fishing vessels they totalled 640 merchant ships. Nearly half of them were sunk, the major part in the Atlantic Ocean, over 3,000 officers and men losing their lives. I believe that, materially, the war effort of our merchant navy has been the most important Dutch contribution to the winning of the war and I believe that this should not remain unsaid.

Second, I want to point out that the Dutch West Indies, to wit Dutch Guyana, Surinam, and the Dutch islands of the Antilles, were also of importance to the war effort. Most of the bombers of the Royal Air Force flew on petrol that had been shipped from the refineries of the islands of Curaçao and Aruba and two-thirds of the bauxite that the Americans needed to build tens of thousands of aluminium airplanes, was mined in Surinam.

In the third place I feel that I should say a few words on the Netherlands-Indies, now the Republic of Indonesia.

The future of that part of the Kingdom of the Netherlands was one of the major concerns of the Dutch government in London. Three phases may be distinguished: (1) the period before Pearl Harbor; (2) the period of the Japanese onslaught, ending with the occupation of the Indonesian archipelago; (3) the years of Japanese occupation. In the first period Queen Wilhelmina and the Gerbrandy cabinet were firm in their determination that the Japanese expansion should be stopped. They did not bow to Japanese pressure to increase raw material deliveries from the Indies, beginning with oil, and I would like to stress that this attitude was adopted and maintained despite the fact that the American and British governments were unable to state that they

11

would come to our aid if the Japanese decided to stage a separate attack on the Indies. One might say that, when Japan struck, the principal prize they intended to gain was the oil in the Indies. They attacked Pearl Harbor, Hong Kong, the Philippines and Malaya before attacking the Indies; indeed they never declared war on us. However, a few hours after Pearl Harbor the Dutch government was the first Allied government to declare war on Japan. During the months of fighting we were given such assistance as was possible in the circumstances – assistance by the Americans, the British and the Australians who, together with us, set up the American-British-Dutch-Australian Command (ABDA). To no avail. The Japanese were too strong and the Indies were incorporated in what the Japanese optimistically called the Greater East Asian Co-Prosperity Sphere.

In that third period the aim of Dutch policy was to speed up the liberation of the Netherlands Indies from Japan and to prepare for the restoration of Dutch rule. We were unsuccessful on both counts. All major decisions which determined Allied strategy in the war against Japan were taken by the Combined Chiefs of Staff and the American Joint Chiefs of Staff. The Netherlands were represented on the Pacific War Councils in London and Washington, but these bodies had no influence whatever on Allied strategy, and the Dutch mission attached to the Combined Chiefs of Staff was merely consulted from time to time without being asked to take part in the discussions in which Allied strategy was hammered out. The American government was not interested in the restoration of Dutch rule in the Indies. In 1945 General MacArthur's plan to land on the most important island, Java, was vetoed by the Joint Chiefs of Staff, soon to be followed by the decision of the American and British governments – the Dutch not having been consulted – to turn over the entire area of the Indies to Admiral Mountbatten. By that time the Netherlands had been liberated, but the new Dutch government was refused permission to use its own ships to transport troops to the Indies. Winston Churchill, who time and again had given the assurance that Dutch sovereignty would be restored over 'every inch' of the Indonesian archipelago, was succeeded by Clement Attlee, and *his* principal concern was not to get involved in too much heavy fighting. I believe that both the Labour cabinet and Admiral Mountbatten were wiser than the Dutch government and the overwhelming majority of Dutch public opinion in understanding that an agreement with the government of the Indonesian Republic, which was proclaimed two days after the surrender of Japan, was imperative, but that was not how things were viewed at that time by most Dutchmen. They felt let down by their wartime Allies and some of them still do.

In a way this is a sad end to a story of cordial co-operation which found its clearest expression in the excellent personal relations between Churchill on the one hand and Queen Wilhelmina and Gerbrandy on the other. The fighting spirit of both was warmly admired by the British Prime Minister. With regard to Western Europe there was but one cross he had to bear: the cross of Lorraine, and he may have felt cheered from time to time that his own roar was echoed by that of the Dutch Lion – a small lion, I admit, but roar it did.

Sir John Peck

It is a privilege to address you on the subject of my personal experiences and impressions of the tragic and stirring and heroic times which began in 1940 – and perhaps of the unhappier prelude to 1940. By definition history is the study not only of the who and the when, but also the why, and one of the purposes of studying this period is to consider what, in terms of European history, went wrong, and how we can stop things from going wrong in the same way again.

I have to put the events of 1940 in a general context with which you are all familiar; nevertheless let us look quickly at the time-table. January 1933, Hitler became Chancellor in Berlin. March 1936, German re-occupation of the Rhineland. February 1938, significant fact, the resignation of Anthony Eden and, under Chamberlain's leadership, the rebuff of an important initiative from the USA concerning the future interests of Europe. March 1938, the German rape of Austria. September 1938, the rape of Czechoslovakia, and what we must admit was the humiliation of Munich. I, at the time, was an assistant private secretary to Mr Duff Cooper, the First Lord of the Admiralty, who resigned over the Munich issue. Not only I think because I was young and impressionable, but also from my own convictions formed during undergraduate days at Oxford, I felt very bitterly indeed about Munich, and it almost cost me my job, because Duff Cooper's successor as First Lord of the Admiralty was very much a Munich man. However, in March 1939, to continue this dismal story, the German occupation of western Czechoslovakia and its incorporation into the Reich, and the significant fact that with the carve-up of Czechoslovakia, Hungary and Poland seized eastern provinces of Czechoslovakia, at which – surprise, surprise – Mr Neville Chamberlain withdrew his guarantee to Czechoslovakia; and then he, on 31 March, somewhat inconsequentially, as it has always seemed to me, guaranteed Poland, one of the countries which raped Czechoslovakia, a country which we could in no way hope to defend directly. Then 23/24 August the Nazi–Soviet Pact, and the two dictators, Hitler and Stalin, drew their demarcation line for the partition of Poland. Now, we have the advantage of course not only of hindsight, but of the captured documents given in evidence at the Nuremberg trials, which included the memorandum of 23 May 1939 from Hitler to his Chiefs of Staff quoted in translation:

England is our enemy. Dutch and Belgian air bases must be occupied by armed force. Declarations of neutrality must be ignored. If England intends to intervene in the Polish war, we must occupy Holland with lightning speed. We must aim at securing a new defence line on Dutch soil up to the Zuider Zee.

Well, that was the situation on 3 September 1939. At which point, as appeared later from the Churchill papers, Winston Churchill received a letter from a former Dutch Prime Minister, whom he does not name: 'In Holland, 300,000 men, still somewhat weak in artillery, are standing by.'

Now, as you know, we declared war on Hitler on 3 September 1939. In November 1939 the British war cabinet discussed Holland and agreed that the aim of a German invasion would be to attack the UK. Dutch islands at the mouth of the Rhine would be the base for putting London in range of medium bombers and fighters. That is significant, because it has to be borne in mind that at the time of the Munich Agreement, the German Luftwaffe did not have a single bomber capable of dropping bombs on London from the bases then under German control, and it was not until Hitler had overrun most of western Europe that he was in a position to bomb London at all. Then, as you know, he made up for lost time. However, it was decided by the cabinet in November 1939 that there was no way the British and the French could prevent the German occupation of southern Holland if it were invaded and that the only thing to do would be to retaliate by bombing the Ruhr.

In his summing up at the beginning of 1940, Churchill noted: 'It was thus clear that Hitler had a detailed plan involving both Belgium and Holland for the invasion of France.' Now, the thing to remember is that during this period Winston Churchill was First Lord of the Admiralty. He had been brought into the government by Chamberlain at the outbreak of war in response to popular demand. It was not an appointment that was viewed with any pleasure by many members of the Conservative party, who mistrusted his record in the First World War and didn't like him as a person; and altogether he was a disruptive influence as far as comfortable Baldwin-and-Chamberlain England was concerned. He was also not a member of the Conservative party – he was an independent conservative and remained as such until well into his premiership, when he was rather reluctantly persuaded to take on the leadership of the Conservative party.

However, to revert to the war, there was a bizarre incident which occurred on 10 January. For some reason, the complete German war plans for the invasion of France and Holland and Belgium had to be transported from Army Air Force headquarters in southern Germany to the north. The Luftwaffe pilot who was entrusted with this charge and wanted to get home to Berlin rather quickly, for some private assignation, took a short cut across Belgium, and unfortunately had to make a forced landing. He was promptly apprehended, hurriedly trying to burn his aircraft and the documents, but they were captured by the Belgians and copied and handed over to the British and the French. They contained the *entire* plan for the German invasion of France, Belgium and the Netherlands – a document from the 'horse's mouth' of what was going to happen. As Churchill remarked, 'None of the governments concerned believed it.' They thought that this was a deception plan to put us off, and the thing was ignored. But as Churchill pointed out, anything more idiotic than to hand the enemy your invasion plans in the hope that they would think it was a double bluff is simply not on. However, nobody took the slightest notice. In point of fact, it was rather difficult to know, in the circumstances, what could have been done that wasn't done.

Now, things were happening on other fronts. The Norwegian campaign, that primarily British and French operation, to try and cut off the iron-ore supplies coming round from Sweden to Germany by an invasion of Norway which was approved by the British cabinet and launched in early April, had run into great difficulty, partly because of bad planning, partly because of the weather, and mainly because of a total failure on the part of the naval authorities, including Winston Churchill, it must be admitted, to appreciate the impotence of naval forces in the face of air attack if they do not have air cover themselves. There was also the problem that they had not appreciated the state of the weather and the snow in northern Norway. The Germans riposted very quickly; they had overrun Denmark and were attacking Norway, apparently in reaction to the evidence that we were planning to cut off the iron-ore trade and to mine the Norwegian coast. But anyway, by the end of April, it was clear that things were going badly. The British public was uneasy; they didn't know if the war was going right or not and there was a growing lack of confidence in Mr Chamberlain's leadership and in his government as a whole. This found expression in the famous debate in the House of Commons on 7 and 8 May which ended in a division in which a substantial number of the Conservative members voted against the Chamberlain government and the whole conduct of the war was in question. I was present in the House of Commons as one of Winston Churchill's assistant private secretaries, when he was First Lord of the Admiralty, when he made his winding up speech in defence of the government and it was the first time I had heard Churchill in action in the House of Commons. It was a brilliant parliamentary performance, a vigorous defence of government policy; but to my mind there was something slightly forced about it, as if he was conscious of the fact that if the vote was so hostile to the government that Chamberlain felt obliged to resign, then he, Churchill, was likely to be called for to form a government. It was a paradoxical situation, and of course it went so badly that by 8 May Chamberlain was discussing with Lord Halifax and with other Conservative leaders whether he should resign and whom he should advise the King to send for. It turned between Lord Halifax and Churchill, and on the evening of 9 May nobody knew what was going to happen. Chamberlain had more or less made up his mind to resign and to go to the King and then he thought it over until the next day, and that was the situation on the morning of 10 May. In effect, Britain had no government – at least not a government capable of governing.

Churchill was still First Lord of the Admiralty. He was waiting in Admiralty House when the Dutch ministers arrived from Amsterdam, bewildered and dazed as if they simply did not know what had hit them. Even with the recent overrunning of Norway and Denmark in their minds, the Dutch ministers seemed unable to understand how the great German nation, which up to the night before had professed nothing but friendship, should suddenly have made this frightful and brutal onslaught. Churchill then writes: 'Early in the year, I had, in a published interview, warned these neutral countries of the fate which was impending upon them, and which was evident from the troop dispositions, and road and rail development as well as from the captured German plans.' And he adds: 'My words had been resented.' And I may add, not only resented by the countries concerned; he got into great trouble with his cabinet colleagues, particularly Lord Halifax, the Foreign Secretary, for stating publicly in broadcasts the delusions which the neutral countries were suffering from. Now this wasn't aimed at Holland or Belgium in particular, but at all the neutrals, and by then Denmark had learnt what it meant, and now this calamity had overwhelmed Holland and Belgium.

Now luckily there were ships in the Royal Navy which were able to give a little help in firing at the German troops advancing across the front of the Ijssel Meer, but anything that we could do at that stage was negligible. The next immediate Dutch contribution was a few weeks later, in the retreat across from Dunkirk. There were available a considerable number of those Dutch vessels whose name the English had some difficulty in pronouncing, and therefore called 'shutes'.

These were immediately pressed into service and assisted in the evacuation from Dunkirk.

At this stage, with the members of the Netherlands government re-forming in London, and Hitler rapidly becoming master of most of western Europe, the records of overt business between British and Dutch governments just disappear from view. Everything after that is the history of the underground movement, the resistance – of the whole problem of keeping hope alive in Europe. It largely disappears from the overt history of the war; and under the very strict rules of 'need to know', which I had to apply, I could add virtually nothing more to the history of Anglo-Dutch relations during the war. But after the war, I was able to transfer to the foreign service, and in 1947 my first overseas post was as Head of Chancery in the British Embassy in The Hague, where I spent three years. There I was able to see at first hand the speed and vigour with which the Dutch government and people were trying to restore their country from the devastation of the war, and in a very minor way to experience some of the privations and the difficulties that even in that post-war period they were enduring.

Before that, after the fall of the Churchill government, Mr Attlee, as Churchill's successor in No 10, took over the livestock with the premises as you might say, and some of us were asked to stay on as Mr Attlee's private secretaries. That's how it happened that, one weekend down at Chequers, I was present when Mr Attlee received the Dutch ministers who had come to invoke his aid on the problems of how to settle the Netherlands East Indies after the war, and it became apparent on the one hand, quite apart from military requirements, that Attlee's government was concerned, ideologically if you like, with decolonization and the winding up of empires, not least our own. It was a very difficult meeting indeed with Mr Attlee, and it was quite clear that if any of the Dutch ministers had hopes of restoring Netherlands sovereignty over Indonesia, they were going to be doomed to dis-appointment. As a matter of fact, after that, when I was stationed in The Hague, an immense amount of the time of the Dutch government was spent in a succession of couriers going to and fro between Jakarta and The Hague negotiating what the Netherlands could salvage from the wreckage.

If you look back over the period of which I have been talking, one or two considerations do occur which I think are worth raising for dis-cussion. The principal one is, to my mind, the obvious one, that the experiences of the war must have destroyed once and for all the illusion that under modern conditions there can be such a thing as neutrality as a political posture or status in international politics. But there is something else, there is a state of mind called neutralism, and under present-day conditions this is a much more insidious thing and I encountered this, curiously enough, during my years in Holland.

This period, 1947–50, marked the start of what we call the 'Soviet peace campaign'. Stalin had built up, through the communist parties and through their sympathizers, an elaborate international network of peace organizations. There were the World Federations of Democratic Youth, of women, of trade unions – all dedicated to the concept of peace; and it wasn't until you thought rather hard, and delved a little bit, that you found, of course, that the whole apparatus was there to propagandize for peace on Soviet terms. In The Hague, there was a lot of peace propaganda going around, ranging from some fairly sophisticated stuff, a lot of it emanating from France; there were some eminent French intellectuals who, consciously or unconsciously, were following this Soviet line – down to crude propaganda on walls, 'Yankees go home', on which somebody went round adding under every notice, 'Yankees go home – by Pan American', a piece of advertising opportunism which was quite handy. But the pressures of neutralism throughout western Europe were quite heavy at that time, and that was what made particularly impressive to me – both at the time and in retrospect – the wholeheartedness with which the Netherlands people devoted their energies to ensuring that their neutral isolation should never recur. Starting with the formation of Benelux and going through all the stages that led up, not only to membership of NATO, but also to the European Community in its present form, the Netherlands government and people have always been prominent. This is where this term of neutralism is still, I think, relevant; if you compare the Dutch record since the end of the Second World War with the British record, without any disparaging of my own country's efforts in this respect, I think that there is a dangerously large element in British public opinion which is prepared not to know about Europe. They take extraordinary attitudes to a mysterious thing called Europe which we are separate from, without realizing that we are already an integral part of it. Living as I do, for fortuitous reasons of family history, in Dublin, I do have a slightly different perspective.

I can just add, on a personal note, that when I first went to the Netherlands, I was able to appreciate and sense the admiration and respect that the Dutch people felt for their Queen, and to confirm the belief that the foundations of a staunch friendship, both universally and in the European context, were forged by those terrible experiences of the war years and it is an experience which I for my part shall always cherish.

Gerard Beelaerts van Blokland

The partnership of the United Kingdom and the Netherlands came as a consequence of the German invasion and both parties had to adjust themselves to the new situation. A unity on all essential subjects had to be established.

The Netherlands had the political traditions of a small power. The best way to preserve their independence was to avoid any conflict and to count on the interest of Great Britain in preventing subjugation of the Low Countries to one or another great power. This political tradition had served the Dutch well during the First World War.

Neutrality mesmerized the thinking of the Dutch government in 1939. This was fully accepted by the Netherlands parliament and by public opinion. Nazism was seen as a danger but the people hoped to muddle through thanks to neutrality. Strict neutrality was observed to placate the 'Nazi devil' while in secret there was a hope that, if the country were invaded, the Allies would come to our help.

Our legation in Berlin gave numerous warnings that an invasion was coming, but people stopped believing this.

Allow me to mention a personal experience: I was due to leave for Geneva on 6 May 1940 for a League of Nations conference. During the night of 4 or 5 May I was on duty at the Foreign Ministry. The counsellor of our legation in Berlin came in, telling me that he would return on 9 May, but that by then we would probably be at war. The next morning I told my chief, asking if I was to go. He answered: 'Berlin has often reported this. You just go tomorrow and, if there is an invasion, you come back.'

Queen Wilhelmina was not surprised. She expected an invasion. When it came she was resolved to fight until the end. When she saw the position was hopeless she left.

The cabinet followed her a day later.

This cabinet had been formed shortly before the war. It was a national cabinet with all the major political parties represented. The Prime Minister, a good man in peace-time, was however at heart a pacifist, unprepared for war. The Minister for Defence was a sick man. When the war broke out the ministers were forced to spend the first four days in a situation fraught with uncertainty, amidst rumours about attack by paratroopers and fifth columnists, lacking proper communi-

20

1. The exiled Queen

2. One of her subjects listening out for her

3. Parachutists at Oosterbeek

4. Pause in battle: a jeep at Arnhem

cations and information. Then they followed the Queen to London, where they felt utterly lost. They had all learned English at school and they could read it. But speaking English was another matter! They had arrived almost without civil servants and – still more important – without their wives, except for Mr van Kleffens, the Minister for Foreign Affairs.

As the invaders were overrunning France many ministers lost heart. Several of them fell ill. The cabinet met very frequently. There, amongst colleagues, the ministers felt they were doing their duty.

The Dutch community in London looked scornfully at the cabinet. Some young men made an ABC, from which I will quote:

'M stands for Ministers, the shivering sisters,
N stands for Neutral, as we all are.'

It was a very trying time for the dispirited ministers and equally for the Queen who was full of fighting spirit.

There was no parliament to force a change. So what could the Queen do but tell the vacillating Prime Minister that she had lost confidence in him?

The Prime Minister resigned and the Queen requested the Minister for Justice, Professor Gerbrandy, a determined fighter, to form a new cabinet. Under Gerbrandy's leadership the cabinet recovered from the shock of the month of May.

The picture of the first months after the invasion also had a brighter side. In matters of finance, naval co-operation, the use of the merchant fleet, the formation of ground forces, etc. all necessary decisions were promptly taken and full collaboration with our British Allies was quickly established.

The first efforts were made to get information from the home country. Naval Lieutenant van Hamel was landed in Friesland and a secretary in our legation in Bern made a few useful contacts, that were broken, alas, on his transfer to Lisbon. The secretary in Bern was Mr Luns, later Secretary-General of NATO.

Looking back at the first months of the war one can state that all that was necessary was done but that both the government in London and the people at home needed a time of about three to four months to recover from the shock of the invasion.

The common people were quicker to know where they stood than many of those who carried great responsibilities. Take this case: when the war broke out there were Dutch ships in British ports. Immediately the crews started painting their ships grey. This greatly alarmed the port authorities who asked them to stop this activity immediately for fear of strikes!

I must add that the sailors and soldiers I met from Holland had little sympathy with the British trade union system, which in their view obstructed the war effort. On the other hand they were full of praise for the British women who did such wonderful work during the war.

Let us now return to the Queen and the cabinet. It is true that the experience of the first months of the war led the Queen to feel that it was necessary for her to have more influence. It was influence rather than power she was after.

In my humble opinion the questions in London arose from the fact that there was no Dutch parliament and that the only powers left were those of the Queen and the cabinet. Both wanted to do what the people of the Netherlands wanted. The cabinet in London could only guess what parliament's opinion might be. It was handicapped by lack of a trained civil service, by the lack of courts to settle legal questions and, in a way, by the low esteem it had earned in 1940 at the outbreak of war. The Queen on the other hand had become the symbol of the nation at war. People who felt wronged by the government turned to the Queen for justice. The old maxim: 'the King is the fountain of justice' proved to be quite strongly alive. According to constitutional law the Queen could only refer the claimant to the minister concerned. In practice the Queen ordered one of the members of her household, if she thought the complaint might be justified, to go to the ministry concerned to try to find a solution.

Another factor that played a role was the Queen's belief in the power of moral forces. The years before the war had shown much moral and intellectual confusion. When in 1938 an appeal for moral rearmament to prevent Europe from sliding into a war was made by a number of prominent men in *The Times*, Her Majesty wanted a similar movement in the Netherlands. This movement did not develop owing to the speedy advent of war, but it shows the spirit of the Queen's speech quoted by Dr de Jong describing the war as a struggle between good and evil.

I would also like to point out that it is a general characteristic of mankind in time of war to long for a better world. Queen Wilhelmina was certainly hoping for a brighter future for her people at home, who were suffering in so many ways. She hoped for a nation regenerated and purified by the tribulations of war.

The escapers from the Netherlands shared these ideals. They thought they knew what should be done. Unhappily they failed to realize that, as no free exchange of ideas was possible during the occupation, each of them proclaimed ideas that he thought were shared by the nation, though in fact they were restricted to his home and his friends. The ministers perceived this and paid little attention to these ideas.

The Queen, who received all the escapers, understood them better though she too could not get coherent ideas. She sensed however that the escapers felt very lonely in London. So the Queen rented a house to serve them as a club. There the escapers debated the future of the country and became aware of the relativity of their personal points of view. Once they were able to start their war-work they became slowly integrated in the curious society of the Dutch colony in London or in the forces.

In a way this was a disenchantment for the Queen who had hoped that the escapers would help her to build the regenerated nation she longed for. When by the end of the war men who had been in the Netherlands during the occupation had joined the cabinet, and the Queen again had hopes of rebuilding the nation, she suffered a similar disillusionment.

At the beginning of the war Queen Wilhelmina had been sustained by her ideals, but at the end she was worn out by the clash between her ideals and the realities, of which she was well aware. She did advise her ministers and on occasions strongly pressed her opinion. But she had sworn to uphold the constitution and she stood by that oath.

She certainly clashed sometimes with Professor Gerbrandy who was a most loyal servant of the crown and of his country. He was with his Queen whenever he could be, and he stood firm whenever he thought it was in the interest of Queen and country.

DISCUSSION

The Chairman, to open the discussion, invited K. H. D. Haley to comment on the analogy between Queen Wilhelmina and King William III of England.

Professor Haley

Obviously there was no question of William III coming to this country as an exile. It was a matter of obtaining an extra ally in his efforts to resist the domination of north-west Europe by France, and it was extremely important for both our countries and for north-western Europe that the history of Europe should not be continued on a French model – politically, nationally, religiously or in any other way. Certainly it is true that between 1689 and 1713 the core of the resistance to Louis XIV was in the Anglo-Dutch alliance – there's no doubt about that at all; and it is quite significant that in the recent war one of the tasks of the Soviet government was to read the account of the combined effort in the war of the Spanish succession, in which both countries were effectively led by Marlborough. The standard biography was written in the 1930s by Winston Churchill, and he too was very sensitive to the idea of Anglo-Dutch co-operation as a continuation of the work of his ancestor against Louis XIV, of another Grand Alliance against the ascendancy of the leading continental power. So there are points of comparison to be made there, though not exactly with a government in exile. Equally, of course, William III had to intervene in English domestic politics in order to obtain the alliance which I have mentioned. One could also say as a point of contrast that in those days, in 1689, the countries were much more colonial rivals than allies; it is curious that the recent war should be followed by the liquidation of the Dutch overseas empire, to which the English were so hostile at that earlier time.

Chairman

Followed immediately by the liquidation of the British empire, I believe.

Professor Haley

Yes indeed, and I think that the two things were linked: if the British empire in India and Pakistan was to be liquidated, it would hardly have

24

made sense for the British government to attempt to restore another colonial empire in Indonesia.

Sir John Hackett

I would like to come to what Sir John Peck told us and perhaps clarify a point about this astonishing ditching of an aircraft in Belgium carrying the plans for what I would assume would be operation 'Sichelschnitt'. The whole of 'Sichelschnitt' was, I would take it, in those plans which were landed by accident in Belgium; for 'Sichelschnitt' was the 1940 variant of the Schlieffen plan, depending on the violation of the neutrality of Belgium and Holland in the first instance, but with one very important variation from the Schlieffen plan. The Schlieffen plan aimed to move through Belgium and Holland and then swing left and encircle and capture and occupy Paris. 'Sichelschnitt', which was the 1940 variant, started in the same way but it paid very little attention to the occupation of Paris – that was to be a windfall later. What it aimed to do was to go for the Channel and separate the Belgian and Dutch forces such as still were in being in the north east, and some French, from the British expeditionary force and the rest of the French in the south west, and by driving for the coast and separating these two out, effectively to neutralize any effective opposition. The crash landing of this aircraft was on 10 January. The whole thing was put into operation in the first fortnight of May. It was on 10 May that the unexpected moves through the Ardennes started the whole thing off under Guderian's tank command with Rundstedt behind him and with Rommel beginning to carve out a spectacular career as an armoured division commander in the crossing of the Meuse, which nobody believed possible. The speed with which things moved after that was really startling. The 12 May saw the crossing of the Meuse at Monthermé and Dinant and for 24–48 hours it would have been possible by a strong earlier reaction to prevent further development. Rommel, in the lead, was cautious, not having been able to get his infantry up to support his armoured thrust. But such was the degree of disagreement and vacillation on the French side, that there was no early adequate response, time went quickly by and virtually the whole thing was settled in about five days and when Weygand was brought in from the Levant to join Pétain, one burnt-out case joining another, the thing was already lost. He arrived on 17 May, and already it was two days beyond the time when any useful intervention could have brought the invasion to a halt. Now, what I would like to know here, if I may ask, is whether Operation 'Gelb', the *coup de main* attack on Fort Eben Emael and the defences on the frontier – was that by any chance included in what was handed on?

Sir John Peck

I don't really know the answer. I have never seen the text myself of what the German officer obligingly provided, but the only gloss on it that Churchill records, is that as a result of that mishap Hitler did modify the plans in some respects. In other words, the final orders did not correspond exactly with what the German pilot mislaid. But what the differences were, I am afraid I don't know.

Sir John Hackett

Of course, it was a critical aspect of the whole operation that the frontier defences, including the most modern and most difficult fort to attack in Europe, Eben Emael, should be taken by a total airborne, glider-borne surprise and I'd be interested to know whether there was a leak of Operation 'Gelb'. It was Hitler's own plan, prepared in the very greatest secrecy, and I've never heard that any of it got out.

Professor Bond

One point needs correcting. The two majors who landed at Mechelen only had the part of the plan which concerned the airborne boys, but enough of it to give some indication – and they did try to burn it, as Sir John Peck said. But the Belgians did not pass on the full plan to the British, they only gave a summary of it; this made it that much harder for the British and French to decide whether it was genuine or not. I think Sir John Peck also said that he couldn't see what could be done afterwards. Gamelin, the French commander-in-chief, had two or three months then with quite a lot of different information from aerial reconnaissance and other intelligence, with which he could have revised his plans, seeing that the Germans were clearly switching their main effort towards the Ardennes. He didn't do so and that does seem to be a great criminal error on his part.

There's one aspect that didn't come up; Sir John Peck also mentioned the problem of neutrality. As I understand it, and I am not an expert on this – there may be people here who are – the Dutch and Belgians who researched this were both in danger of a German attack. Both prepared independent defences, hoping they would remain neutral, but I think they did very little to co-ordinate their own efforts, and that might be something that someone here might cast some light on.

Chairman

In effect, why did the Dutch and the Belgians not co-ordinate their activities more carefully in view of the German danger which they must have foreseen?

Professor de Jong

There was, in fact, some measure of co-ordination. We had a military attaché in Brussels, who was in touch with the Belgian general staff. I would like to add, because the concept of neutrality is constantly being stressed here, that although the Dutch pre-war cabinet insisted on a very strict implementation of its neutrality policy, our military leaders clearly understood that some measure of agreement prior to any attack on the part of Hitler was imperative. So fairly full information on the state of Dutch defences, and on the first moves the Dutch general staff intended to make, was put at the disposal of General Gamelin and secret information was also exchanged between the Dutch and the British Admiralties. The fact for instance that members of the Royal Family and the cabinet were able to go to Britain aboard British destroyers was a consequence of all the prior arrangements that had been made. So it would be wrong to say that a 100 per cent policy of neutrality was conducted by the Netherlands until the morning of 10 May 1940. I do feel that our military leaders should be praised for the initiatives they took; on the other hand, I think that we must always keep in mind that one of the reasons why the Dutch government insisted on maintaining its policy of neutrality was that both the French and British governments for various reasons would be unable effectively to come to the aid of the Dutch whenever Hitler would be given the pretext by the Dutch government to invade the Netherlands. The state of weakness, principally on the part of Britain, but also to a certain extent, on the part of France was the cause of constant concern on the part of every pre-war Dutch government.

Chairman

I can add one curious footnote to this history. The War Office was worried, in the late autumn of 1939, and got the Admiralty worried also, about what was going to be done with the oil stocks should the Germans attempt to overrun Belgium and Holland. In the end in May 1940 150 sappers from the Kent Fortress Company Royal Engineers went over to the Netherlands and spent a happy day setting fire to the oil stocks in Rotterdam, returning in considerable disarray without having lost a man and having started a colossal fire. A similar colossal fire was started by one sapper subaltern at Le Havre three weeks later, finding for once a use for the Boyes anti-tank rifle. It was quite good at punching holes in oil tanks though it couldn't punch holes in much else.

Sir John Peck

On the question of the significance of European neutrality, specifically the Netherlands and Belgium: a much greater pre-occupation, in the mind of Winston Churchill in the period between May 1940 and Pearl Harbour in 1941, was American neutrality. Part of the great struggle that Winston Churchill and President Roosevelt had to wage was the attitude of the United States Congress and the strong isolationist influence, especially in the middle west, of such journals as the *Chicago Tribune*. The question that I have constantly been asked is whether in my opinion, without Pearl Harbour, the United States would have come into the war, given the pressures of isolationist and neutralist opinion in the United States, and the best considered composite opinion that I have been able to obtain is that the answer would have been 'No', and that, of course, was of far greater significance in the course of the world war than the neutrality of Holland and Belgium.

Chairman

The most important thing that the Special Operations Executive ever did, it did before its political wing had been shorn away from it. Very gently, very discreetly, its political wing managed to change the minds of a majority of US newspaper owners and broadcasters during the winter of 1940–41 on the question of which was the more constitutional attitude to take – to be isolationist or to be anti-Nazi. If you look through the files of the US press, which are scattered round the libraries of all the American universities, you will find that most newspapers, the *Chicago Tribune* always excepted, during that winter did shift over from being isolationist to being anti-Nazi, though this was by no means only SOE's work. It was aided by such people as Edgar Morrow, Raymond Gram Swing, William Shirer, who were present as reporters this side of the Atlantic, particularly perhaps by Shirer, broadcasting from Berlin, and Swing broadcasting from London during the blitz, with his talks punctuated by the sounds of bursting bombs, that convinced the Americans that perhaps the anti-Nazi horse would be the better one to back. This was, I believe, an important and a major shift in American opinion.

Sir John Peck

I wholeheartedly agree with that. Overtly, it was part of Brendan Bracken's duties as Minister of Information to keep the Prime Minister posted on visiting American VIPs, influential characters informing public opinion in America, to make a point of seeing them and giving them his pep talk.

Baron d'Aulnis

My question is to Professor de Jong. I hear from him that the Queen had hopes of gauging the development of political thought in Holland by consulting political people there on the continent. Now my question is: Do you think that the government in London had sufficient possibilities of gauging the political thought of the majority of the Netherlands people in occupation?

Professor de Jong

My answer would be 'No'. There were no possibilities of gauging the state of political opinion in the Netherlands. The Queen did not dispose of these possibilities, nor did the government. But, on the other hand, although no one knew what might be the result of post-war elections, a pronouncement on the part of all the pre-war political leaders of all the major parties, a pronouncement which occurred in April 1942, was decidedly of some importance. I would like to stress that this opinion did not only involve Prime Minister Gerbrandy, but also Queen Wilhelmina. The answer – no changes in the constitutional position of the Crown – was known to both of them, but evidently this answer did not deter Queen Wilhelmina from entertaining the high hopes which I tried to illuminate in my address.

Baron d'Aulnis

May I ask then, do you think that this National Committee we had in the first years of the war, did any good in this field? They were in Holland, they had communications, but of course also they had to live in secret and they had to form their opinions in secret.

Professor de Jong

One might say in general that although by the end of 1941 all pre-war political parties had been forbidden and dissolved by the German Reichskommissar, as required, the leaders of the pre-war political parties had been able to keep in touch with the members of the parties, cadres, not the ordinary members, but the people who really had been the principal members of the party concerned either on the provincial, on a district or on a local level. A man like Drees knew exactly the state of feeling among the people who had belonged to or who had voted for the Socialist party before the war – slightly over 20 per cent of the electorate. The same is true of the leading members of the anti-

Revolutionary party, the Calvinist party. It is remarkable that this party, which at the start of the German occupation totalled only 80,000 members, grew to a quarter of a million within a year, and this testifies to the fact that many people, not all, but certainly many people, clung to the party ties that had been established before the war.

I would say that anybody with real political insight living either in London or in the occupied nation could have guessed by 1942 and 1943 that, although no one knew what the results of the post-war elections would be, there would be a socialist party after the war. There would be a communist party after the war, there would be a Calvinist party, and the fact alone that there would be a Calvinist party, would mean that there would also be a Catholic party and two Protestant parties. I won't give you all the details, but it was clear as the war progressed that the main political distinctions which had occurred in the Netherlands before the German invasion, and the start of the occupation period, would manifest themselves again after the war, although the spirit of co-operation between these political parties would be far stronger than was the case before the German attack.

David Snoxall

Professor de Jong, in the interests – very properly I believe – of a complete account of Anglo-Dutch relations in the war, did refer to the Netherlands East Indies theatre, and I just wanted to add a very small historical footnote from personal experience. I served in that theatre, briefly, in 1945–46: Sir John Peck indicated with an interesting remark about Clement Attlee's attitude, the origins of the unhappy events of that time. There was a particularly unhappy aspect which affected me as a junior officer, and that was, that when I was posted to rejoin my unit on Christmas Day 1945, the unit participated in a small mutiny, because it was an Indian unit, and I think it is not generally recognized in the contemporary histories, that because of the shortage of other nationalities of troops in that theatre, Indian troops were in fact used in that period, and I must admit I felt at the time that it was an extremely impolitic step on the British government's part to involve British Indian troops in that highly delicate operation. This was the time when Subhas Chandra Bose was active through the Indian National Army in subverting Indian troops and that was the origin of this brief and unhappy event in my own battalion. I am pleased to finish by saying that thereafter they served very loyally and I believe very effectively in the difficult task they then had to perform.

Anna Harvey-Simoni

We have well-deserved tributes to Dutch sailors and land forces who participated with the Allies. I would like to add the Air Force. There were at least individual Dutchmen who came over and joined the Air Force. They may have done so independently of the Dutch government in exile; I don't know how they came to join, but I remember dancing with one on the night of VE-Day on my Air Force station.

Sir John Barnes

May I for a moment lower the tone from these weighty contributions and add a tiny tailpiece to what Sir John Peck said to begin with? On 10 May 1940, a friend of mine, John Addis, who will also be known to John Peck, was one of the private secretaries serving in 10 Downing Street when the telephone went, and a fruity voice said 'Will you tell the Prime Minister that the Germans are bombing Rotterdam, good-bye', and he heard the receiver go down. He thought he recognized this fruity voice as that of Sir Neville Bland, who was one of my predecessors at The Hague, and is probably known to a great many of those present. But, he thought that on the strength of this caricature of a telephone call, he'd better not tell the Prime Minister anything too deadly. So he got back on the telephone and got hold of Neville Bland and said, 'Did you ring me just now and say that the Germans were bombing Rotterdam?' 'Oh, yes, buzzing around all over the place, good-bye', and down went the receiver again. And on that John Addis thought he could tell the Prime Minister.

Leo Marks

I would like to ask Sir John Peck: When you were one of Churchill's private secretaries, did you ever see any of the reports sent to him by SOE's minister, Lord Selborne, particularly with relation to the Dutch, and if you did not, Sir, would it be your impression that those reports would have been seen by Colville or Morton, or which of his private secretaries would handle highly confidential SOE reports?

Sir John Peck

I myself did not see any of those very highly classified reports, and I do not think that any other of the four private secretaries would have seen them, because Winston Churchill had Desmond Morton on his staff for the specific purpose of dealing with all matters relating to MI5, MI6,

SOE and all that side of the war, on which we operated on a very strict 'need to know' principle.

Chairman

There was moreover a strict rule in Downing Street that when C himself – the head of MI6 – came round to see the Prime Minister, nobody, nobody, nobody else was present, not even an admiral of the fleet, not even a member of the war cabinet, not even his wife.

Colonel Powell

Could I add to what Mr Snoxall had to say about the use of Indian troops in 1945–46 in the Netherlands East Indies? I was Brigade Major of an Indian brigade at the time, which consisted of three Indian battalions and one British. It's an extraordinary thing that with all the pressures on those Indians, both religious and political, they were absolutely first class in every way. Their discipline was quite impeccable, and this was at a time when a British parachute brigade mutinied in Malaya. Adding to that, about three or four years later, about 1950, I was in Arnhem, late at night, drinking with a lot of very worthy senior citizens of Arnhem. My relations with them were, I think, perfect. When I mentioned the fact that I had fought in the Netherlands East Indies – the atmosphere changed immediately and I realized the depth of the bitterness at the loss of their colonies, which they blamed then on one man, on what they saw as Mountbatten's intrigues to remove the empire from an old ally.

Professor Janssen

I would like to come back to the first part of Dr de Jong's speech about the Queen. I remember being a student in the war, and we had several discussions about the position of the Queen. I was a student of Professor Geyl in Utrecht, which will tell some of the audience something, and the problem was always the difference between the attitudes of the Queen and King Leopold. I think one of the things which gradually over the first year of the war became clear to us was that the Queen chose the right way, though at first view most people were inclined to see the decision of Leopold as the right decision. I think that enormously strengthened the popularity among the students of Queen Wilhelmina, and I think we honoured her because she was wiser than most of us had been.

Chairman

I owe it to King Leopold's memory to remark that Lord Keyes, son of

Lord Keyes of Zeebrugge, is busy writing a new life of Leopold, attempting to revise the popular view of Leopold as a tremendous catastrophe, which seems to be datable back to a campaign launched by Paul Reynaud, the perishing prime minister of the perishing French third republic, taken up almost equally ardently by Reynaud's ally, Winston Churchill.

Sir Roger Cary

I would like to ask a question of the members of the panel, about the miracle of getting the Queen out so quickly, with the bombs falling, upsetting our ambassador there. And also getting the money out.

HRH Prince Bernhard

Well, Sir, I left with my wife and children, on 12 May, intending to return the next day, instead of which the Queen came over. And that was that. And then I went back over to Dunkirk, to the south of Holland for a couple of days, and came back via France.

Mrs Olivia Mitchell–Stas

Mine is a very frivolous comment. I was an employee of the Royal Netherlands government in the Department of Home Affairs in 1943. I was only a youngster at that time, but I was very much impressed that it was not all gloom during those times while we were working. We had invitations galore to celebrations at some of which Her Majesty Queen Wilhelmina was present.

Sir John Peck

A very quick one on the attitude of Winston Churchill, to, shall we say, those of whom he was a less fervent admirer than some, such as the King of the Belgians. He had a phrase, 'He has the root of the matter in him', which was really his highest praise for those whom he admired under difficult circumstances, and it was rather ostentatiously not used in the case of those for whom he had less considerable respect. In the tense period we were going through, and in accordance with his own temperament, it is extremely improbable that he would have said that King Leopold had 'the root of the matter in him'. Whereas, for example, General de Gaulle, with all his tribulations, did 'have the root of the matter in him'. As he once tried to explain to another French general – I forget who it was – at Chequers, he was airing his inimitable French, and he said, 'Mon Général, Général de Gaulle a la racine de la matière dans lui' – received by a polite and slightly quizzical silence.

CHAPTER TWO

THE DUTCH ARMED FORCES IN EXILE

Robert den Boeft

INTRODUCTION

My subject today is the Dutch armed forces in exile in the United Kingdom in the Second World War. I will in particular look at the importance of this period for the armed forces in their transition from isolated existence in strict neutrality in the pre-war years, to the fully integrated NATO role they fulfil today. I will do this with the background of an officer who joined the Navy two years after the birth of NATO and ended his career recently after a four-year term as NATO Chief of Staff in the NATO joint Maritime Headquarters in Northwood, close to London. Furthermore, although I am a genuine naval person, I served six of my last 10 years in inter-service jobs, the last one as Deputy of the Chief of Defence Staff, which left me with a healthy respect for, and some insight into, the efforts of armies and air forces. I will in sequence deal with

— the consequences of the long period of neutrality for the state of our armed forces in 1939
— briefly, with the period when the UK was at war while the Netherlands were still neutral, from September 1939 until May 1940
— the birth of some Anglo-Dutch co-operation during hostilities in the Netherlands in May 1940
— the evacuation of some of the Dutch armed forces to the UK
— the restructuring of Netherlands armed forces in the UK and the integration of their operations into those of the British forces
— the rebuilding of independent Dutch armed forces after the liberation of Dutch territory

and finally

– the integration of Dutch forces into the Western European Union and NATO.

It is worth remembering that in 1939 the Netherlands still possessed large colonies in the West and East Indies. The former were relatively little affected by the war, and I will touch only briefly upon the East Indies, because my back-up speaker, Dr J. A. Scholte from the University of Sussex, will cover that area.

I hasten to say that as an officer who, mainly thanks to NATO, has not seen combat action in his 37 years of service, I have the greatest respect and admiration for the numerous courageous individual and collective feats of arms during this period, involving many people. Having said that, I hope they, and you, will forgive me if I consider those outside the scope of my presentation today, but I am sure that the subjects of other speakers will make up for this.

THE NEUTRALITY PERIOD AND ITS CONSEQUENCES

First then the neutrality period and its influence on the armed forces. It is in this context essential to realize that since the defeat of Napoleon at Waterloo, the Netherlands had been independent and neutral. Apart from a brief campaign during the secession of Belgium in 1831, and two mobilizations for three months in 1870, during the first German–French conflict, and a prolonged one during the 1914–1918 war, the Dutch armed forces saw no real action. During that last period we kept an army with a strength of 200,000 men in readiness, to show that Holland would be no easy prey if one of the belligerents wanted to improve its strategic position at our cost.

This long period of aloofness and neutrality had of course its inevitable effects on the Dutch people, their governments and last but not least, their armed forces.

For those forces it meant in 1939 inadequate material, ambiguity of aim and consequently limited fighting spirit, the country open for espionage, inadequate preparation for Allied co-operation if drawn into conflict, and inadequate preparation for evacuation and functioning thereafter.

The main roles of the forces in 1939 were: for the Netherlands Army to guarantee Dutch neutrality and to defend Dutch territory if necessary; for the Dutch East Indies Army to defend their islands; and for the Navy some tasks in relation to defence of the homeland and the sea lines of communications, and a major role in the defence of the Dutch East Indies.

There was as yet no air force as such, because all these forces had their own air component.

Inadequate materiel

As far as materiel is concerned, after the First World War the Netherlands, like most countries, were happy to reduce their forces, due to the severe economic burden of their maintenance. In the early 1930s, when growing German rearmament cast its shadow on things to come, the mood changed somewhat, but strengthening and modernization of the armed forces did not get any real momentum until the late 1930s, when it was obviously too late. This although as a neutral the Netherlands could buy both British and German equipment. Furthermore, after 1919, to evade the restrictions of the Treaty of Versailles, a number of German companies moved some or all of their activities to the Netherlands, such as the aircraft industry of Fokker. In 1921 Siemens started with Hazemeyer a firm specializing in fire control systems in the Netherlands. Both are still flourishing today, the latter as part of Philips. Other firms specialized in optics, searchlights and shipbuilding.

But the bulk of equipment had of course to be purchased abroad, and at this stage there was a lot of competition from other nations which had to catch up as well. The component that probably suffered relatively most was the air side. When obviously some of the air forces in neighbouring countries were undergoing spectacular developments, there were in Holland very few high-ranking political or military authorities who had the foresight to see their rapidly growing influence. This is particularly sad, as with hindsight those developments can be pinpointed as one of the principal factors that precluded continued Dutch neutrality. Air Marshal Göring, for example, was keen to take possession of the whole country for his operations.

Air defence was sadly neglected. Only one prototype air warning radar set was operational in 1940. The air observation posts all over the country did not have sophisticated communications and had to use public telephones. Searchlights lacked equipment to point them in the right direction and there were no anti-aircraft balloons. Anti-aircraft guns had been obtained from nine different countries with too little ammunition and there were six types of fighter aircraft, of which only two types (Fokker D2 and G1) with 50 aircraft had the required speed. The bomber situation was even worse. There were 11 Douglas bombers which had to be modified for use as fighters, because there were no bombs, and 16 T5 bombers, the majority of which had no proper bomb racks, or sights to aim their bombs properly.

Machine guns malfunctioned at higher altitudes due to the wrong oil and there was a shortage of fuses for heavy bombs. The need to adjust airfields to modern aircraft capabilities was sadly underestimated. Last, but not least, a last-minute chance to acquire 36 modern American fighters was bungled due to indecision in the cabinet. All in all not a pretty picture. The naval air side was no more encouraging. Fifty aircraft, all old, were meant to use small bombs and torpedoes against landings, but the torpedoes were not yet available; 24 Dornier aircraft were ready in Germany but were for obvious reasons not delivered. Only seven of a bunch manufactured in the Netherlands became available. Germany on the contrary had 260 bombers and 240 modern fighters ready for use against Holland, as well as transport planes.

The Army did not have much to show for itself. No tanks and only 18 armoured vehicles. Orders for some 300 were placed at the time. Too late! The communications were very poor. Philips had excellent equipment on offer, but it was only purchased for the artillery. The remainder of the components of the Army relied on field telephones with ground cables, which are of course very vulnerable and not much good in moving battles. All in all, the picture in headquarters, including the main HQ in The Hague, was seldom up-to-date. Motorization was still limited and bad uniforms and packs hampered mobility. Most rifles were from 1890 and there were far too few hand grenades. Thirty-eight types of gun were in use, mostly of First World War vintage, and Germany was superior in machine guns and mortars.

The least gloomy picture was offered by the Navy. Some modern ships had been constructed and more were being introduced. Because of the ingenuity of a number of naval scientists, inventions had been made in the fields of radar, stabilization of guns and fire control, and snorkels for submarines, to enable them to recharge batteries while remaining submerged, as well as for firing torpedoes without release of air to the surface. The naval headquarters were connected by good communication systems and the Navy was the only government organization with equipment for coding and decoding. But again the overall picture was not good. Introduction of the new equipment had just started and most ships were ill equipped for modern war. Again, too little too late!

Ambiguity of aim and limited fighting spirit

Theoretically Germany, Britain and France were possible opponents as nations that might invade Holland for strategic reasons. During and after the First World War many people, in particular in army circles, were admirers of the German Army's professionalism but others, like Queen Wilhelmina, had from the beginning of German National Socialism never been in doubt where the real threat was. In the 1930s the armed forces were also, with few exceptions, thinking in terms of a German threat.

In particular, the Chief of Intelligence of the armed forces, Major General J. W. van Oorschot (who had an English wife – which may be irrelevant) was convinced that Germany would attack sooner or later. However, the government, and in particular the Prime Minister, clung to the idea that all could blow over. Therefore, it was Dutch policy that anything that could be considered as contrary to the spirit of neutrality should be scrupulously avoided. An Allied invasion was considered as a hypothetical case by the cabinet, but it was known that most ministers felt that we should then put up armed resistance. There was, however, also a strong faction of the opinion that we could never, not even informally, take sides with Germany. All in all, neutrality was the name

of the game, more or less closing the eyes to other options.

As far as the armed forces were concerned this contributed to inadequate motivation and insufficient training. This was worsened by the fact that senior officers had no experience in leading larger formations. Staffs had been cut down in budget savings, and so had fuel for training. It did not help much that countries such as Britain did not accept foreigners on their staff courses, thus contributing to Dutch isolation. Conscript time was shortened below an acceptable minimum.

However, as a recent newcomer, the Air Forces had some glamour, as well as the Navy. Airmen and in particular submariners were therefore the most motivated. As was proven later in the war the large majority of Dutch people, when properly motivated, could be excellent soldiers. But in 1939 not all was well.

THE NETHERLANDS OPEN FOR ESPIONAGE

Dutch neutrality meant that the boundaries were basically completely open for crossing by individuals, leaving substantial room for espionage. Both Germany and the UK were active in Holland for different reasons – Germany in view of its plans to attack Holland, which had been definite since September 1939, and Britain used Holland as a base to get information from Germany. In this area also, Holland was strictly neutral, but Major-General van Oorschot worked closely with the British intelligence people in Holland, who by the way were not top class. In the end this led to a severe incident in November 1939, when one Dutch and two British intelligence people were framed and hijacked at the Dutch border by the Germans, who claimed this at the highest level as proof of the Dutch siding with the enemies of Germany. This was the 'Venlo incident'.

It was fairly easy for the Germans to obtain all sorts of Dutch uniforms (although in the end this was detected), which they used in the early stages of the war to send in saboteurs in advance parties. The German attaché could roam around freely and even the Major-General commanding one of the divisions which had to attack the first main Netherlands line of defence could personally and on the spot, dressed in civilian clothes, get a good impression of the layout of the defence some five weeks before the attack. A high viewing tower in a zoo overlooking the area was very useful to him. The Prime Minister had recently refused to demolish this tower on the grounds that a neutral country had nothing to fear! The months before the German invasion of Holland were also a busy time for British and German air activity over Holland. I will come back to that later.

INADEQUATE PREPARATION FOR ALLIED CO-OPERATION

The stringent policy of neutrality prevented the preparations that would have been required for co-operation with the Allies after a German invasion. The defence posture of the Army was centred on the western provinces, where the government, the harbours and the economic centres were situated. But the flanks could well have been co-ordinated with Belgium and France, if it had not been considered provocative to the Germans. This would have been particularly useful, because one reason for a German invasion would be circumvention of Belgian and French defences. In the late autumn of 1939 the requirements for assistance from France, Britain and Belgium were formulated and deposited in Dutch embassies in the respective capitals in sealed envelopes to be opened on the day of German aggression. As far as France was concerned the requirement consisted of four divisions to be transported overseas to Holland. The Chief of Intelligence had already on his own initiative discussed this in Paris, and the military attaché accredited to both Brussels and Paris also opened the envelope immediately. He made it clear, based on information from the Belgian attaché in Paris, that the divisions would probably be available, but that the plans of General Gamelin, C-in-C of the French forces, and the Dutch plans were geographically incompatible. During the following informal contacts through the attachés no agreement could be reached. The same applies to the Belgians, who were approached in February 1940 on army level, even though the Ministry of Foreign Affairs was still against this on neutrality grounds. There was no army attaché in London and it was fortunate that the post of naval attaché in London had been re-established in 1936. This attaché was repeatedly approached to suggest UK/Dutch staff talks, and the British naval attaché in The Hague urged this too. The requirement for Britain consisted of one division to defend the Southern Dutch province of Zeeland, a large quantity of AA guns, eight squadrons of fighters and two reconnaissance squadrons. In retrospect it is obvious that considerable consultation and substantial preparation, including disclosing Netherlands' defence plans, would have been essential for all this assistance to become effective. It is of interest to note that although the majority of the reinforcements had to come from overseas, the C-in-C of the Netherlands Navy was not informed. This was due to the fact that organizations of the Navy and Army were separated. Virtually only within Dutch European territory was the Navy subordinate in its activities to the C-in-C of the Netherlands Armed Forces. In some way this was an advantage.

Whereas everything directly related to defence of the Dutch territory was under strong political control, the Dutch Navy's relative freedom allowed them to make some preparations with the Royal Navy, which they had never doubted would be their closest ally. The most important arrangement was establishing a radio link between the admiralties in London and The Hague for emergency use. It was tested on both sides by listening in to transmissions of each station to other stations in the same country. This link proved to be invaluable for co-ordination of operations and evacuations during the war. Some other important measures were taken, such as providing the main Dutch warships with sealed envelopes containing British harbour charts, safe routes and rescue signals. Other important measures were preparation of escort by British destroyers for transfer of the remainder of the Dutch national bank's gold to Britain in May 1940, and prevention of mutual interference of British and Dutch submarine operations and minefields. In February 1940 the Dutch chief of naval staff also ordered his flag lieutenant to be ready to go to Great Britain at short notice with the

Dutch naval cipher codes. As a conclusion at this stage, I would suggest that the deepest wish of the government to avoid any violation of neutrality was understandable and in line with the wishes (or dreams) of the Dutch people, but from a military point of view it prevented the bare minimum of preparations for the very probable future co-operation with Britain, France and Belgium.

EVACUATION

If all had been well, careful evacuation plans would have been made and co-ordinated with the Allies to ensure continuation of the Dutch war effort and to prevent valuable assets falling into the hands of the enemy. In some cases this had been considered, but no co-ordination took place with the countries concerned. This concerned the following groups.

The royal family

It is certain that the Queen had given considerable thought to evacuation. With good co-ordination over the aforementioned naval communications, evacuation was effected on board a British destroyer, when the need arose.

The government

There were no evacuation plans or preparations for communications with Dutch occupied territory. On the day, evacuation of the cabinet proved to be no real problem. At the outbreak of hostilities the Ministers of Foreign Affairs and Colonies went by naval plane to London to press for assistance and to enhance communications with the Dutch colonies. The rest of the cabinet followed a few days later in a British destroyer. However, most ministers were not accompanied by a skeleton staff with which to rebuild their organization.

Military leaders, staff, personnel and equipment

There were no plans in the Army for evacuation or retreat into Belgium, other than the evacuation of the two flying training schools and their instructors, trainees and equipment. The naval staff had given the idea some thought. The naval attaché in London had provided them with a report on the evacuation of the Polish Navy. The Royal Navy repeatedly urged the Dutch Navy to co-ordinate these matters. But only when Mr Churchill personally raised this matter did it really stir up the naval staff. In February 1940 the intention to evacuate the old cruiser *Sumatra* to Britain had been communicated to the Royal Navy. But even the chief of naval staff (who was, incidentally, also C-in-C) did not give his personal evacuation much thought until the hostilities were so far advanced that defeat was inevitable. Fortunately some subordinates were able to convince him that he had to go in order to continue the war with the evacuated assets and the fleet in the East Indies, even though the C-in-C Armed Forces remained opposed to his departure until the end. He was accompanied by a good staff element which proved to be invaluable to ensure early continuation of operations of Dutch naval units. The Army and in particular the air component suffered badly in the years to come from the lack of good staff expertise, denying them enough clout in the restructuring of their forces. So far as they were not lost in hostilities, nearly all operational ships and naval aircraft, as well as ships under construction, could be evacuated.

However, particularly when they were still in civilian hands, there were regrettable cases when ships under construction could be completed by the Germans. Furthermore there was no firm plan for transfer of ammunition and spare parts to Britain, which could now only in part be improvised. It is worth mentioning that the big companies, Philips and Unilever, had been preparing evacuation for years, by making legal arrangements to transfer ownership from Holland and by safeguarding industrial secrets (documents, reports and models) from capture by the Germans. Philips had also prepared to evacuate 150 people, directors and staff, including their wives and children, to England. General Winkelman, the overall C-in-C, had assisted them to draw up these plans before he was called back from retirement. But as C-in-C, he remained faithful to the neutrality idea to the end, thus missing a chance to evacuate more of the Army and the air component, in particular, staff and pilots, and this, much to the dismay of the last category, who with great reluctance had to carry out the order to destroy the aircraft with which they wanted to escape.

BRITAIN AT WAR, HOLLAND NEUTRAL
(3 SEPTEMBER 1939–10 MAY 1940)

Although the burden of war is very high, neutrality is not necessarily peaceful and effortless. For example, during the 1914–18 war neutral Holland kept 200,000 men combat-ready, and lost 121 merchant ships and 96 fishing vessels with a total of 1,200 seamen. When Mussolini occupied Albania during the Easter of 1939, the Dutch government called up the troops charged with strategic security (including the frontier battalions). A hundred thousand men were now combat-ready. The full armed forces of 250,000 men were mobilized on 28 August 1939, shortly before the German invasion of Poland. The situation remained thus until Germany invaded Holland in May 1940. I have already described the espionage in the Netherlands. In the wake of the air war activities, extensive violations of Dutch air space took place, roughly 170 by Germany and some 70 by Britain, in particular, on the routes to and from the German Bight and along the Dutch North Sea coast, but sometimes straight from the UK to the German Ruhr area and vice versa. Many violations were unintentional, due to poor navigation, weather (such as fog) or battle damage. However, about one-third were due to high-flying reconnaissance aircraft, which took photographs from Holland or Germany to make maps or check troop concentrations and defence works, depending on their future intentions. This art had become highly developed! It was Dutch policy to intercept the intruders and force them to land. The Netherlands air defence was however ineffective due to the absence of radar, lack of capability of Dutch aircraft to intercept modern high-flying aircraft and the small size of the country, leaving little time to intercept after warning.

In all the actions of anti-aircraft guns and aircraft only one British Whitley bomber, which ignored warning shots, was damaged and forced to land with one fatal casualty. The pilot stated that he was convinced he was over France! In this period 10 German and four British airmen were interned in the Netherlands. The activities described were very helpful for training purposes, thus steadily improving the Dutch air defence capability. Their experience had obviously given the Germans cause to underestimate this capability, for during the following hostilities they incurred severe losses, as will be described later. The Netherlands raised many protests but the Germans soon blatantly denied the violations, whereas the British were more apologetic. The Germans even fired back when they received warning shots.

At sea the Dutch merchant navy again suffered from mines, submarines and one air attack, losing 21 ships and 240 men. For the remainder, apart from some blockade activities and the protection of the routes through Dutch territorial waters, and apart from an incidental British attack on a Dutch submarine (which survived) and some violations of territorial waters, there were no major incidents at sea. During this period there were many instances when Hitler intended to attack, but cancelled for various reasons, resulting in false alarms. On 10 May, however, Dutch neutrality was ended by the German attack.

ALLIED CO-OPERATION DURING THE WAR IN THE NETHERLANDS (10–15 MAY 1940)

Before hostilities started, the Netherlands Army had expected to hold out for two to three weeks. Unfortunately, the German estimate of four to five days proved more accurate. The Dutch Army did what they could, but the Germans were simply vastly superior in equipment, armour, air power, training and fighting spirit, as described earlier. They complicated the Dutch Army's problem from the outset by occupying the most important airfields near The Hague and Rotterdam with paratroopers and airborne troops, altogether two divisions. The main aim was to seize The Hague and thus the Royal Family, the government and the high command. The airfields around The Hague were soon retaken by the Dutch, but for this troops had to be extracted from the main defence lines in the East, where they were badly needed, and the German occupation of the Rotterdam airport, Waalhaven, remained a thorn in the Dutch side. A factor that contributed to the loss of the airfields was that a substantial part of Dutch air assets had been destroyed on the ground, including 75 per cent of the modern fighters. The German bombers had first overflown Holland at high altitude simulating a transit to Britain, but shortly after leaving Holland they turned round, thus achieving a surprise attack. However, from then on the air defence put up a tough resistance. Although the Luftwaffe remained superior they incurred heavy losses – 328 planes, which is 35 per cent of bombers, fighters, reconnaissance and transport aircraft they used against Holland. Of particular importance was the loss of 220 Junkers transport aircraft (i.e. 51 per cent), which severely diminished the capability of Germany to use airborne troops, for example against Britain.

As far as outside assistance was concerned, during the months before the war there had been consultations between the French Army staff and the British Expeditionary Force. Neither country had much faith in Dutch strength, and France felt that Britain had a greater interest in saving Holland. Britain's military build-up was not advanced enough to enable large-scale assistance. The French Seventh Army was therefore instructed to defend the Scheldt estuary and link up with the main Dutch forces in Holland. They covered some 325 kilometres in 18 hours, but could not contact the main Dutch force and had to retreat the next day to Zeeland, threatened by the advance of German troops in

Belgium. It was then already clear that French–Dutch Army co-operation was difficult. Reconnaissance groups could not co-ordinate with Dutch commanders and other operations also could not be integrated. With the RAF there were similar problems. Dutch airfields and ground organizations were not geared to handle British planes, which also used petrol of a different octane rating and different fuel hose couplings. On the naval side it was agreed, on 11 May, that the Dutch C-in-C and the British naval attaché would lead Dutch partici-pation in Allied operations as joint admirals. The possibility of German naval activity in connection with the invasion in Holland was not excluded.

Therefore 12 Allied submarines operated in the North Sea and extensive minefields were laid. The British admiral responsible for North Sea operations had a large number of cruisers and escorts at his disposal and as the German Navy did not appear, could comply with almost all requests for escorts, such as for a Dutch ship with 1,500 captured German paratroopers. The British and French ships assisted with gunfire support for the land battle and each provided four mine-sweepers. Near the Hook of Holland there was a temporary landing of British Army and Marine units. In this town many British refugees embarked, as well as the British and Norwegian legations. In the north the Dutch Army skilfully defended the easterly end of the *Afsluitdijk*, the dike that connected Friesland with Holland, but the main defence in the centre of Holland steadily weakened. Therefore the royal family and the government evacuated. On 14 May, after a heavy bombard-ment of Rotterdam, with hundreds of people killed and with the other cities of Holland threatened with the same fate, the High Command capitulated, except for the province of Zeeland, where fighting by Dutch and French forces continued until 19 May supported by Dutch, British and French naval gunfire. On that day the French withdrew across the Scheldt. The Dutch Army virtually ceased to exist, with 5,000 military killed and wounded and 2,000 civilians killed. The penalty for ill-prepared co-operation with other forces was paid dearly!

RESURRECTION OF DUTCH FORCES IN BRITAIN
AND THEIR WAR OPERATIONS

With what then did the Netherlands restart in Britain? First, with the royal family and the government, the latter with very limited staff, which also applied to the Minister of Defence. Then, with the Chief of Naval Staff, who could count on a reasonable staff element. Of the Army, around 1,500 men (0.5 per cent of the previous Army strength) arrived in a number of groups along a variety of routes, and with a variety of means of transport, such as cars, bicycles or even walking, and then, wherever they could hitchhike to, by any type of boat from Belgium or France. You can imagine how eventful those trips were in the fog of war. There was no coherence whatsoever. Two hundred arrived guarding German POWs, the rest mainly retreated from Zeeland, the biggest group of 473 men under the leadership of a medical doctor. The rest were mainly 100 gunners, 420 Royal Military Police, various smaller groups or individuals and last but not least 179 men from the flying schools, who had to leave their aircraft in France. There were hardly any staff or senior officers.

The Navy had arrived with some 24 combat ships including two cruisers, one destroyer, seven submarines, gunboats, torpedo-boats, mine-sweepers, mine-layers and some 20 smaller auxiliaries. Not an impressive fleet, but important enough in a period when every ship counted. The Naval Air Arm flew across with 24 aircraft after some operations from France, accompanied by some supporting staff and technicians. By ship, by aircraft and by individual means, 300 officers and 2,700 men arrived (about 20 per cent of naval strength). It was fortunate that some Dutch radio, radar and fire control boffins, who were in the front line of new developments, could also be persuaded to go to Britain, where they worked closely with the Royal Navy.

It was less fortunate that the invention of the submarine snorkel fell into German hands. They were quick to spot the equipment's advantages, which stood them in good stead for later submarines. It is ironic that the Royal Navy felt that the snorkel made the submarine hull too vulnerable and removed it from Dutch submarines under construction.

What then happened to the Dutch forces? First, it is appropriate at this stage to highlight the invaluable role for the armed forces of His Royal Highness, Prince Bernhard, whom we are fortunate to have with us today. Before he was appointed as Commander of part of the Dutch forces later in the war, he tirelessly visited all elements of the armed forces, from airbases to command units and submarines, inspiring them with his leadership. This was particularly valuable for the Navy, whose leaders in London, not detracting from their other qualities, sadly neglected to motivate the men in the operational units. For the Army and its air element he played a vital part in getting the training on the right track, as well as securing an independent role for the Dutch contingent.

Thanks to the excellent preparations of the naval attaché, the first part of the armed forces that started refunctioning was the naval staff under the Dutch Navy's CNS, who also quickly got himself appointed as the C-in-C, with authority to mediate directly with the British authorities. As early as three days after the capitulation, they restarted their work on one of the floors of an office building of C. & A. in London.

Because the Minister of Defence had difficulty in rebuilding the proper staff, the Navy became more and more independent; in July 1941 this resulted in the Dutch Chief of Naval Staff being appointed as Minister of the Navy. In any democracy this would be a monstrosity, but under the circumstances it was a very clever solution to facilitate his dealings with both British politicians and admirals. The overall arrangements for the operations of the Dutch forces were soon agreed. They all remained under Dutch administrative command, responsible for personnel and materiel, but their operational use was decided by the appropriate British commanders. British naval forces could also be under Dutch command in the East Indies if appropriate. Britain also agreed to assist in rearming, training, and supplying them, when feasible. Financial and legal arrangements were also concluded.

Under this arrangement the smaller Dutch naval units soon settled down in their local tasks and the first Dutch submarine went on patrol on 12 June as part of a British squadron.

From then on Dutch ships operated fully integrated with the Royal Navy in the Norwegian Sea, the Atlantic and the Mediterranean. They took on the role of escort command over British ships where appropriate. During the war the Netherlands acquired three British destroyers, three British submarines (plus one on loan) and a large number of motor-torpedo boats and mine-sweepers. They also manned three French ships, when the Free French could not provide the crews. The British called them 'Her Netherlands Majesty's French Ships'.

After December 1941 most of the major ships went to the Pacific. The Navy fought well, and at the end of the war they had lost 3,000 men – a large percentage in relation to the total.

Since the war the Dutch Chief of Naval Staff has stated that co-operation with the Royal Navy worked extremely well. In the sub-marine world there were at the beginning some differences of opinion about the use of the Dutch submarines and their tactics, which had used markedly different philosophies before the war. But the younger generation of Dutch submariners soon fell into line with the British. Some Dutch ships had to be re-equipped to achieve standardization with the Royal Navy. Spare parts for submarines also posed a recurring problem. But apart from those initial hitches the transition from isolation to Alliance went very satisfactorily for the Navy. The Dutch Naval Air Arm was also soon able to be integrated as an entity into RAF Coastal Command.

The RAF was by that time already quite experienced in taking part of other Air Forces under its wing, such as Polish, French, Czechoslovakian, Belgian and Norwegian. The foreign forces were not independent but were, wherever possible, granted their own identity within the RAF. No. 320 Dutch Naval Squadron was the first fully non-British unit in the RAF, soon followed by 321 Dutch Naval Squadron. They started their anti-shipping patrols as early as 20 June 1940 from Wales with their own aircraft.

Mainly owing to lack of spare parts, the old Dutch aircraft could not be kept operational. In the autumn of 1940 both squadrons moved to Leuchars, combined as 320 Squadron, equipped with American Hudson bombers. They operated happily and impressively in Coastal Command until March 1943, when they were transferred to Bomber Command and equipped with B25 bombers. After the invasion they supported the Allied armies and went to Belgium in October 1944. They were stationed on nine different British airfields and flew some 4,600 sorties, building up an excellent war record, but losing about one-third of their flying personnel. Dutch naval pilots also flew from British aircraft carriers and Shell tankers.

For the Army Air Arm, the way to independence was much more arduous. They had not brought their aircraft or their leaders, and the Minister of Defence was irresolute about their destination. The most logical plan was to create a Dutch training school and to take it from there. Canada seemed to be a suitable place, because most RAF training was carried out in that country. However, the only offer received was to start a school in Newfoundland, and it is doubtful if its climate provided the minimal conditions for flying training. The Minister wavered between various other options, such as integrating them into the RAF in British service or sending them to the Dutch East Indies to strengthen the Air Forces over there. It must have been a very unhappy time for all those young men eager to get to grips with the Germans.

After some months, a large percentage, in particular technicians, were transferred to the Dutch Naval Air Arm to fill gaps in those forces; 68 went straight away and 63 others via training in the Dutch East Indies. The remainder were for the time being sent to the Army, which was not a popular solution, because the Army was not actively participating in the war, and yet when their chances for flying training came up, the Army was reluctant to release them. Fortunately, mainly thanks to Prince Bernhard, events took a turn for the better. The prince first arranged RAF training for himself and got his wings in April 1941. He negotiated an agreement with the Air Ministry in December 1940 to provide training for Dutch airmen in Britain. Dutch pilots joined all the various commands of the RAF in bombers, fighters and transport planes. For them it was an overwhelming experience to be integrated into a vast professional organization such as the RAF. It produced in them the strong conviction, that in future there would be no room for smaller air forces. They could only function in a larger, Allied context. Another solid step from isolation to Allied integration! With the growing number of experienced Dutch airmen the creation of a Dutch squadron became a distinct possibility and, in particular thanks to the efforts of Prince Bernhard, 322 squadron was established in June 1943, equipped with Spitfires. In the first months 50 per cent of the squadron was British and later it also always included a British contingent. The first Dutch CO was appointed in March 1945.

The squadron had an important role in escorting bombers, attacking the hideous German V1 missiles and supporting the Allied forces on the Continent. They returned to Holland in October 1944. Sixty-five Dutch pilots did their flying in fighters or bombers of other squadrons. Altogether, they completed more than 12,000 flying hours. They made an excellent contribution, fully integrated in the RAF, but more than 30 per cent of Dutch flying personnel lost their lives.

The story of the Army was at the beginning one of sheer frustration. The incoherent group that had arrived in England formed the basis of the Dutch Legion, in 1941 renamed Princess Irene Brigade. They were supposed to have two basic tasks: to assist in the defence of the territory of Great Britain, which was not necessary, and to take part in the liberation of Holland, which was not yet possible. They initially counted some 750 people, but in the autumn of 1940 the government decided to call up Dutch citizens all over the world as conscripts. This was also a condition of the British government for assistance in re-equipping the Dutch armed forces. The main sources were Canada, the United States and South Africa. There were great expectations that the Brigade would quickly grow to some 5,000 men, but for various reasons the total was not more than some 1,550. The Brigade further suffered from only moderate leadership, to say the least, and came to be used as a pool for various purposes such as security detachments, guard duties and gunners for merchant shipping.

Many therefore tried to get more active jobs in Special Services – the Dutch commando group, created in mid-1942, the RAF or the Navy. It was not until July 1943 that the motivation returned under the firm leadership of Marine Colonel de Bruyne. In mid-1944 they were reinforced by 100 marines, to reach the number required by Field Marshal Montgomery to be accepted as part of 21st Army Group. They played their part in the liberation of Holland, having landed in France in August 1944 and entering Holland one month later.

So, on the level of the forces, co-operation with the British was excellent and steadily improving during the war. On the highest command level, however, the situation was less satisfactory. In December 1941, Mr Roosevelt and Mr Churchill had decided to establish a combined US–British Chiefs of Staff Committee to direct the overall conduct of the war. In particular in view of the Dutch East Indies, the Netherlands had obtained President Roosevelt's agreement to be represented in this group. In practice, the committee remained very reluctant to accept this, and when the Netherlands had lost the Dutch East Indies and most of their fleet, any influence virtually disappeared. For any sovereign nation in an alliance, this was an unsatisfactory situation.

Regarding the Dutch East Indies, I will restrict myself to a few remarks about the lessons learned since 1940. First, it was a great step forward from the posture of neutrality that the Dutch government decided to go to war with Japan simultaneously with Great Britain and the United States. Second, this time they had the wisdom to allow military staff talks with the British, the Australians and later the Americans, even before the start of hostilities. This resulted in co-ordination of peacetime patrols, exchange of secret airfield data, a common coding system, exchange of liaison officers, etc. Third, participation in the American–British–Dutch–Australian (ABDA) Command put the Dutch further on the road to Allied thinking, although as you will hear later, this organization had substantial teething problems. Fourth, it was disappointing to see that although the right proposals had been made, the evacuation from the Dutch East Indies of valuable assets and manpower for further action was again unsatisfactory. But overall the neutrality philosophy had begun to change drastically.

REBUILDING THE DUTCH FORCES AFTER THE LIBERATION OF HOLLAND

Relatively early in the war the Dutch government started planning for the future liberation of the Netherlands, including a further build-up of Dutch forces. Clearly this could not be done independently from contributing to the on-going war, both in Europe and in the Pacific, and in particular to the liberation of the Dutch East Indies. It was obvious that the Princess Irene Brigade would form the nucleus of the Army, augmented with the troops that had been organized in Holland in the final months before the liberation, with the help of the resistance movement. It was decided that recruitment bureaux would be established as soon as a substantial part of Holland was liberated. Discussions with the British government were started about equipping and training these forces. At the beginning the British War Office had evidently other priorities, but two days after the invasion of Normandy they approved as a first step arming 24 battalions to re-establish internal security in Holland. Further negotiations, also involving the Joint US/British Chiefs of Staff Committee and Supreme Headquarters Allied Expeditionary Force, were sometimes delicate, due to the diverging interests. Changing circumstances made everything also somewhat unpredictable, such as the partial liberation of Holland. Ambitious plans to form divisions for the liberation of the Dutch East Indies had also to be scaled down. Dutch forces remained part of the Allied forces in Germany until spring 1946. In Holland the British Army assisted in particular with training and organization in the rebuilding of the Dutch Army, obviously based on the British concept. Later, when Marshall Aid got under way, the Army adopted a more American concept. This was also caused by some disagreement about the way to go, because the British Army was more geared to carrying out tasks in the colonies, and therefore different from most European armies. A clear vision for the future was also missing, but through WEU and NATO it was later firmly established that the Dutch Army would fit into the forces of the Atlantic Alliance.

The Dutch Navy did not have an easy time either in getting their future plans in order. They were strongly of the opinion that they should first make a substantial contribution to the liberation of the Dutch East Indies, and then rebuild a much bigger fleet than before. For the first task they considered 24 extra ships necessary. But the Joint COS Committee considered the request premature in April 1944 and suggested further dealings with the British chiefs of staff on the matter. Stretched as they were at the time by the war effort, they could only agree to provide an aircraft carrier in due course – which happened after the war. Only the formation of a Marine Brigade of about 5,000 men, started in the United States in October 1943, went ahead and this was completed in 1945. Rebuilding the Navy after the war became, apart from the British aircraft carrier, on the whole a national matter with some generous US assistance, but the excellent ties with the Royal

Navy continued to exist, and co-operation received renewed impetus when the WEU and NATO were created.

Last but not least, the plans for the air component started later than those for the other force components because of lack of expertise. The air community clearly aimed for an Air Force that would fit into an international structure, inter-operable with the RAF and therefore organized, equipped and trained by the RAF. A high-level committee, including Prince Bernhard, was tasked to map out the way ahead through consultation with the RAF which strongly supported the plans.

The majority of the committee were in favour of a strong independent Dutch Air Force, absorbing all existing elements, but the strong Navy and East Indies lobbies were against this. There were also ambitious plans for a large Air Force, but because of economic circumstances, progress in the post-war years was slow, although assistance by the RAF remained considerable. In the end an independent Air Force was born in March 1953, with the Navy keeping their maritime patrol and shipborne aircraft. It is no exaggeration to state that the RAF provided a cradle for the Dutch Air Force, and indeed an excellent one.

In summary it can be said that the plans for rebuilding the Dutch forces after the war were over-ambitious. Neither the Netherlands nor Great Britain had the economic resources on which they so heavily depended for assistance in this process. But British assistance was instrumental in getting the Dutch forces off the ground in the post-war years. The ill effects of neutrality had been overcome and the Netherlands were on a steady course to an alliance role.

CONCLUSION: INTEGRATION INTO WEU AND NATO

In conclusion, the Second World War was a crucial period for the Dutch armed forces. The contribution they made individually and collectively was of a high standard although due to the occupation of Holland and the Dutch East Indies, it can only be called modest in numbers.

But the main importance of this period lies in the transition from armed forces that had existed in neutral isolation for over a century, to becoming valuable members of an alliance which they are today. Since Germany invaded the Netherlands in May 1940, they have never looked back. Even before the end of the war the Netherlands concluded an economic treaty with Belgium and Luxembourg, creating the Benelux, soon followed by the Treaty of Brussels in 1948, establishing the Western European Union, including Britain, France and Benelux. Far-reaching commitments for mutual defence assistance were agreed in case of attack on one of the members. Work was soon started to create integrated staffs for future planning, but the appearance of the North Atlantic alliance soon overtook these developments. The WEU gave their members a solid basis for their participation in NATO. The initial set-up under the overall direction of the Council of Ministers and the Military Committee included Regional Planning Groups, one of which was for the WEU area. When General Eisenhower was appointed Supreme Allied Commander Europe this structure was changed basically to the shape it has today. The area of the North Atlantic Ocean was also placed under a US naval commander, but the WEU countries held on to their independence in the North Sea and Channel area in the Channel Command under a British admiral. The regional planning groups were replaced by truly integrated international staffs, based on the first models generated in the WEU. Since then integrated military planning in NATO has progressed steadily and at present we have reached the stage where long-term NATO force planning is becoming meaningful.

Today we find the Dutch Air Force solidly embedded with the RAF in NATO's Second Tactical Air Force commanded by a British Air Chief Marshal.

The Dutch Army is an integrated part of the Northern Army group, commanded by a British general, defending the northern half of the central sector of Europe. The Dutch Navy closely co-operates with the Royal Navy in the Atlantic and Channel commands. NATO can claim a success story in its 40th year of existence. But, as always, there remains room for improvement, and we can and must make progress in combined armaments planning to reduce the proliferation of incompatible weapons systems which still exist in NATO today. In this area Great Britain can also certainly do better.

I have described the developments in the co-operation of British and Dutch forces in Europe. I now hand the floor to Mr Scholte, who will cover the same subject for the Far East.

IMPERIAL ALLIES?
RELATIONS BETWEEN
BRITISH AND DUTCH ARMED
FORCES IN ASIA 1941–1946*

Jan Aart Scholte

INTRODUCTION

Rear-Admiral den Boeft has guided us through the relations between the British and the Netherlands armed forces during the Second World War in Europe. With this back-up paper the focus shifts away from that continent to the other main region of operations, the Pacific theatre. Rather different themes emerge with regard to the British–Dutch military bond in Asia. In Europe, these armed forces represented nation-states defending their 'homelands'; in Asia, they fought to preserve imperial claims which were becoming unsustainable. In Europe, their general experience of the war was one of victory and confident hope for a new and better post-war order; in Asia, the Allies' defeat of Japan came in the context of the decline and, not long thereafter, the end of colonial rule. Not surprisingly, perhaps, the relationship between the Dutch and British armed forces in the twilight of empire in Asia was not always a happy one. The frustrations of weakness and the insecurities of a period of change tended to make their relationship in Asia rather tense.

In this fleeting – and, it is perforce extremely fleeting – overview of collaboration and conflict between Dutch and British armed forces in the Far Eastern theatre of the Second World World War, I will first note the slow and halting emergence of the British–Dutch alliance against Japan in the late 1930s and early 1940s. Then I will review the

*The author is grateful for a grant from the University of Sussex which partly funded the preparation of this paper. The help and hospitality of Professor Dr Albert Kersten and his colleagues at the Rijksbureau voor Vaderlandse Geschiedenis were also invaluable.

experience of this Anglo-Dutch military partnership in terms of three phases: first, the campaigns of December 1941 to May 1942 which drove the British and Netherlands colonial regimes from most of South East Asia; second, their joint operations from positions in exile, between 1942 and the capitulation of Japan in August 1945; and third, the re-occupation of Indonesia by British and Netherlands armed forces, beginning with their first landings on Java and Sumatra in September–October 1945, and ending with the departure of the last British occupation troops from the Dutch colony in November 1946. The same broad theme of uneasy co-operation holds for each of these time periods.

THE FORMATION OF THE ALLIANCE

Although no British–Dutch military alliance against Japan was explicitly proclaimed before December 1941, the London and Hague governments had a long prior history of close ties in Asia. By the twentieth century the bond between Britain and the Netherlands in South East Asia was so long-standing and so deeply entrenched that many on both sides regarded it as given that the two states would align together to defend their imperial positions, even if this strategic connection had not been formalized in a treaty.

Dutch business figures and officials expressed concern to the British authorities regarding Japanese penetration of the Netherlands Indies as early as the time of the First World War. Military co-operation between the two states against a possible Japanese invasion was already discussed on a number of occasions between 1936 and 1940. However, no formal bilateral talks towards the formation of an alliance occurred at this time.

Following the Nazi incursion into Holland in May 1940, a British–Dutch alliance was sealed in Europe, but the mutual commitment was not yet extended to Asia as well at this juncture. After considerable debate amongst Dutch ministers during the summer of 1940, the Netherlands government raised the issue of a British–Dutch alliance in the Far East with the UK Foreign Office. By the autumn of 1941, the Dutch cabinet in exile had gone so far as to decide that it would regard a Japanese offensive against British or American territories in Asia as a *casus belli*, even though the Netherlands had received no similar assurances from either London or Washington in respect of the Indies.

On the UK side, meanwhile, although there was a general opinion that the Netherlands Indies were an important, even vital, British interest, the Churchill government gave no affirmative reply to the

Dutch overtures of 1940 and 1941 for a formal military bond. The prevailing view was that British power and resources were already overstretched, and that the UK's strategic priorities should be accorded to Europe and the Middle East before the Pacific. London moreover argued that any British promises regarding the Dutch East Indies would be empty so long as the US government maintained an ambiguous policy with regard to Japanese expansion.

For its part, Washington remained largely unresponsive to both the Dutch and the British approaches for military collaboration in Asia between the three states. It was not until 1 December 1941 that President Roosevelt finally declared to the UK Ambassador to Washington 'that in the case of direct attack on ourselves or the Dutch we should obviously be all together'. The British Foreign Office thereupon immediately proffered a military guarantee in Asia to the Netherlands government. However, Japanese forces attacked Pearl Harbor and Malaya a few days later, before any specific alliance arrangements could be concluded.

This is by no means to say that Dutch–British military collaboration was entirely absent in Asia during the years leading up to the Japanese offensive of 1941–42. Indeed, it appears that the respective Army and Navy commanders in Singapore, Batavia and Bandung were generally quite willing, even eager, to develop bilateral co-operation, even if their civilian superiors refused to formalize the relationship. Joint British–Dutch strategic planning in South East Asia began in November 1940. However, the resulting schemes for co-ordinated military movements were fairly restricted in both scope and detail, especially with regard to land operations. Moreover, the British government refused to confirm even these limited arrangements in the absence of a complementary American strategic commitment.

In sum, then, collaboration between the Dutch and British armed forces in Asia was quite limited prior to December 1941, in spite of ample indication that a Japanese invasion of their colonies was possible, if not probable. Thus Britain's traditional pose as the protector of the Netherlands Empire in Indonesia had already developed shaky foundations even before the outbreak of war. True, there was never any suggestion that Britain and the Netherlands would be on opposite sides in a Pacific War. However, active military co-operation – whether in the form of alliance arrangements, strategic plans, shared facilities, co-ordinated procurement, combined training, or joint exercises – was largely absent, too. The co-ordination of Dutch and British military efforts was therefore for the most part a matter of improvization when global war came to the Pacific in December 1941.

JAPANESE INVASION AND OCCUPATION, DECEMBER 1941–MARCH 1942

The campaigns in South East Asia between December 1941 and March 1942 were, in a word, a débâcle for the new British–Dutch military partnership. The Allies' land forces abandoned the Malay Peninsula at the end of January after a seven-week campaign. Presumptions about Singapore were shattered when that island fell to the Japanese invaders in less than one week on 15 February. The Netherlands Indies commander ordered the Army on Java to surrender on 9 March, eight days after Japanese units had landed on the main island of the Dutch colony. The Royal Netherlands Indies Army (the KNIL) capitulated in Sumatra on 28 March. Thus, with the exception of a few isolated enclaves which remained in Dutch hands, three centuries of European empire in insular South East Asia were ended in three months.

By a crude quantitative comparison, the strength in troops and weaponry of the invading Japanese armies would not seem to have been superior to that of the combined Allied forces. The question might thus be raised whether – as some commentators suggested at the time – earlier and more thoroughgoing Dutch–British military collaboration could have allowed Allied resources to be employed more effectively, thereby significantly changing the course of the battles in 1941–42. Yet there were so many other factors working against the tardily concluded alliance – such as poor intelligence, misjudgements with regard to tactics, inappropriate training and organizational structures of the armies, demoralization of the troops, the relative absence of support from the autochthonous populations of Malaya and Indonesia for the beleaguered imperial forces, and so on – that it seems unlikely that a closer British–Dutch military bond could have altered the outcome very much.

It was certainly the case that British–Dutch relations were sometimes strained during the short and rather desperate defence of their colonies in South East Asia. For example, the Dutch government very much resented having been excluded from the British–American deliberations which produced the combined American–British–Dutch–Australian Command (ABDA) to direct operations against Japan in the South West Pacific. Relations between Netherlands and British staff officers at ABDA headquarters, hastily set up in Java in January 1942, appear to have been amicable for the most part. However, the operation of the command was hampered by various technical and strategic mismatches between the Allies. Fraught with organizational problems and undermined by the sorry performance of its forces in the field, ABDA was disbanded within six weeks of its creation. Many Dutch in the Indies felt that the British left them in the lurch with the early dissolution of the Allied command: Java fell a fortnight later.

The British force commanders in South East Asia made a number of strong expressions of gratitude for the willingness of the Netherlands armed forces to participate in the Allied defence of Malaya in 1941–42. On the whole, however, the British military were impressed more by their Dutch ally's goodwill than by the concrete contributions that Indies forces made to resisting the Japanese advance down the Malayan Peninsula.

For their part, the Dutch authorities were generally disappointed with the amount, and in some cases even the spirit, of British military assistance to the Netherlands Indies in early 1942. Some Netherlands officers drew what they saw to be a stark contrast between large and noble support for the British by the Dutch in Malaya on the one hand and desertion of the Dutch by the British in Java on the other. Meanwhile, a number of British accounts of the Japanese invasion of Java highlighted the defeatism of Dutch forces as one of the chief causes of the swift collapse of Allied resistance on the island.

Yet allocations of blame between the Allies of this kind do little to explain the rapid fall of the British and Dutch colonies in South East Asia before the Japanese advance of 1941–42. Such mutual recriminations as there were seem mainly to reflect the two Allies' frustrations at their weakness and defeat. A more fundamental cause of the rout would appear to be that the Netherlands and British Empires were – like worldwide European colonialism in general – on the wane. It seems unlikely that the adoption of an alternative military strategy or different tactics by the allied British and Dutch forces during the months of this short campaign would have prevented the Japanese occupation of the region.

RELATIONS IN EXILE, MARCH 1942–AUGUST 1945

After the fall of Java, the venue of the British–Dutch military relationship in the Far Eastern theatre of Second World War moved from South East Asia to positions of exile in Ceylon, India and Australia. The Netherlands armed forces now found themselves in an even weaker position in relation to their British, and still more to their American, ally. Most of the Dutch Royal Navy and a substantial part of the Indies merchant marine had been lost in the campaign of 1941–42. Only a small portion of the Indies Air Forces remained. And no more than a few hundred KNIL troops managed to escape to Australia ahead of the Japanese advance.

With these extremely limited resources, the Dutch armed forces in exile in Asia could give their British ally little support in the operations to recover the imperial territories. The only two notable Netherlands contributions to the Allied military effort came in the form of leases of Dutch merchant shipping and the participation of evacuated Indies Air Force aircrew in Allied bombing raids. Yet even those few parts of the Indonesian archipelago which the Allies recovered before the Japanese surrender were re-occupied by armies which were almost entirely American and Australian in composition. Allied naval attacks on Japanese-held Indonesia, carried out under British and American direction from the middle of 1943 onwards, also involved only minor Dutch participation.

This position of weakness and dependence in military affairs was often highly frustrating for the Dutch forces in exile. The Netherlands commanders in Asia henceforth did not even direct their own small forces: this competence was transferred to British and American military chiefs. The Dutch moreover found themselves on the sidelines of Allied decision-taking. Netherlands Indies territory was now operationally divided between the American-led South West Pacific Area Command and the British forces' Indian theatre, reorganized as South East Asia Command (SEAC) in late 1943. The Dutch government's protestations that all of their colony should be kept within a single Allied command region went unheeded. At the end of the war against Japan, on 15 August 1945, SEAC's territory was suddenly extended eastwards to cover the whole of the Indonesian archipelago. With regard to this critical move, too – one which was to have far-reaching consequences for the British–Dutch military relationship in colonial South East Asia in the wake of the Second World War – Netherlands officials were shut out of the decision-taking.

Not only were the Dutch authorities often disheartened by their subordinate position to the British and the Americans in the alliance structure in Asia; they were also unhappy about a number of the policies which the Allied commands adopted. For instance, the re-capture of the Netherlands Indies was consistently accorded the lowest priority amongst the Allied objectives in South East Asia. However, having only negligible military or other resources of their own, there was little that the Dutch could do to alter this situation.

The Dutch armed forces in exile did seek to improve their position somewhat by attempting to form new Netherlands military units for the eastern theatre, but these schemes made little headway. During the second half of 1943, Dutch staff officers drafted proposals (a) to rebuild the Netherlands Royal Navy; (b) to construct an Expeditionary Force to participate in the war against Japan; and (c) to form new Internal Security battalions to support the colonial regime in the Indies after re-occupation. The naval plan got nowhere with the British–American Combined Chiefs of Staff, and implementation of the scheme for the Expeditionary Force, which would be equipped and trained by the British Army, did not come into full swing until 5 August 1945: that is, just before the Japanese capitulation. The Dutch had pressed the British commanders to begin the construction of the Expeditionary Force earlier, but without success. The plan to train Internal Security battalions similarly made little progress during the period of exile. Netherlands Indies authorities repeatedly petitioned the Combined Chiefs of Staff for the necessary shipping space from Europe to Australia, where the training was to take place, but these pleas went largely unanswered. As a result, only a handful of Dutch Army troops were available to receive the Japanese surrender in Indonesia in the autumn of 1945. This fact, coupled with the change in Allied command boundaries on 15 August, meant that the bulk of the forces for the post-war re-occupation of the Indies had to be drawn from British rather than Dutch armies. Needless to say, the Netherlands authorities were not happy with this situation, and some of them specifically faulted British policies with regard to troop training and transport for creating the dilemma.

Reviewing the 1942–45 period of exile, it cannot be said that the British military were unsympathetic to the predicament of their much-weakened Dutch ally. However, in Asia as well as in Europe, the Netherlands armed forces were so small that they were easily over-looked in Allied policy-making. Moreover, British officers had problems enough of their own which distracted them from attending to Dutch desires in the Far Eastern theatre. The resources of the British Empire too were being sorely depleted by the war, and the longer the hostilities against Japan continued, the more the British armed forces found themselves in a position of dependency on the United States. The Dutch authorities were looking to Britain to play patron to the Netherlands Empire in Asia, but the UK no longer disposed of the means to fulfil that former role.

POST-WAR RE-OCCUPATION,
SEPTEMBER 1945–NOVEMBER 1946

As has been indicated above, relations between the British and Dutch armed forces in the Second World War in Asia did not always follow an easy course before and during the hostilities with Japan. However, this partnership experienced what was perhaps its most difficult stage with the Allied re-occupation of Indonesia in 1945–46. As noted earlier, the British-led South East Asia Command was given responsibility for the entire Indonesian archipelago at the very moment of the Japanese capitulation. Yet SEAC had no plans ready for landing on and administering the Indonesian islands aside from Sumatra, and the command lacked adequate numbers of Dutch, or even British, troops to undertake the tasks of re-occupation. Moreoever, only very limited civilian supplies had been stockpiled to meet the emergency requirements of the local population, many of whom were left destitute by the war. And SEAC had next to no intelligence available concerning the current situation in the territory which it was newly mandated to control. On top of all these problems, SEAC also had to contend with a large anti-colonial uprising and a variety of attendant social revolutionary movements which erupted in Indonesia when Japan surrendered. Given these explosive circumstances, in which the Dutch and British armed forces became more aware than ever before of their limited power in colonial Asia, it is not surprising that the Second World War alliance between them now went through its most trying phase.

For one thing, many Netherlanders were distressed about SEAC's slow despatch of occupation troops to Indonesia. Once again, Java and Sumatra came at the bottom of the list of priorities, behind the shipment of contingents to Burma, Singapore, Malaya, Hong Kong and other Chinese ports, Japan itself, Indo-China and Siam. The arrival of Allied troops in Indonesia was further delayed by the order of General Douglas MacArthur, the Supreme Commander Allied Powers in the Far East, that no re-occupation of Japanese-held territory should be undertaken before the general surrender document had been signed in Tokyo. As a result of these decisions, the first Allied troops did not disembark on Java until 29 September: that is, six weeks after Hirohito's broadcast and the Indonesian nationalists' declaration of independence. Indeed, SEAC did not begin to form a command organization for the occupation of Indonesia until Allied Forces Netherlands East Indies (AFNEI) was created at the end of September. There were at the time many Dutch recriminations against the British armed forces for their slow arrival in the Indies in the autumn of 1945. It was widely maintained that SEAC's tardiness had allowed what most Netherlanders then regarded as a 'collaborationist' Indonesian nationalist regime, the newly proclaimed Republic of

Indonesia, to establish its roots. On the other hand, it can equally be argued that, without the support of the British armed forces, the Dutch colonial administration, having only minimal military and other resources of its own, could not have established the foothold in Java and Sumatra that it did in the autumn of 1945.

Many Dutch were further dismayed by the narrow brief which the British gave to the AFNEI force. AFNEI limited its presence in Java and Sumatra to half a dozen major towns: the re-occupation of the rest of the two islands was left to the Dutch themselves. Moreover, the scope of AFNEI's responsibilities was restricted to that of (a) taking the Japanese surrender of the Indies; (b) disarming the enemy troops and organizing their repatriation to Japan; and (c) rescuing the Allied prisoners of war and civilian internees. SEAC accepted no further responsibilities regarding the re-establishment of Dutch colonial administration in Indonesia. These and other British decisions produced what the leader of the Indies government later described as a 'black cloud of estrangement from our closest ally' in many Dutch quarters.

Yet the Dutch condemnations of AFNEI and SEAC which were widespread in 1945–46 took little account of Britain's precarious position in Indonesia and in the world generally at that moment. As Ernest Bevin, Britain's Foreign Secretary, lamented when opening his remarks to the House of Commons concerning UK involvement in Indonesia, 'All the world is in trouble, and I have to deal with all the troubles at once.' Moreover, the British government had to contend with the considerable sympathy which existed abroad for the cause of Indonesian nationalism. From a number of domestic quarters, too, the Attlee government faced persistent charges that the AFNEI occupation of Indonesia amounted to a 'colonialist' intervention. Further, the great majority of the Allied occupation troops were drawn from the Indian Army, and the British imperial authorities in Delhi were under much pressure from nationalists there to halt the use of Indian troops for, as the National Congress leader, Jawaharlal Nehru put it, 'doing Britain's dirty work' against fellow Asians in Indonesia. In short, whatever their formal obligations to their Dutch ally may have been, the British armed forces were constrained by the circumstances to disappoint Dutch hopes and expectations of a full restoration of Netherlands authority in the Indies by the British military.

On the other hand, it should not be concluded that British forces carried out a decidedly anti-Dutch, anti-imperial policy in Indonesia in 1945–46. On the contrary, after adopting something of a wait-and-see attitude during the first month after their arrival, SEAC troops took many actions to contain the nationalist Republic and to suppress some of the more violently anti-Dutch groups on Java and Sumatra. In total, AFNEI suffered 2,400 British–Indian and British killed and wounded during the 14 months that the Command operated in Indonesia. The cost to the British Exchequer of maintaining the garrison in Java and Sumatra during this period reached 15 million in direct expenditure alone.

The British military also did much at this time to prepare the Dutch armed forces to take over from AFNEI in Indonesia. For instance, SEAC trained and equipped many recently released Dutch wartime prisoners in Malaya, Singapore, Indo-China and Siam. In addition, nearly 11,000 Dutch officers and other ranks were trained in the UK during 1946. Furthermore, when the British and British–Indian units departed from Java and Sumatra between March and November 1946, they left behind sufficient munitions and stores for an army of 62,000. It was thus no gross exaggeration to conclude, as one Netherlands minister is reported to have told a press conference at the time, that there would not have been a single Dutch soldier in Indonesia had Britain not provided the equipment.

As Netherlands troop strength grew, control in the areas occupied by the Allies was gradually handed over from the British military command to Dutch civilian government. The transfer of authority was completed in Borneo and eastern Indonesia in July 1946, and in Java and Sumatra on 30 November. A final dispute in the rather troubled British–Dutch military relationship in South East Asia in the Second World War concerned the speed with which their joint operations were terminated. SEAC began to reduce British–Indian troop strength in Indonesia as soon as Dutch reinforcements began arriving in Java. The Netherlands government complained that the British exodus was premature; however, the UK government felt that post-surrender tasks should henceforth be undertaken using Dutch troops. On 30 November the last British soldier departed from the island, and with that step SEAC, the final remaining Allied command of the Second World War, could be dissolved.

CONCLUSION

So the relations between British and Netherlands forces in the war against Japan in many ways do not form the happiest chapter in the history of British–Dutch collaboration. While the wartime link in Asia was an intimate one, and included a substantial measure of co-operation, considerable conflict is no less apparent to the historian who looks back on this relationship nearly half a century later. For the British, the link with the Dutch in South East Asia was generally seen as an unwelcome added burden for their already overstretched empire. British armed forces lacked the resources to make good a guarantee of the Netherlands Indies; and it was not thought that the Dutch military in Asia had a significant contribution to make first to the defence and later to the re-occupation of British imperial territories in the region. In contrast, the Dutch generally held the expectation that Britain would, as in the past, underwrite their imperial claims in the Indonesian archipelago. There was thus considerable disappointment in Dutch quarters when the United Kingdom, first, did not conclude a military alliance with the Netherlands in Asia prior to December 1941; second, when British armed forces retreated – overhastily in some Dutch eyes – from Java in early 1942; third, when British decision-takers did not accord a high priority to the re-occupation of the Indies during the rest of the war against Japan; and finally, when British armed forces were not employed to the full in order to help reinstate the Dutch colonial regime in Indonesia after the Japanese capitulation.

Yet, problematic though this military relationship may have been in many respects, neither side – the British nor the Dutch – can really be 'blamed' for the limitations and the failures of their collaboration in the Second World War in Asia. Even a completely harmonious relationship between them and a full commitment of their respective military resources to each other would not, one suspects, have allowed them to perpetuate their imperial administrations in South East Asia beyond the middle of the twentieth century. Colonial regimes were passing from the world scene, and British and Netherlands armed forces had the experience – generally for them an unhappy one – of discovering that fact together. It is indicative of the strength of the underlying British–Dutch bond, however, that these strains in Asia during the 1940s did not undermine the wider partnership between London and The Hague. At the same time that the two states withdrew their armed forces from South East Asia, they consolidated a military partnership of unprecedented closeness in Europe, as Rear-Admiral den Boeft has indicated in his address.

DISCUSSION

Dominic Flessati

Did the pre-war Dutch government assume that its posture of neutrality applied in the Far East?

Rear-Admiral den Boeft

Well, in fact, in the beginning it applied all over the world. It was fairly clear, of course, that if anything happened it would occur first in Europe. But the posture was really that they wanted it to last until the year 2000. That was what the people hoped; they had succeeded in sticking to neutrality for 127 years, and although the circumstances had changed, the majority still hoped that it would blow over. After the German invasion groups of people, like the Minister of Foreign Affairs, fairly quickly turned away from the idea of applying the same system to the Dutch East Indies (Indonesia). And there were others – the Queen, for example – who also had different ideas; so after May 1940 the neutrality posture changed.

Jan Aart Scholte

Neutrality was a policy in the Far East as well as in Europe. It was one Netherlands kingdom, and neutrality applied to the whole. In the summer of 1940, there were quite a few discussions back and forth, and in fact the Minister for the Colonies and several of his leading officials were actually still inclined to favour the fairly defeatist wish to stay neutral in East Asia as well. When they finally approached the British, hesitatingly, for an alliance to be extended to Asia, the British answer was, 'No, we cannot.' So the Dutch fell back on the position, 'Well we can't commit ourselves either.' There was a will after, say, about October 1940 to commit to an alliance and to abandon neutrality in East Asia as well as in Europe, but not before that, and there was hesitation before the move away from neutrality.

Dominic Flessati

May I then ask a supplementary question – did the Dutch fight any campaigns in the Far East between the battle of Waterloo and 1941?

Jan Aart Scholte

Those were not international campaigns, they were colonial wars. This is an important point, since it ties in with the earlier comment about defeatism, and part of the reason I think for the defeatism of the Dutch forces, such as there was, derived from their being an internal security force. They were not organized and they didn't have the plans or the equipment for defence against a foreign invasion; and so once the naval and air cover on which they depended was wiped out within a couple of weeks, what did they do? One can say what they might have done, or should have done. I don't know. There are also stories that as the Japanese forces approached the British contingents in Java at the time ran for the hills to try and let the Dutch commander defend what was left of it. One has to remember that the Dutch forces had little support from the internal population, they had few plans and things ready, and so, one wonders if they could have been anything but defeatist.

Dominic Flessati

I'd just like to comment, that I carry away from this session the notion – rather new, to me – of a neutral empire. It strikes me as rather bizarre.

Jan Aart Scholte

Yes, but if it succeeds for over a century, then whether bizarre or not, it looks attractive to some people.

Chairman

Has Mr Flessati considered the case of the neutral empire of the Soviet Union, 1939–41?

Laurence Le Quesne

A short factual question. What proportion of the Netherlands armed forces in the Indian East Indies in 1941 were native troops?

Jan Aart Scholte

I can't commit myself on that, because I am not entirely sure of actual numbers, but what I can say is that the dividing line is sometimes a bit thin in the Netherlands Indies, because there was a lot of intermarriage, and so for many people, where do you put them? Also, there was a question of citizenship; some who were racially Indonesians were Netherlands by citizenship and nationality, so there were all sorts of problems in that area. The other thing is that Indonesians are not one nationality, or were certainly not at that time, and so there was a division of the island's population into many different groups. Just as the British in Burma tended to draw on the Karens and in Malaya on the Chinese, there tends to be a tradition in Empire to draw on one or other of the ethnic groups. In Indonesia it was the Ambonese who were often drawn into the Netherlands East Indies Army. They were therefore quite antagonistic towards the other majority groups, such as the Javanese and the rest, and they also held themselves in a certain esteem and were somewhat affiliated to the Netherlands Indies regime. There was not much question of their deserting, as a matter of fact.

CHAPTER THREE

HOW DUTCH RESISTANCE WAS ORGANIZED

Harry Paape

INTRODUCTION

It was eight o'clock in the morning of Friday 10 May 1940. Already for the past four hours German troops had been pouring into the Netherlands across its Eastern border. The whole of Holland had been woken up hours before by the noise of huge numbers of German aeroplanes. German aircraft had landed on the aerodromes in the west of the country, especially in the neighbourhood of the centre of government at The Hague and near Rotterdam while parachutists had been dropped in the same areas. One of the German intentions, to capture members of the Royal House and the government in the first hours, had actually failed. This was due to the fact that the plan of attack, including routes to the palace and to government centres, had been discovered in a crashed German aircraft.

The Air-attack Warning Service had for hours been passing on the most alarming reports through the radio. The two Dutch broadcast transmitters normally came on the air at eight o'clock – and so they did on this day too. Immediately after the time signal, the well-known voice of one of the news-readers started to read out a proclamation from Queen Wilhelmina:

> After our country has, with scrupulous conscientiousness preserved strict neutrality for all these months, and whilst we had no intention other than to adhere to this absolutely and consistently, the German Army last night, without the slightest warning, launched a sudden attack on our territory. This occurred in spite of the solemn undertaking that the neutrality of our country would be respected as long as we ourselves maintained it. I hereby

issue a fiery protest against this unexampled violation of good faith and against the outrage done to the conduct customary between civilized nations. I and my government will now also do our duty. All of you must do yours, everywhere and in all circumstances, each one in the place assigned to you, with the utmost vigilance and with the tranquillity of mind and the assurance to which a clear conscience gives you every right.

(signed) Wilhelmina

It is a moving and impressive text. At the same time, however, it was a naive text with its reference and appeal to Dutch neutrality, the expression of anger that the attack had not been preceded by a proper declaration of war and the indignation at 'solemn undertakings' given earlier.

Naivety, insufficient insight – even after seven years of the Hitler regime in Germany – into the nature of National Socialism and its inevitable consequences. It was a naivety which, especially during the first years of the German occupation of Holland, was to play a part both among the great majority of the Dutch population and the slowly emerging resistance.

In the image of the occupied Netherlands, as this was gradually to develop, a number of factors play a role, and these are of particular significance when considering the growth, the structure and the activities of the resistance. I shall briefly indicate them:

(1) Since the Napoleonic period, the Netherlands had not experienced any war or any occupation of its territory by a foreign power.

(2) As a consequence of a long tradition of neutrality, there was in the Netherlands, in contrast to Belgium and France for example, no experience whatever of underground activities. No one had the faintest notion of underground techniques and tactics. Everything had to be learned in the hard experience of the occupation. No preparations had ever been made.

(3) Compared with the other territories occupied by Germany, Holland was both geographically and logistically ill-suited to underground activities, let alone actions by armed resistance groups. In an area of little more than 30,000 square kilometres, nearly nine million people lived closely together. Nearly all the land was cultivated; there were scarcely any forests of an appreciable size; the highest 'mountain' rose but 300 metres above sea-level. The land was intersected by a dense railway network and by innumerable roads, mostly of excellent quality. A rural telephone system existed, which extended into the smallest villages. The organization of a semi-permanent armed resis-

tance group, after the model of the French 'Maquis', was a practical impossibility – quite apart from the fact that until well into 1942 the Dutch resistance had hardly any serviceable weapons at its disposal. On the other hand, the geographical situation enabled the army units and police troops of the German occupiers to appear within a few hours at any place where it was considered desirable or necessary.

(4) At the same time, Holland was the most isolated of all those western European countries occupied by the Nazis. Beyond the long eastern frontier lay Germany; the Scandinavian countries, of which only Sweden was not occupied by the Germans, could only be reached by sea, and the western border, which provided the only route to England, faced the North Sea. This coastal area, mainly dunes and beaches, was guarded by the Germans, both on land and by patrol-boats in the waters alongside, and from 1943 Dutch people were forbidden to enter the entire coastal zone. In the south, before neutral territory could be reached on the road to England, three borders had to be crossed – or four if one includes the demarcation line between occupied and unoccupied France.

In my view it must be seen as a singular mark of initiative and courage that in the years 1940–44 about 2,000 Dutchmen succeeded in escaping to England from their occupied homeland in order to take up posts in the administration of the Netherlands government, now settled in London, or to serve in the merchant navy or the Netherlands Army units which, under the name 'Princess Irene Brigade' had been brought into existence. At the start the brigade consisted of Dutch soldiers who had escaped to England in 1940, supplemented later by other Dutchmen who had remained in the free world. How many of those who attempted to escape to England from occupied Holland drowned in their bid to cross the North Sea, or how many fell into German hands on their long journey (and this brought with it at least one year in a concentration camp), I can only estimate; some hundreds drowned and about twice as many were arrested while on their overland routes. As a general proportion, one out of every three or four attempts was unsuccessful.

I now return to May 1940. After five days of fighting between the inadequately armed Dutch forces, ill-prepared for a modern war, and the superior German powers, culminating in the terror-bombing of Holland's second town, Rotterdam, and the subsequent German threat that other Dutch towns would also be subjected to this fate, the Dutch Commander-in-Chief brought the fighting to an end. The articles of surrender were signed on the following day, 15 May 1940.

RESISTANCE: THE BEGINNING

In the evening of 14 May, four men were sitting together in a small town not far from Rotterdam. That afternoon they had seen Rotterdam burning. They had gone there together, had been able to offer some help here and there, and had felt great anger rising against the perpetrators of this evil. They had only just got back when they heard the report on the radio that the fighting was to end. Grief and anger struggled within them for supremacy. 'One should be able to do something about this riff-raff; help to throw them out again,' one of them sighed. They all nodded. 'Yes. But what?'

Their question was quickly answered. In a neighbouring parish there lived a teacher whom they all knew. When they voiced their sorrow to him, they found that he shared their feelings, and the following evening he provided the answer to their question. He took a pen and a writing-pad and wrote a message: a call to resistance. He copied the text about ten times and posted these, while his son pushed other copies into letter-boxes in the neighbourhood.

This message has been lost. However, his second message, dated 18 May 1940, has been preserved. It is headed 'Geuzen Action – Message Number Two.' It contained, first of all, a notice which makes it clear that the writer had even then understood that underground activity must seek to mislead the enemy. It starts: 'The Geuzen action has started on 15 May in Amsterdam', instead of his real place of residence. Moreover, he provided evidence that he had some idea of what awaited the people of the Netherlands: 'All our stores will be taken away: food, clothing, shoes ... Our young people will be forced to work elsewhere for the usurper' (of course at that time no one had heard of *Arbeits-einsatz*, forced labour). Then the writer pointed to a character from Dutch sixteenth-century history who would be well-known to every Dutchman: the cruel governor appointed by Philip II of Spain and Margaret of Parma: 'We'll soon be getting a new Duke of Alva with executions and the inquisition.' The name which the teacher had given to his action was also based on the same period; the very first who in 1572 wrested a small Dutch town from the domination of the Spaniards were the freebooting seamen who operated under the title of *Water-geuzen*, sea beggars.

'Courage and trust', continued the writer. 'The Geuzen action will gradually bring an organization into being, and one day we will recapture our liberty, just as happened in the 80-years war [1568–1648]. Our country shall not become a part of Germany!'

There followed an exhortation to copy out several times the papers that had been received and distribute them further. 'Secret agents are being placed everywhere. You will soon hear more. Let everyone do his duty as a Geus!'

The teacher, Bernard Ijzerdraat, promised more and pretended to more than he could make come true. During the month of May, he wrote one Geuzen message after the other, but that was as far as it went, until about the end of the month, when he received a visit from a former colleague. This man was much more practical than Ijzerdraat. He was not only an enthusiast, but wanted much more: sabotage and espionage, and saw the need to pass information of all kinds to England.

The colleague now took the lead. He made contact with the other four men who reacted equally enthusiastically. The hand-written sheets of paper were replaced by typed ones, and shortly these became stencilled mini-newspapers which contained news apart from the exhortations to the readers to start practising resistance: sabotage, spying, but above all to recruit new members for the Geuzen group: tens, hundreds, several thousands, mainly from the area of Rotterdam and district, but also from elsewhere: The Hague, Leiden, Amsterdam and other places.

What did they really do? The news-sheet was produced by a small group; a further number were concerned with the distribution; there were others, particularly from the enterprise group, who undertook simple sabotage: the cutting of German telephone wires and on one occasion the cable of a German searchlight to safeguard over-flying British aircraft.

Some drawings were made of the sites of searchlights and anti-aircraft guns; simple sabotage acts hit German ships which lay at berths for maintenance, repair and reconstruction. That's where it stopped; but the Army of Geuzen grew. The oath of secrecy which had to be sworn when membership was accepted was now and again forgotten. During the summer and autumn, one could sometimes hear whispering in trams and trains; 'The Geuzen ... sabotage ... spying ... England.'

Of course, this could not continue to prosper, and already in November 1940 it went wrong. The proud indiscretions of a young man who had only just been admitted to membership led in November 1940 to the arrest of more than 200 Geuzen, among them all those who had been involved in special enterprises.

OPEN RESISTANCE: ONE DEMONSTRATION AND THREE MASS-STRIKES

I am aware of the fact that in Great Britain knowledge concerning the details, and even the general outlines of the period of occupation of the Netherlands and of the resistance is comparatively slight, both among the general public and among historians; much slighter than knowledge of like facts in most of the other countries occupied by Nazi Germany. It is clear that the language problem has here played the most significant part.

In the very comprehensive international library of my institute (we believe it to be the largest specialized library in the world dealing with the Second World War) one cannot find a single monograph by a British historian which deals with the resistance in the Netherlands.

It therefore appears proper to me to provide you with a picture – brief and sketchy though it may be – of developments, both of the policies of the occupying power and of the actions and reactions of the population of the Netherlands. I intend to do this with reference to one mass-demonstration and three large-scale strikes which in their nature and extent have no parallel in the history of occupied Europe.

The Austrian Nazi, Dr Arthur Seyss-Inquart, who was appointed by Hitler as *Reichskommissar* (Governor-General) for the occupied Netherlands and Head of the civil occupation administration, gave an inaugural address in the Hague on 29 May 1940. From this it became obvious that he saw it as his most important task to persuade (not to force) the Dutch people – after all a people of Germanic brothers – to embrace National Socialism. It was a very soft approach which, however, in the course of the years deteriorated until there was a regime to which only the terms 'complete lawlessness' and 'terror' can be suitably applied. In the first period, however, some optimism on the Dutch side could be justified for, in contrast to the case of the French and Belgians, Seyss-Inquart arranged for all Dutch prisoners of war to be released as early as June 1940.

Carnation Day

Seyss-Inquart had to suffer his first disappointment as early as 29 June 1940 on the birthday of Prince Bernhard. Before the war there existed the custom (which incidentally still exists) of celebrating the birthdays of members of the Royal Family with solemn ceremonies, but also with some exuberance. This was to happen now for a member of the Royal

Family who had been forced to live in exile overseas. From shortly after his arrival in Holland, the Prince had adopted the habit on all public occasions of wearing a white carnation. Without preparation, without consultation, without organization, there appeared on the morning of his birthday vases with one or more white carnations in the windows of innumerable dwellings in towns and villages, and if carnations could not be obtained, there were orange blossoms. White carnations and orange blossom decorations were also worn everywhere in the streets. In Amsterdam, it came to a large-scale demonstration at the monument to Queen Wilhelmina's mother, who had died in 1934. Many hundreds of people almost buried the monument under flowers, again white carnations or orange blossoms; thousands came to watch and, almost automatically, a birthday atmosphere developed just as in the years before the war. In The Hague, the Court Chamberlain of the Royal Palace laid ready the customary congratulatory register, and people came from all over the town to the Palace to sign it, and long queues formed of those waiting to sign.

The reaction of the Germans was moderate; there were no interventions in the demonstrations on that day. Merely (and one must use that word in the light of what would eventually happen), the former Commander-in-Chief of the Dutch forces, General Winkelman, was taken away as a prisoner of war; the Mayor of The Hague was dismissed and two organizers of the demonstration were arrested, but were released after some months. Demonstrations on the forthcoming occasion of the royal birthday of Queen Wilhelmina on 31 August were strictly forbidden.

In the meantime, the first measures against the Jews, albeit to a limited extent, had already been carried out. In the autumn, the Germans went a step further: all Jewish officials had to be dismissed. This fate also befell some professors at the University of Leiden and their dismissal led to a large demonstration in the hall of the university, where one of their colleagues gave a masterly address. After this, the multitude in the large chock-full room spontaneously burst into the National Anthem, a most profound and moving experience. The professor was arrested and kept in prison for 'only' eight months.

Already some days earlier, the students of the Technical University of Delft had decided to go on strike; in Leiden the same decision was reached. One day later, after Delft, the University of Leiden was also closed down on the orders of the Germans.

These were all the measures that were taken. It would be the last occasion that a reaction from the German side could be considered as falling under the heading of the maintenance of peace and good order in the occupied territory without moving towards the extremes of terrorization.

The February Strikes, 1941

Three months later, they were to drop their masks fully; actually in two phases, one shortly after the other. A new development in the measures against the Jews provided the first inducement. Instigated by the Germans, uniformed Dutch Nazis, who had placed themselves alongside the Germans with their unconditional support and were now wholly outside Dutch society, started to indulge in provocative activities against Jewish citizens. They forced the owners of cafés and restaurants in the centre of Amsterdam to put up signs saying: 'Jews not wanted', provoked fights and caused damage in cafés which Jews were in the habit of visiting. They marched into the Jewish quarter in the old centre of the town and molested its Jewish inhabitants. The Jews defended themselves vehemently and were assisted by workers from other neighbourhoods; during the fights, one of the Nazis was killed. The disturbances became continuous, as did the provocations and the destruction caused by the Nazis, which spread to other parts of the city.

In an ice-cream parlour in the south of the city, owned by two German-Jewish emigrants, the windows had also been smashed by members of the NSB (the Dutch Nazi organization), and further provocation was anticipated. A strong-arm squad consisting of Jews and non-Jews waited inside, prepared for anything; they had a bottle of ammonia gas which stood ready to spray into the faces of possible attackers. The blinds had been drawn over the windows. One evening there were loud thumps on the door and those inside thought it was the Dutch Nazis. The ammonia gas cylinder was turned on, and they all took to their heels. However, it turned out to have been a patrol of German *Sicherheitspolizei* (security police). The Germans kicked the door in, the ammonia drove them back for a short time, and then they found the premises empty. In the next house they came across the members of the strong-arm squad, and a short time later the two owners were arrested in the flat of one of them. All were seriously maltreated.

Three days later, on 22 February, the Germans took their revenge with the personal agreement of Himmler, the *Reichsführer* – leader – of the SS. It was Saturday afternoon. Six hundred *Ordnungspolizisten*, regular German police, hermetically sealed off the old Jewish quarter. During that afternoon and the following morning, 400 young Jewish men, mostly between 20 and 35 years old, were arrested, ill-treated and taken away to Buchenwald concentration camp. Forty of them died there in the next four months. The others were transferred in June to the extermination camp Mauthausen, and before the end of the year only one of them remained alive. He had succeeded, with the help of fellow-prisoners, in remaining hidden in the tuberculosis block and he managed to survive the war.

News of these round-ups had immediately spread throughout the whole town; Amsterdam seethed with indignation, fury and yet a feeling of impotence. Were they really impotent? Some communist workers, on the evening of that Saturday, immediately reached for the traditional weapon: the strike. Preparations were quickly made. On Monday evening, in a square in one of the working-class areas, a large, ostentatious meeting took place which issued a call to strike. No German was to be seen. By Tuesday morning, 25 February, everything had been arranged. In the tram-depots, drivers were called on to strike, and they did not refuse. The call to strike spread among the shipyards and other large industrial works in the north of the town; within a short time, work here also ceased, and a large crowd of strikers from Amsterdam-North marched into the city-centre. The number of strikers continued to grow. Businesses and workshops, offices, stores and shops all emptied and closed their doors. Within a few hours, the strike had taken on a general character and large crowds remained in the town walking around shouting and singing. In the afternoon, it became known that strikes were also taking place elsewhere in the environs of the capital; the rumours that circulated spoke about The Hague, Rotterdam, even Antwerp. The atmosphere remained grim, but became almost euphoric because of the mass participation and the fact that there was no German to be seen.

The Germans were indeed completely surprised by the strike, but from The Hague they took their counter-measures. The local authorities in Amsterdam were put under pressure, threats were uttered. The battalion of the *Ordnungspolizei* in Amsterdam was placed in readiness and given orders to fire no warning shots, but to aim and fire directly. Two battalions of the SS *Totenkopf Standarte*, the death's-head brigade, who were stationed in nearby towns, as well as 250 men of the Dutch military police, were ordered to move into Amsterdam. A curfew was imposed: after half past seven no one was to be allowed on the streets. These measures were made known by broadcasts and also by loudspeaker vans. Because he was afraid of German reaction, the mayor of Amsterdam, who was no Nazi, sent a notice to all municipal officials instructing them to return to work immediately or face punishment and dismissal.

As a result of these measures, the strike collapsed rapidly, and on the next day the tram service had largely returned to normal. However, for many others there were visible signs of what was happening. German police and soldiers cruised through the whole town, shooting wildly in all directions; many citizens dropped dead or were wounded. Those who continued to strike mostly remained in their homes as a precaution.

By Thursday morning the strike had completely fizzled out. The estimates of the number who took part in the strike vary from between 200,000 and 300,000 out of a total population of not quite 800,000. The February strike, as it quickly became known, the first general strike of the whole population of a town in human history against the deportation of a group of Jewish fellow-citizens, is still remembered annually on 25 February by thousands who meet in the square where the original round-ups had taken place.

About 200 people were arrested. All had taken part in the strike; several had been involved in the preparations. Some of them were badly ill-treated. One of the owners of the ice-cream parlour, where it all started, was given a summary trial and was shot on 3 March. Thus a Jewish emigrant from Germany became the first person to stand before a German firing-squad in the Netherlands. His colleague was sentenced to ten years' imprisonment, which he did not survive. The others who had been arrested were released after a number of weeks, except for three, to whom I shall return shortly.

First of all, the fate of the Geuzen deserves some notice. Those who had been arrested, about 200 of them, were locked up in Scheveningen prison, the first of several thousand resistance fighters who were to find themselves there between 1940 and 1945. During the course of the war, this institution became popularly known as the 'Orange Hotel', a name which is still in use among the older generation of Dutchmen.

There followed protracted and intensive interrogations during which torture was not eschewed. One of the prisoners did not survive this treatment. Ultimately 43 Geuzen were selected for trial. It was meant to be a show-trial and, as a special exception, some members of the press – carefully chosen by the Germans – had been invited.

On 24 February – one day before the February strike – the trial began. After six days of lengthy cross-examinations, the prosecution made its demands: the death penalty for 22 of the accused, terms of imprisonment for another 17. Four were recommended to be acquitted.

It cannot be said whether the feeling of amazement was stronger than that of horror. All those death sentences? What were they actually supposed to have done? On 4 March, in the presence of hundreds of

German officers and police officials the sentences were read out: 18 Geuzen had been condemned to death, six were acquitted and the others received sentences of hard labour or imprisonment. The appeals for clemency that had been submitted were rejected by the *Wehrmachtsbefehlshaber*, Army Commander-in-Chief, with three exceptions: the sentences of death against the three accused who were not yet 20 years old were commuted to imprisonment for life. On German instructions, very full reports were given in the press of both the trial and the sentences.

An ironical footnote can be added to the prisoners' fate: the proverbial German thoroughness and literal-mindedness led to one of the three boys whose sentences had been commuted – and the only Jew among them – being dragged from one concentration camp to another for four years, including camps with such dreadful names as Auschwitz and Mauthausen. He was saved from the gas-chambers because he had been sentenced officially by a German court, and it was thus considered correct that he should serve his sentence in full. He survived the war, occupied a number of posts in the administration of middle-sized towns, and has been for some years the chairman of the Dutch federation of former resistance fighters.

On 13 March 1941, the 18 who had been sentenced to death, 15 Geuzen and the three February strikers whom I have previously mentioned, faced the firing-squads in the dunes near Scheveningen. Is it a coincidence that they were brought together here? Had the February strike, which had led to such dismay among the Germans, been to some extent responsible for the harshness of the sentences against the Geuzen? The question cannot be answered with any certainty, but the supposition is easy to support. It was felt necessary to make examples. The Geuzen and the February strikers had made it clear to all Germans, and certainly to the *Reichskommissar* Dr Seyss-Inquart, that the Dutch people were not prepared to be re-educated into becoming Nazis. The policy of the velvet glove had failed and had been abandoned – the whole of Holland could now realize that.

Shortly after the trial, 157 Geuzen were transported to concentration camps in Germany; 54 of them would never see liberation.

April–May strikes 1943

The situation of the war had changed considerably. The entry of the United States into the war, although this was at first directed towards the fight against Japan, had reinforced the powers of the Allies considerably. By early May the Germans had finally been completely defeated in North Africa; landings in Sicily and on mainland Italy appeared imminent. It was also recognized, even at that time, that Stalingrad would lead to the final retreat of the Germans from Russia.

In the Netherlands also, far-reaching developments had taken place during the past two years. In connection with the requisition of labour, tens of thousands of men had been transported to Germany to work there in the armament and other industries; the deportation of Jews to the extermination camps Auschwitz and Sobibor had since the summer of 1942 been operating at full speed; more than 50,000 had disappeared in deportation trains to Westerbork Jewish Transit Camp in a thinly populated part of the east of the country. The Nazification of all kinds of administrative organizations had increased considerably; new bodies under Nazi direction had been set up in local government and other organizations. The underground resistance had revived, although quite slowly in some areas, and involved itself in every imaginable activity. The German apparatus to counter this had grown at the same rate; its actions had hardened and were generally efficient: resistance groups were rolled up, death sentences were passed, and many of those arrested disappeared into the concentration camps of the Third Reich.

Then suddenly and totally unexpectedly on 29 April 1943, Holland was shocked by an announcement from the German military commander: the entire former Dutch Army, released from prisoner-of-war camps in the spring of 1940 'through the generosity of the Führer' (this reference was stressed), would again be taken prisoner and transported to Germany.

This order did not affect just one section of the people, just one town. The measure would touch the entire population of the country, for everyone was acquainted with those concerned: in 1940 the Dutch Army had consisted of about 300,000 men.

There were no preparations. There was hardly any discussion. Immediately the news had been read, just after the hour of midday, the workers streamed out of a number of factories in Hengelo, an industrial town in the east of the country, and left them empty. It was felt that here there was just one answer: to strike. On the same day practically the whole area around Hengelo went on strike and, thanks to the alarm being given over the telephone, nearly the whole province of Overijssel. Travellers on the trains carried the news into the neighbouring provinces and even further. At the Philips factories in Eindhoven the action that day was restricted to sit-down strikes; serious disorders broke out in the mining area of the province of Limburg: the night-shift in one of the mines refused to go down. More than 10,000 Limburgers altogether went on strike. Factories, mines and other businesses emptied, as did municipal installations. Farm-workers left the estates. In the province of Friesland and other places the farmers refused to deliver milk to the dairies. Schools were empty. Buses and trams ceased to run. On the following morning 18,000 men at Philips in Eindhoven went on strike, nearly 40,000 in the mines of Limburg.

The manifestos and proclamations which were quickly distributed by underground groups were in fact superfluous since they called for a strike. Their use lay in the first place in providing further stimulation to the spirit of resistance by which the entire nation had been moved. Only in the large towns in the west of the country did it remain peaceful.

The Germans, however, at first surprised and bewildered, just as they were by the February strike, rapidly hit back. They feared that the strikes might spread to Belgium and perhaps even to France. The following morning two measures were announced by means of posters; in the afternoon and in the evening they appeared in the newspapers. The *Höhere SS-und-Polizeiführer*, the head of SS and Police, had given orders to his SS and police troops to fire without warning on any assembly, and the *Polizeistandrecht*, martial law, to be carried out by the police, had been proclaimed in five towns, Hengelo among them. On the following day, Saturday 1 May, this was extended to cover the entire country. The strike had to be broken without delay.

A lot of wild shooting did indeed take place, and some innocent people were hit. Death sentences were carried out after only the most perfunctory hearings. Notices giving the names of those executed were exhibited in profusion everywhere in the country. Among those shot was a 13-year-old boy.

And London remained silent, while hundreds of thousands sat in Holland in the evening to listen to the BBC and to Radio Orange. The Dutch government in exile and the British knew of the storm that raged over the Netherlands. Only on Sunday afternoon, 2 May, a long telegram was received from Holland, but this had been drawn up by a resistance organization of which nothing had ever been heard in London. They did not dare trust it. It was considered that the proclamation of a general strike would only be meaningful shortly before the Allies carried out landings. The Dutch Prime Minister took the matter up with Churchill who replied that the invasion could not be brought forward.

The strike, in the meantime, was diminishing. German terror reached a new height on Monday 3 May. The miners in Limburg remained stubborn longer than most, and in the countryside there were places where the strike continued, but many went back to work on that

Monday. On Tuesday another 19 executions were carried out. Then it was all over.

The strike had cost 80 deaths by execution; 95 people had been shot dead in the street, and more than 400 seriously wounded. Some thousands of strikers were arrested and of these, 900 disappeared into concentration camps in Holland and Germany. More than a hundred officials and holders of public offices were dismissed, among them 15 mayors, mainly of towns where the strike had been intensive.

Some days later it was announced that all students who had refused to sign a declaration of loyalty to the occupying power would be transported to work in Germany; that all men between the ages of 18 and 35 likewise had to report for *Arbeitseinsatz*, labour duty, in Germany; and finally that all Dutch people, with the exception of the Nazis, had to hand in their radios to prevent their being further influenced by the BBC and Radio Orange. It must be clear that this last regulation was not in any way connected with special activities during the period of the strike.

The strike and the German reaction to it had a new and decisive influence on the further development of the nature of the German occupation; the resistance certainly received significant impulses from it. I shall return to this matter presently.

The Railway Strike – 1944

I now turn to the third extensive strike which, incidentally, was quite different from the other two. The war scene had changed considerably. The Dutch coastal region had seen the Germans strengthen their defences since 1943: thousands of bunkers had been built, gun sites installed and all sorts of provisions made against landings, both from the sea and the air. Tens of thousands of Dutch people had suffered a forced evacuation from the coastal strip; houses had been demolished, tank-traps dug.

After the Allied forces had rapidly rolled through France and Belgium in August 1944, Antwerp, only some ten kilometres from the Dutch border, was liberated on 4 September. It seemed as if the advance could not be arrested. A whirling current of rumour swept across the country on the morning of the next day, Tuesday 5 September. The border was said to have been crossed; Breda liberated; a short time later Dordrecht, Rotterdam, there was no stopping the rumours. Along the approach roads, in towns, villages, even in Amsterdam, stood tens of thousands of delighted people, many carrying flowers, waiting for the first Allied soldiers to show themselves.

Flags were put out, patriotic songs were sung; 5 September 1944 has since then been known as 'Mad Tuesday'.

The Allied troops did not come. It was not to be until 13 September that the first soldiers reached Dutch territory and then at its most south-easterly point in the province of Limburg.

Shortly after midday on Sunday 17 September, hundreds of thousands of people in the Netherlands were surprised by the squadrons of British and American aircraft on their way to Arnhem. Their great number, the routes they flew and their low altitude, all seemed to point to one conclusion: the hour of liberation was near.

For some time, contact had existed between a member of the general administration of the Netherlands Railways and the government in London. That company had something to make up for. For four years it had run both passenger and freight traffic in excellent, punctual order, as much for Dutch passenger and goods traffic as for the Germans. Some thousand Dutch trains had undertaken the transport of half a million Dutchmen who had been forced to work in Germany; more than a hundred thousand Dutch Jews had been transported by Dutch trains, under German orders, to the assembly camp Westerbork, whence German trains, using the Dutch railway vehicles, had taken them to the extermination camps in Poland. As late as 5 September 1944 a train carrying 5,000 political prisoners had been sent to Germany. When in the course of 1942 the number of sabotage attacks on railway lines increased, the Netherlands Railways satisfied a German demand to bring into existence a so-called Railway Guard of 2,000 men who examined the lines eight times every 24 hours. The railway company had, further, always taken great care to repair any damage done by sabotage as quickly as possible. Furthermore, the leadership of the largest (socialist) union of railwaymen had during the first part of the occupation not remained free from the taint of Nazism.

Some hours after the landings at Arnhem, the railways management was surprised by a message from the Dutch government, passed on through the BBC, and issued after consultation with the Allied high command: 'The government considers that the moment had come to give orders for a general strike of railway personnel in order to interfere as much as possible with enemy traffic and troop concentrations.'

The management was completely startled by this order, and was not in a position to provide central direction for the strike. During the night the strike developed on a local level and, it must be said, not everywhere with equal enthusiasm. Fear of German reprisals, with the April/May 1943 strike still very much in mind, had much influence on many individuals, and urgent persuasion, sometimes even threats by resistance organizations were needed in some cases to make the railwaymen leave their stations and yards.

However, on the following day railway traffic had ceased for all practical purposes; for at the most a few weeks – so it was thought. But it was to extend to more than seven months. Nearly all railwaymen went into hiding. There were no round-ups, no shootings and no executions; in this last period of the war, the Germans had other worries. For their own transport they brought 4–5,000 railwaymen from Germany who dealt solely with their own needs: troop movements and the transport of supplies and food. They further assisted in the plundering of the Netherlands; a massive quantity of trams, trains and factory installations were shipped to Germany.

There now came large-scale round-ups of Dutch men; the most extensive took place in Rotterdam on 10 and 11 November. Some 50,000 men were taken and used mainly to work on the preparation of defences, and the total so employed came to more than 120,000. During these round-ups, striking railwaymen were also caught, but they were treated in exactly the same way as the other detainees.

Public transport in Holland had come to a complete stand-still. After a few months food, electricity, gas and coal could scarcely be made available for the people. Particularly in the thickly populated centres in the west of the country, these developments were to lead in the final four months of the war to what has become known as the 'Hunger Winter'.

OPEN AND UNDERGROUND RESISTANCE

In 1976 I was involved in a discussion with my predecessor, teacher and friend, Louis de Jong. In his manuscripts for Part Seven of his long series of works on *The Kingdom of the Netherlands during the Second World War*, he made an explicit distinction between the concepts 'resistance' and 'clandestine actions'.

Especially after the war these concepts were often quite generally used interchangeably in a somewhat careless and indifferent manner, particularly in the names given to associations of former resistance fighters.

De Jong's starting point is his own formulation of the four aims of the Nazi administration in the Netherlands, and he defines 'resistance' as 'any action which sought to prevent the national-socialist occupiers from realizing their aims'. He goes on to point out that his term 'resistance' has a wider meaning than the term 'clandestine action', which he defines as 'an activity which had been officially prohibited by the Nazis'. It is my view that de Jong here bases his case too much on formal judicial principles in a situation which constantly declined towards a condition of the total abrogation of law and unpredictability on the part of the German occupation forces. It might well be said, for example, that from the point of view of the rightful Dutch government in London, all these activities could be regarded not only as of the strictest legality, but even as a moral duty.

De Jong provides further difficulties for himself when he enumerates groupings which, as he formulates it, still contend that they 'had been the real clandestine workers'. He commences this with 'the secret organizations which laid the foundations', the resistance by the churches, implying therewith that he divides church resistance as such into two categories. Yet this resistance was principally expressed in messages from the pulpit and letters of protest to the German authorities for which the organizers provided the preparation, and these were not infrequently the same people who also expressed themselves in public both from the pulpit and as co-signatories of protest letters. The same could apply to the resistance in the Protestant schools and the resistance of various professional associations such as doctors, pharmacists and dentists, and to a part of the resistance by students and professors. And, if one continues this splitting-up, what can be said about the producers of underground news-sheets and leaflets which, according to German records, as the war went on, proceeded to a position where more and more copies of their publications were sent to one or other of the German authorities? Did the production of these fall under the heading of 'clandestine' and the circulation under that of 'resistance'? I do not wish to drag the matter into the ridiculous, but such is the ultimate consequence of the distinctions introduced by de Jong.

I further want to add here that the carelessness in the use of the Dutch language by those involved, when they refer to the activities carried out by them and the groups to which they belonged as 'the resistance' and 'the clandestine workers', or even farther 'the underground', does, as it were, invite this kind of exercise. Fortunately, as far as I am aware, this carelessness has remained limited to the Netherlands; where French is spoken, I believe, they speak only of *la résistance*. In German-language areas they speak of *Widerstand* and in Eastern Europe the various languages provide a similarly uniform term. I must merely make a reservation regarding Norway and Denmark, where the labels in use are not known to me.

Thus in the following part of my paper, I shall speak exclusively of 'open' and 'underground' resistance. In my view this will serve clearly to indicate the distinction between the nature of the different actions, some of which were made deliberately visible to the Germans, while others fundamentally had to be secret and invisible, in the hope that they would always remain so. At the same time, some legal qualifications and consequences, juridically including the criminal law (mostly predictable), should be left out of consideration, as the victims of immediate German reactions as well as of punitive measures fell under both categories.

Open resistance

It will be obvious that the demonstration on 29 June 1940 with its emphatically defiant character of support for the House of Orange, as well as the spontaneous strikes of February 1941 and April/May 1943, both voicing popular anger and public protest, belong to the first category. The 1944 railway strike was of a different nature; after all, an order from the government in London had been needed for it to start. In the beginning, pressure had to be exerted in some places on railway personnel by members of underground groups; here and there even threats had to be resorted to. Nevertheless, after little more than 24 hours the strike assumed a general character with 30,000 participants, none of whom could guess how the Germans would react.

There was a massive move to go into hiding, often at addresses in the close neighbourhood. The German threat, 'Whoever goes on strike will be shot', was not carried out; the battle against the Allies had priority for all available German military and police units. On the other hand, the whole of Holland, and of course also the strikers, were convinced that the war would come to an end within a few weeks. The 30,000 strikers saw it through for nearly eight months with support from their management, especially to prevent them and their families from suffering financial hardship. I shall return to the last point later. One thing can be certain: the railway strike belongs to the most important demonstrations of mass open resistance in occupied Holland.

There was still considerably more public resistance in the Netherlands, and many more activities which endeavoured to impede the aims of the German rulers, who only had the total support of the Dutch Nazi Party, the NSB. These aims, formulated much earlier by de Jong and further elaborated, I shall only summarise briefly here:

- the transformation of Holland into a National Socialist state;
- the utilization of the Dutch economy, including its work-force, in the service of the German war machine;

- the deportation to concentration and extermination camps of more than a hundred thousand Dutch Jews, as well as the gypsies who remained in Holland and others who in Nazi parlance were termed 'anti-social elements';
- the prevention of assistance being given to the Allies, and countering resistance against the first three aims.

Resistance against the first aim can be found beyond the spontaneous demonstrations and strikes which, in fact, voiced a broader feeling of protest on the part of the participants. It can be shown in the very small number of Dutch National Socialists and other pro-Germans, all of whom accounted for no more than a few per cent of the population. Moreover, the broad mass of the population gave expression to their feelings through all kinds of behaviour – perhaps some of it looking rather childish when viewed 50 years after the events. There was the wearing of coins on their clothing showing an emphasized portrait of Queen Wilhelmina, and carrying matches with their heads showing thus demonstrating a double meaning, i.e. 'Keep your heads high' and 'Up the Orange'; but this action was limited to the first year and was later replaced by the 'V'-sign.

Officials and members of many kinds of commercial and professional organizations gave clear signs of what they thought of the German plans and aims. The leaders of the six large political parties emphatically held on to the ideas of 'Orange' and 'independence', and the membership of the largest Protestant political party grew from 70,000 to 250,000 during the first year of the occupation. However, the continued existence of the political parties was soon made impossible. Earlier on, the central organization of employers had chosen to disband rather than co-operate with the Nazi union movement, and after that about 70 per cent of the members of the Socialist federation of trade unions, 96 per cent of the Roman Catholic and 75 per cent of the Protestant federations ostentatiously cancelled their membership when these organizations were incorporated in the Nazi Netherlands' *Arbeitsfront*, trade union.

Various church denominations protested repeatedly through official messages from the pulpit as well as letters and telegrams to the German occupation authority against many developments. In one instance this led to disastrous consequences. In the summer of 1942, when the deportation of Jews had just begun, the churches once again sent a fierce protest to *Reichskommissar* Seyss-Inquart, and the content of this telegram was read out in the Catholic churches. In revenge for this, the 700-odd Catholics of Jewish origin were arrested and transported to the extermination camp at Auschwitz, among them the internationally famous philosopher Edith Stein.

The great majority of those responsible for the Protestant schools refused to carry out a duty laid upon them by the Nazis: to submit the names of teachers to be appointed for approval. Countless artists refused to join the guild of the Nazi *Kulturkammer*, chamber of culture, established in 1942, although this refusal robbed them of all income because publication or appearances were now forbidden to them.

More than 160,000 farmers, nearly half of the total number, refused to pay a compulsory contribution to the Nazi organization for farmers, the Netherlands *Landstand*; thousands of young men refused to listen to the order to report for the *Arbeitsdienst*, a Nazi organization on para-military lines for carrying out reclamation and work on the land.

About 75 per cent of doctors in general practice and consultants refused to join the Nazi organization for doctors, the *Ärtztekammer*, and when they were informed that they had automatically been made members, they replied that they had given up their practice, and removed their name-plates from their house-fronts. Notaries and advocates were able to prevent the setting up of a chamber of lawyers. Of the total of 14,000 university students, 11,000 refused to sign a so-called declaration of loyalty; they were not allowed to continue their studies and promptly received an order to report for the *Arbeitseinsatz*, forced labour, in Germany. Most of them went into hiding.

The term for going into hiding was *onderduiken*, diving under, and that soon became one of the most frequently used words in Holland. It meant leaving one's normal place of residence and finding another which, one hoped, would be safe. The Register of Population in the Netherlands was traditionally one of the best, if not indeed *the* best, in the world. Each municipality had its own card-index in which everyone had to be included: names, addresses, dates of birth, composition of family – every alteration was precisely and carefully recorded, and all these details were further brought together in a central index in The Hague. Everyone who remained at his 'official' address could be found instantly.

Immediately after the fighting in 1940, some people had already left their registered addresses; their position before the war had been such that they feared, often with justification, that they might be included in a German list of people to be arrested. At the beginning, the number of people in hiding remained limited. All the Geuzen had been arrested at their normal addresses, even those who were collected weeks after the first wave of arrests.

All this changed in the course of 1941. The *Arbeitseinsatz*, the forced labour in factories and other works in Germany, produced the first considerable number of *onderduikers*. By the beginning of 1942, 165,000 Dutch workers had been forced into Germany; more than 60,000 had then returned to Holland without permission – many of them not to their own addresses. Apart from this small group mentioned above, some resistance fighters, but not more than a few dozens, considered it safer to alter their addresses.

The number of people in hiding then started to grow apace: those who had been called up for work in Germany, Jews and resistance fighters. During the last half-year of the war, their number exceeded 330,000. A large proportion of them remained inactive, others took part in resistance activities of various kinds and thus ranged themselves into the ranks of what I have termed 'underground resistance'. The organizations which looked after the *onderduikers* will later be considered further.

Underground resistance

The underground resistance went through a slow process of growth which was conditioned by:

– the lack of experience of war and/or occupation already mentioned;
– the increasing pressure by the occupation authorities through which ever larger groups of Dutch people were threatened in their barest existence;
– the understanding of the course military warfare should take.

It goes without saying that the techniques and tactics of resistance had to be learned by trial and error. Not surprisingly, a great drive towards resistance was provided both by the participation of Russia in the war in the summer of 1941 and by the German defeats in the winter of 1942–43. Moreover, the start of the deportation of Dutch Jews in the summer of 1942 and the plans outlined earlier to re-imprison all Dutch soldiers as prisoners-of-war, as well as the driving of students into forced labour, created the bitter need to lend help to these threatened groups.

Already in the summer of 1942 a beginning had been made towards providing this help in an organized manner. At first its scale was limited, but by the first months of 1943 a nation-wide network had been built up, and the so-called National Organization of Help for those in Hiding could extend its activities considerably. These activities varied greatly:

- willingness had to be stimulated throughout the whole country to assist those in hiding;
- those who were potential *onderduikers* had to be found and put in contact with the families who were willing to take them in and, if necessary, to accompany them to their new address. This was specially needed for Jews who were no longer allowed to use public transport;
- money had to be provided to support both the family remaining behind and the families that had given shelter;
- provision had to be made for the necessary distribution of food, for those in hiding could after all neither request nor collect this;
- if the relationship between the hosts and those in hiding did not turn out to be good, efforts had to be made to improve the atmosphere or to find another safe address.

The National Organization of Help for those in Hiding ('LO' after its Dutch initials) rapidly realized that a particular problem arose from the acquisition of food distribution cards which could not be solved by the people normally providing help.

This led to the setting up of special units, called strong-arm squads, whose task it was to carry out raids on food distribution offices which existed in all municipalities, in the smaller ones often in the town halls. Often there was co-operation, active or passive, by the officials themselves. After a short time the offices concerned were guarded night and day by the police, and thus it was necessary to provide weapons. Once weapons had been obtained, these were also used for raids on prisons, which were under German supervision, and where arrested members of underground organizations were locked up awaiting trial – which often resulted in the death sentence. In some cases prisons were broken into to liberate particular prisoners; sometimes it came to gun-fights with the guards, when the strong-arm squads got the worst of it.

These squads were distributed over the whole country, but they were in contact with each other, so that if the need arose, other groups could be called on for help.

I must also point out to you that the image of these strong-arm squads in the Netherlands is entirely different from such groups in most of the other occupied countries: the geography of the country made it in reality quite impossible for them to stay together permanently. Each member had his own address – either a permanent residence or a place of hiding. They only came together to prepare actions and carry them out. They were mostly provided with forged identity documents and certificates of exemption from work in Germany, supplied by experts in that field. In the course of the years, moreover, they had come to have at their disposal many hundreds of German rubber-stamps, either stolen or ingeniously copied. The occupations and/or dates of birth recorded on these identity documents often led to the bearers being left in peace during the frequent controls and round-ups by the Germans on the streets and, since 1943, with increasing frequency on the trains.

I must give a further explanation of my more or less incidental remark that the National Organization also cared for the financial needs of those in hiding. The money was indeed distributed, but how was it provided? This provision happened after it became obvious that time-consuming and risky individual collections only realized a very small proportion of the money required, and was due to the initiative of a number of bankers who were already in possession of the necessary funds which they held on behalf of the families of soldiers and seamen who had escaped to England. They established an organization, the National Support Fund, and extended their help to those in hiding, with the assistance of some 1,900 collaborators. With the help of the London government, which guaranteed these payments, and an ingenious registration system, they were able to make more than a million guilders available for this purpose.

The National Organization ultimately comprised nearly 15,000 helpers, and looked after between ten and twenty times as many people in hiding. The strong-arm squads accounted in total for no more than a few hundred members who, at the same time, were engaged in sabotage actions, especially against the railways, just as some others, including the resistance group which had in 1943 sent the telegram about the strike to London. These actions against the railways were not very meaningful because of the speed with which the excellently equipped railway service could always repair the damage caused and because of the fact that it was the Dutch travelling public which suffered in the first place. Naturally these acts of sabotage reached a climax in the first half of September 1944, and then they were perceived as most useful, in view of the rapid approach of the Allied armies.

Further enumeration of the many resistance organizations and independent groups would create needless complications without adding a great deal to the general picture of the resistance as such. The activities of a military nature which were carried out in the liberated south of the country by some thousands of so-called war-volunteers between the autumn of 1944 and May 1945 will be left out of account.

However, I want to turn to just one more very extensive resistance activity which, especially in the Netherlands, was of particular importance. At the same time, because of its nature, it displayed clear parallels with the most significant actions directed towards the Netherlands by the Allies and particularly the British – obviously quite separate from the military conflict.

For those in Holland who understood English, and even 50 years ago there were many who did, the names BBC, Home Service and European Service were not meaningless noises. Already during the battles of 10–15 May there had been many in Holland who apart from listening to the Netherlands radio stations had tuned in to the news broadcasts of the BBC. This habit was continued after the capitulation; the daily broadcasts from Radio Orange were quickly added, thanks to the facilities also provided by the BBC. It was not long before many families hardly listened to the Dutch news broadcasts; whenever they did listen, they were filled with a feeling of aversion.

During the early years, there was little stimulating news to pass on, but there were two elements in these broadcasts which, certainly during the first half of the war, were of a significance that should not be underestimated: the news was reliable, and on every occasion it gave a clear picture of the resoluteness and the optimism of the British – however much they may have been out of place particularly in 1940. Of course, the propaganda element was recognized, but it was also accepted as a part of the common struggle. Perhaps the latter was the most important: every day new *hope* came from the other side of the Channel.

I pointed to a parallel activity earlier, and you will understand that I was referring to the underground press. No occupied country in the Second World War came to know such an extensive underground press as the Netherlands, which had for centuries enjoyed free and uncensored newspapers.

At the time of the arrest of the Geuzen at the end of 1940, the number of underground papers had risen to about 60; they were bulletins, but they also dealt with considerations of a general and fundamental kind. Still produced very primitively and with limited editions ranging from tens to several hundreds, they appeared at intervals of between a week to a month.

The number of newspapers increased rapidly, techniques developed and the problem of paper supply was solved every time, although the business world as a whole suffered from an increasing shortage. Many papers could sustain themselves for only a short time; some even disappeared after just one or two editions. Others carried on and, according to the requirements of the war, appeared in wider circulation and at shorter intervals. With the increase in circulation, the distribution network had also to be widened and the transport techniques perfected. The hunger for news had become ever greater since the spring of 1943 when the Germans had ordered all radio sets to be handed in as one of the measures taken after the strike. Only the underground press could fill the need for news, for even the bulletins dropped in great numbers by British aircraft could not satisfy this news-hunger in the occupied areas. The places where the drops were carried out varied too much and, more important, many of the copies dropped were lost before anyone could read them. I hope that the Editor-in-Chief of *The Flying Dutchman* was not aware of this during the war.

Here is a single example of what the underground press achieved and what its significance was. One of the first underground papers, already in existence from the autumn of 1940, brought out a special edition on 'Mad Tuesday' (5 September 1944) in Amsterdam, quite apart from its normal issue. This edition, which had been regarded as a one-off event, was continued; in various towns these bulletins, which grew to 100,000 copies, were distributed right up to the moment of liberation. The underground newspaper *Het Parool* is still one of the larger newspapers appearing daily in the Netherlands, together with another daily, a weekly paper and various local papers in the country, all having their roots in the resistance against the Nazis.

Christopher Andrew

I shall concentrate on intelligence rather than resistance. I feel an appropriate sense of humility in doing so – the next speaker this morning, and those this afternoon, will speak from personal knowledge about intelligence during the Second World War. I can't do that. My purpose is more modest: first to put some of the problems of British wartime intelligence in the Netherlands into historical perspective, and second, to raise some questions about Anglo-Dutch intelligence collaboration during the war to which I don't know the answers, but to which I hope the answers may be forthcoming in our discussion.

First, the historical perspective. British intelligence in the occupied Netherlands during the Second World War suffered from at least two very well known problems. First the rivalry between different British intelligence agencies – between the Secret Intelligence Service, usually known as SIS or MI6, on the one hand, and the Special Operations Executive, SOE, on the other. And second, penetration by the Germans. What is often forgotten, however, and what I hope may justify a brief attempt to give an historical perspective, is that both those problems originated not in the Second World War but in the First. During the First World War, the Netherlands played an even greater role in British intelligence operations than they did in the Second. They were the main base from which both SIS in London and GHQ in France gathered intelligence from behind the German lines on the Western Front, and indeed they had little option, since the solid line of trenches made it very difficult indeed to get intelligence directly across the front line. British intelligence had only two options – to go round the end of the line either in the south or in the north. In the south the Swiss were ill-disposed to British spies; they made life very difficult for Somerset Maugham, as he describes in a slightly fictionalized form in the 'Ashenden Papers'. The Netherlands, however, during the First World War, as between the wars (and this was explained in the talk by Admiral den Boeft yesterday), were hospitable to spies of all nations, including ours.

Allied intelligence networks in the Netherlands during the First World War achieved some remarkable successes. The greatest was the network La Dame Blanche in occupied Belgium and northern France – 900 strong by the time of the Armistice – run by SIS from the Netherlands, which provided during the last year of the war remarkably complete and accurate intelligence on German troop movements by rail. But along with those successes were both remarkable organizational confusion and an unacceptably high level of German penetration.

In the Second World War there may have been rivalry between two different agencies, but in the First there was rivalry between three. Three British networks were run simultaneously from the Netherlands. There an SIS network was headed during the last two years of the war by Henry Landauer, the South African son of Anglo-Dutch parents, and by Hugh Dalton. Both, sad to say, later ended up in the rogues' gallery of SIS: Landauer wrote an inter-war volume of memoirs which was about as popular in Whitehall in the 1930s as Peter Wright's *Spycatcher* in the 1980s; Dalton committed suicide in 1936 after embezzling SIS funds. Alongside the SIS network in the First World War, there were two rival GHQ networks, one of them run for the first three years of the war by Sigismund Payne Best, the same man who in November 1939 was taken prisoner at Venlo, and the other run from Folkestone by Major Cecil Cameron who, like Dalton, committed suicide – in 1924, after a scandal of a different kind.

These three British networks were in competition not merely with each other, but with other networks in Belgium run by the French and the Belgian government in exile, and from time to time, the consequences of that rivalry closely approximated to organizational chaos. According to a secret post-war British report about the three British networks:

> They were, in fact, not only in actual if unconscious competition with each other, but also with parallel systems controlled by our French and Belgian allies. In spite of the excellent results produced, there is little doubt that denunciations, buying up other services' agents, duplication of reports and collaboration between agents of the various Allied systems were not uncommon, so that the information arriving at the various headquarters was received in a manner which was not only confusing but sometimes unreliable and occasionally dangerous.

The second problem during the First World War which recurred in the Second was penetration by the enemy of the British intelligence networks in the Netherlands. In June 1916, a series of SIS reports from the Netherlands were seized by the Germans when they captured the British steamer *Brussels* in the North Sea. There followed the collapse of the SIS organization run from the Netherlands in occupied Belgium and northern France, a disaster which bears some comparison with the *Englandspiel* during the Second World War. Among the captured SIS reports was one from the SIS station chief in the Netherlands, Ernest Maxse, which contained a number of disobliging antisemitic observations about Francis Oppenheimer, the British Commercial Attaché responsible for monitoring the blockade of Germany. One of those reports, which describes Oppenheimer as a typical Bosch Jew, was forwarded by German intelligence to Francis Oppenheimer and caused a predictable row in Whitehall. A second example of German penetration of British intelligence in the Netherlands in the First World War, occurred during the beginning of the last German offensive in 1918. On 22 March 1918, the clerk to the British Military Attaché in The Hague, having become suspicious of the Military Attaché's typist, looked through the keyhole into the typist's room. To his horror, but not entirely to his surprise, he saw the typist putting copies of secret telegrams into his pocket. A search of the typist's rooms revealed that for the past three months he had been selling British military intelligence reports to the Germans. So penetration during the Second World War wasn't new. It recurred as a serious problem for British intelligence in the Netherlands in the 1930s.

The Netherlands, as we were reminded yesterday, made life easy for the many foreign agents who operated in it in the 1930s, and some of those agents were operating not against the Netherlands but against the United Kingdom, using the Netherlands as a base. The Netherlands in the 1930s was a major centre for both Soviet and Nazi penetration of the Foreign Office and SIS. The first two Soviet agents in the Foreign Office were both recruited, not at Cambridge University like their immediate successors, but by Dutch illegals working for the KGB (then known as the GPU). Ernest Oldham, a code clerk in the Foreign Office Communications Department, was recruited and run from 1930 to 1932 by a Dutch illegal, Hans Gallini. Though poorly paid, Oldham had unrestricted access both to Foreign Office ciphers and to diplomatic telegrams channelled, as they all were, through the Foreign Office Communications Department, and he supplied both to the KGB. In the end the strain became too much and he committed suicide in 1933.

An even more important Soviet agent in the Foreign Office, Captain J. H. King, was recruited in 1934 and run for the next two years by the Dutch artist, Hans Christian Pieck, also a KGB illegal. Early in 1936 he handed King over to a KGB career officer. More serious from the point of view of the Second World War was the German penetration of the SIS station in the Netherlands. That penetration derived from a disastrous sequence of three SIS station chiefs in the 1930s: Hugh

Dalton, who shot himself in 1936 after embezzling SIS funds; Monty Chidson, who, though he did sterling work in rescuing more than a million pounds' worth of industrial diamonds from under the noses of the Germans in Amsterdam in May 1940, became in 1936, as Dalton's successor, embroiled in a series of disputes which forced him to leave in 1937; and finally Major Richard Stevens, an Indian Army Officer with little experience of intelligence, who later described himself as 'the wrong sort of man for such work', and ended up with Sigismund Payne Best being captured by the Germans at Venlo in 1939. Dalton's assistant, Jack Hooper, and one of Chidson's agents, Folkert van Koutrik, were both turned by the *Abwehr* and used to penetrate the SIS station in the Netherlands. That penetration led to the discovery by the *Abwehr* of the two most valuable SIS German agents. It also led to the planting of bogus intelligence by the *Abwehr* which ended in the Venlo disaster in November 1939.

To guard against penetration and to provide for an independent source of intelligence, SIS set up in the mid-1930s, entirely separate from its main networks, the so-called Z organization run from Bush House (the HQ of the BBC World Service), headed in the Netherlands by Best. But the whole point of the Z organization in the Netherlands was destroyed when it was ordered to combine with Stevens' SIS station at the outbreak of war. The consequence was that Best, as well as Stevens, fell victim to a major German deception. Early in the war, SIS in the Netherlands, as is well known, was contacted by Germans who claimed to be senior army officers engaged in a plot to remove Hitler from power. The alleged plotters were in reality officers of the *Sicherheitsdienst* and they successfully deceived both Best and Stevens.

In arranging their meetings with the bogus German conspirators, Best and Stevens had the co-operation of the head of Dutch military intelligence, Major-General van Oorschot, who assigned one of his officers, Lieutenant Klop, posing as a British officer, to assist Best and Stevens. On 9 November 1939, Stevens and Best were lured to the border town of Venlo, kidnapped, and taken to Germany where they were given starring roles in a Gestapo publicity stunt involving an alleged attempt on the Führer's life. There was a brief exchange of fire at the frontier in which Klop was killed, and when the Germans invaded Holland in May 1940, the support given by van Oorschot and Dutch intelligence to SIS was used as one of the pretexts to justify their aggression. Indeed the German pretexts also cited some of the exploits of British intelligence in the Netherlands in 1914–18. Now ever since the Second World War there has been a tendency to blame the Venlo fiasco simply on the incompetence of SIS and on bungling by Stevens and Best in particular, but Venlo would never have been possible without much more serious bungling by both the Foreign Office and Downing Street.

Since I wrote *Secret Service* I have been able to get access to what remains of the papers of the inter-war chief of SIS, Admiral Sir Hugh 'Quex' Sinclair, which show that in the run up to the Venlo disaster the Foreign Office had the greatest confidence in Stevens. The claim afterwards that it never had very much to do with him was simply a way of 'passing the buck' to SIS. Sir Neville Bland, whose name was mentioned yesterday as the British Minister in the Netherlands, wrote to congratulate Sinclair (his letter is preserved in the Sinclair papers) on the choice of Stevens to run the negotiations with the alleged anti-Nazi plotters: 'Stevens is being quite admirable. You couldn't have done better when you chose him.' Lord Hankey, Minister with special responsibility for the intelligence services in Chamberlain's war cabinet, was equally enthusiastic. He described Sinclair's secret report on Stevens' and Best's negotiations with the bogus German conspirators as 'One of the most cheering documents I have ever read' and he adds confidently, 'Here is someone who is getting results.'

Even after Stevens and Best were kidnapped at Venlo, both the Foreign Office and Whitehall as a whole failed to realize they had been taken in. Ten days after the kidnap, Cadogan, the Permanent Under-Secretary at the Foreign Office, was still drafting notes on peace terms to pass to the alleged German conspirators. Finally, on 22 November, the *Sicherheitsdienst* tired of the charade and radioed a mocking message using the conspirators' call sign to tell SIS that it had been duped. One of the consequences of Venlo was the collapse of the SIS stay-behind network in the Netherlands. As a result of German penetration, British Intelligence in the Netherlands had to start again virtually from scratch after the German conquest, and from that flowed many of the problems of SIS and SOE over the next few years.

With the gift of hindsight, however, it is now possible to see Venlo as a tactical victory but a strategic defeat for the Germans also. The Germans could, and should, from their point of view, have used their penetration of SIS as the basis of a much more dangerous wartime deception of British intelligence. Instead they sacrificed that long-term prospect for the sake of a short-term, if spectacular, success. British intelligence did the opposite. It is often forgotten that one of the greatest British Intelligence successes of the war, indeed one of the greatest successes of British intelligence at any time, the Double-Cross system – the turning round of German agents in Britain to feed false information to the enemy – began on Dutch soil at the very moment when SIS was being deceived at Venlo. In September 1939, Arthur Owens, code-named 'Snow', the first of the *Abwehr* agents in Britain to be turned round by MI5, met his *Abwehr* control, Major Ritter, in Amsterdam, and told him he had recruited a Welsh nationalist named Gwilym Williams, who had agreed to organize sabotage in South Wales. In October 1939, Owens brought Williams to meet Ritter at another meeting in Amsterdam. Ritter was greatly impressed. Williams, however, was a retired Swansea police inspector working for MI5. Thus began on Dutch soil the Double-Cross system, the most successful deception in the entire history of warfare, without which the Normandy landings could not, I think, have taken place in the summer of 1944.

The Dutch defeat in May 1940 had three consequences for the conduct of British intelligence over the remainder of the war. First it provided part of the explanation, though only part of the explanation, for the founding of SOE two months later. The German victories of May 1940, and particularly that in the Netherlands, were interpreted in Whitehall as evidence of the enormous power of subversion and sabotage. The sheer rapidity of the German *Blitzkrieg* victory was mistakenly ascribed to the assistance of large fifth columns working behind the lines. Sir Neville Bland argued that the Dutch defeat in only five days would have been impossible without extensive co-operation between the fifth column and German parachutists. He cited as an example a report that a German agent had led German parachutists to one of their principal Dutch targets. That story seems to me extraordinarily similar to the fictitious spy scares of the First World War, but I would be very interested to hear afterwards if anyone could substantiate stories like that. So, the belief that Europe could be immediately set ablaze in July 1940, to quote Churchill's famous instruction to Dalton, was based I think on exaggerated beliefs of what sabotage and subversion achieved in the Netherlands in May 1940.

Second, the rapid Dutch defeat spread fears within the British intelligence community and more generally within Whitehall, of a dangerous fifth column in Britain as well. Sir Neville Bland insisted that the German fifth column which had sabotaged Dutch defences was at work in England. I quote him: 'The German and Austrian servant, however superficially charming, is a real and grave menace.' Churchill took Bland's alarmist report seriously. He said later:

> After the dark vile conspiracy, which in a few days laid the trustful Dutch people at the mercy of Nazi aggression, a wave of alarm passed over this country and especially in responsible

circles [meaning himself] lest the same undermining tactics and treacherous agents of the enemy were at work in our island.

And it was that fear which led, in the three months after the invasion of the Netherlands, to the internment of 22,000 Germans and Austrians, far greater an internment, as is now recognized, than was justified by the needs of national security.

The third consequence of Dutch defeat in May 1940 was, of course, wartime collaboration, of which we shall hear more authoritative interpretations than my own, between Dutch intelligence and British intelligence. I simply want to put three questions to which I hope some answers may emerge in our discussions. First, it is well known that there was collaboration over what today's jargon now calls Humint, an unnecessary abbreviation of human intelligence. What I should like to know is not merely more about human intelligence, but how far that collaboration extended to Sigint – signals intelligence. We already know that Dutch code-breakers achieved one major success at the beginning of the Second World War. They broke the main Japanese diplomatic code, JN19, better known as 'Purple'. We know that also, in the months before Pearl Harbour, the Dutch Sigint station in Java co-operated with the British and the Americans. I should like to hear more about that, and also to hear what other codes the Dutch broke at the beginning of the Second World War. Second, I hope we may discover how far collaboration in human intelligence took place in the Far East and the Pacific as well as in occupied Europe. The Allied Intelligence Bureau in Australia which, from the moment that MacArthur landed, had an Australian head but an American deputy – the American deputy had all the money so it was effectively American-run – also contained a Dutch contingent. I should be fascinated to discover, and I hope that I may, what Dutch intelligence achieved in the Pacific war as well as in the European war.

And the third question, which I hope may not be too intolerably indiscreet, is this: How far does Anglo-Dutch wartime intelligence collaboration pave the way for post-war intelligence collaboration? One of the greatest intelligence consequences of the war for the United Kingdom within the English-speaking world – the Dutch are, after all, pretty much a part of the English-speaking world – is the emergence of an intelligence alliance unique in history, which has no precedent of any kind in any previous conflict, or in any previous time of peace. I think in particular of the Sigint intelligence alliance which emerged during the Second World War between Britain, the United States, Canada, Australia and New Zealand, formalized in a series of agreements.

From an examination of the Australian records after the Second World War, I am struck by how greatly Dutch intelligence was valued by Australian intelligence, and how close relations remained between Australian and Dutch intelligence right up to and beyond the period of 'confrontation' with Indonesia. Perhaps I can end with a document which, possibly, should not have been published in the Australian press, but since it was published I believe will do no great harm for me to quote now. It is a document stemming from the Australian Secret Intelligence Service, ASIS, in 1977, which bemoans the decline of Dutch intelligence since the great days of the Second World War and the great days of 'confrontation'.

> It is understood that the Dutch no longer conduct intelligence operations outside Europe, and therefore ASIS's liaison with them is now minimal. Contact is still maintained, however, on an occasional visiting basis, and a secure channel of communication still exists between ASIS and the HQ of the Dutch External Intelligence Service, the IDB. Initially, intelligence was provided by the Dutch to ASIS and distributed to consumer departments. In addition during the 1960s the two services co-operated closely on marine intelligence operations in the Far East. This has now ceased. Liaison with the IDB is now intermittent and lacking in substance due largely to the Dutch service's lack of involvement in SE Asia and its declining significance in the Netherlands itself. Some ASIS reports, however, are still passed to the IDB in order to keep open a channel which could later be of value.

I believe that that report expresses enormous nostalgia for the great days of Australian–Dutch collaboration during the Second World War and immediately afterwards, and my modest hope is that we shall hear more of it.

*　　*　　*

Chairman

Living as we both do in the penumbra of intelligence, we get used to collecting strings of acronyms; I'd have hitherto thought that IDB stood for 'illicit diamond buyer'.

Our next speaker was a genuine spy during the war. He is the senior surviving agent of the Bureau Inlichtingen, run by Dutch Intelligence in London – Baron d'Aulnis.

P.L. Baron d'Aulnis

In order to create the proper cloak-and-dagger atmosphere, I will now cover one of my eyes. Before I begin I will apologize to those who know about the past war, that my short speech is necessarily full of generalizations, and everybody here could point to things I forget to mention.

When Holland was occupied in May 1940, patriotic Dutchmen wanted to continue the struggle. They formed large and unwieldy secret societies of like-minded people – often demobbed military and/or students, such as I, who was both. They wanted to be helpful to Britain's war, and expected your armies to return to the Continent in a matter of months. But these societies were not functional and the members were without discipline for secrecy so that in 1941 and 1942, as we heard this morning, many leaders were caught and shot or sent to extermination camps. Nevertheless, out of these amateur beginnings, independent cells found specialized work to do and as the war continued, a quite large substratum of security-conscious underground workers had formed by 1943. Among these cells developed groups that quite spontaneously concentrated on politics, economics or military intelligence as their originators had been inclined or positioned to do best. These were the groups that claimed recognition in messages to London. It was to them that agents were sent to contact and support.

As an example: I was sent to find three men who had let it be known in London that they could create a weather service. I found them and taught them all that I had learned in England. A dropping was arranged and within months three weather stations were in operation in faraway Dutch towns, plus a budding intelligence group in The Hague known as the Packard group, which was eventually deployed nationwide. Other important intelligence groups were Albrecht, Kees, GDN and other names that won't mean anything to you, but I still stand at attention when I mention them. I have a report by a German *Abwehr* officer mentioning 34 specialist underground groups.

This paper discusses intelligence as an organized activity of the Dutch Bureau of Intelligence (which I will now call BI), in co-operation with the Dutch section of MI6, but it remains the story of those many independent groups that together produced the information and got it to England, albeit closely supported by agents and orchestrated from

London. Escape will be mentioned as performed from 1943 in co-operation with MI9's department, IS9. SOE's activities in Holland are not discussed, though their agents worked with the same underground people engaged by agents of BI. Certainly Michael Foot, speaking this afternoon, will point out that after the terrible havoc wrought by the *Englandspiel* among the intelligence community, a new Dutch Bureau for co-operation with SOE was created in March 1944, that from its start achieved much in spite of severe losses. It dropped 56 agents, of of whom 19 lost their lives.

I have been billed as the longest-serving agent, but I was dropped only in June 1943, and you will wonder about the agents who must have been there before me. In all there had been five bureau chiefs, but only 16 active agents, none of whom was operational in 1943. So let us forget the beginnings and concentrate on BI, created on 28 November 1942, and soon led by Major Dr Jan Somer. BI dropped 43 agents beginning in March 1943, of whom 11 were operational at the time of liberation in May 1945 – happily, myself among them.

In May 1940 the government of the Netherlands came to London and soon realized the need for political and economic information from occupied Holland. Our Queen and her ministers wanted to help our people by providing from England the national leadership that was no longer possible at home. Then the Dutch East Indies and the West Indies, our Royal and merchant navies, mostly intact, all expected guidance and also information of developments in Holland. And third, there were speeches to be made on Radio Oranje, the Dutch language service, that must ring true and take recent events in Holland into account. So political and economic information were required. More-over, there was the military leadership in Britain wanting to know what the Germans were up to. Until 1943, however, little intelligence reached England: mostly, by reports sent to Sweden by boat or to Switzerland by incidental traveller.

Only after the creation of BI on 28 November 1942 could the business of professional intelligence be developed in a systematic and long-term manner. In its charter, BI was instructed to provide information concerning political and economic developments, to solicit military intelligence, and to promote the evacuation of escaped POWs, volunteers for service in Britain and fugitives from the Gestapo, and interesting politicians, and of course to train and place agents. Evacuation was a kind word for safe conduct to Allied territory, and agents might be solicited among Dutchmen escaped from Holland; BI had first option to such volunteers. In the course of the war there were some 1,800 escapers from Holland who succeeded in reaching England and BI could cover its need for agents almost entirely from this extremely motivated group. In fact the staff of BI, including its head, Dr Somer, were themselves escapers from Holland, where they had participated in underground work.

Now speaking for the agents, they were young, and their aim was to throw the Germans out without considering politics at all until the war was won; their ambition was to help the Allies – that's what they came to England for. They were therefore thinking of military intelligence first and foremost. However the agents, both organizers and wireless operators, were despatched with orders to find and serve specific existing groups, and when these groups were activated by their official recognition in BI, and by the support of an agent with his communications, then the senior element in their organization saw to it that our government in London got its information along with the Allied military forces. Thus under the direction of a Dutch BI, Dutch groups and Dutch agents provided the information from Holland, but of course the end product was very much an Anglo-Dutch affair.

Your MI6 had the know-how to train the agents and give them codes and equipment. Your RAF Squadrons at Tempsford transported them and dropped them over Holland, losing many planes and men doing so, your central wireless station received and sent the messages, and your code service transposed the messages back and forth. Most important, your MI6 Dutch section translated and distributed the military info to the service departments and sent us the request for specific intelligence. Dr Somer, head of BI, wrote after the war that support from MI6 had been loyal, generous and of the highest quality. I for one have always felt that the spirit of co-operation and personal friendship from Charles Seymour, sitting there, with his crew of Dutch section, were of very great importance to our success.

In 1943, 14 agents were dropped, and some intelligence soon began to flow to England from different sources. From 1940 until May 1943 a total of 68 messages were sent from Holland; in the seven remaining months of 1943, 700 messages, in 1944 almost 6,000, and in the four months of 1945, 3,400 messages went up and down to Holland – and these figures do not include frequent telephone contact between the underground and BI after September 1944 by means of private lines of the electricity board. Only dialogue and urgent information were transmitted by radio.

By far the most intelligence was reported in dossiers, composed of many hundreds of individual and detailed reports and drawings, photographed and then shrunk to be hidden among the personal effects of messengers who would carry them to Sweden or to Switzerland. The latter, of course, in those days had no airline contacts with the Allied world, so in Switzerland you had a further problem getting the dossiers on to England. These dossiers represented the harvest of continuous observation by many scouts touring the country on their bicycles and reporting to centres in Amsterdam or The Hague.

The dossiers found their way to England mainly by the good services of two courier groups. One was grafted on to the pre-war connections between Dutch Protestant churches and the World Council of Churches in Geneva, where the then Secretary-General was a Dutchman. The other had already been developed as an escape line in 1941, when Jewish refugees needed to go no further than Vichy France, it was thought. This line first went therefore only to Lyon. Later, from there both into Switzerland and down to Spain; but the dossiers went mostly to Switzerland and their reports were then forwarded hidden in scientific books through the Swiss mail to Sweden and Portugal. In 1944, an average of 10,000 individual reports per month reached BI in London.

Thus our main problem was not the collection of information. We were all Dutchmen together, and the Germans had to use Dutchmen for every move: to build defences, transport their troops, order food and also beer – Heineken was a very good source for knowing when new troops had arrived! Once London asked for information about the Rotterdam ports. I did not go snooping along the quays, but upon a suitable introduction I asked the Director-General of the port authority personally, and with a sigh he handed me the answers all typed out and said that I was the fourth to come and request them.

Our problem was to get the information into England, across supervised land borders, later on across fighting lines, or by radio signal that the enemy could hear and of which he could plot the source. In Amsterdam alone, there were two fixed radio DF (direction-finding) stations and 13 cars equipped with DF radios trying to identify the transmitters' locations, and throughout the Netherlands wireless operators had been located in this way and arrested together with their host families.

The photographed dossiers, too, presented danger. They went to Switzerland through a chain of individual messengers. Every messenger went over the bit of territory he knew best and where he would work well with the local population, and then handed on to the next man to go across French territory or across the Jura mountains. The messengers were well provided with ever better identity and travel legitimation, but everybody close to neutral borders might be searched. When the Germans arrested a messenger and found the dossier it was almost inevitable that in some reports the source could be identified and then some Dutchmen in Holland would be arrested.

As the land fighting came closer and reached Holland, our efforts intensified and golden security rules were neglected. One such rule was, 'be active in one illegal enterprise only', then when you were arrested your partners would know that they must take immediate evasive action, which was always a bother and disruptive. But if one man participated in many things, even if it were only the distribution of illegal press communiqués, he might be arrested for that and you didn't know whether your own organization was in danger. Another example: the courier lines were now also used to evacuate the Allied soldiers left behind after Market Garden. General Hackett here was one of them and has written a moving book, *I was a stranger*, on his escape through the tidal marshes between the German and Allied lines. This perhaps is a good point to describe the escape, considered in London so important that a special organization was set up, MI9, to mastermind it on the Continent.

Already in 1940, stray soldiers of the BEF had found citizens willing to hide them, and to hand them from address to address into the Vichy zone and so to Spain. Airey Neave escaped from Colditz, together with a Dutch officer, another example of English–Dutch co-operation, and upon returning to London in 1942, was put in charge of organizing escape from Holland, Belgium and France. He was not lucky with his first agent, a girl who fell victim to the *Englandspiel*, but in June 1943, he dropped his second agent in Holland, and thanks to him, and later to other agents, the Dutch escape routes could now check the identity of airmen and POWs by radio before they picked them up and evacuated them. Before this time, German provocateurs had been able to pose as Allied military, for instance, as Polish or Norwegian RAF pilots, and penetrate and get to know whole chains of relay people right down to Spain. Some 500 patriots had been arrested and lost in consequence.

In his book *Saturday at MI9*, Neave figured that some 3,000 airmen had been shot down over north-west Europe and avoided capture. They then had to be found by his organization, by the help of which some 90 per cent had reached the Allied lines, according to Airey Neave, as also had some 4,000 other soldiers. His grandest moment was, no doubt, the evacuation from the Market Garden battle area of some 130 Allied soldiers, in Operation 'Pegasus', arranged by Neave from Nijmegen and by his agents north of the Rhine communicating by telephone of the electricity network right across the German lines.

Now what to say about the results of our intelligence? Some results were seen and enjoyed by our population, such as the bombing of a Gestapo prison or a military headquarters, and some were not immediately evident, such as the destruction of the central registry of all identity passes, as a result of which local authorities could now issue genuine identity papers to underground people without fear of discovery. Some results were only known after the war, such as the negotiations through BI channels between the Germans and the Allies that stopped needless destruction and inundation and prepared the surrender of all German forces in the Netherlands on 5 May, at which ceremony HRH Prince Bernhard was rightly present as our C-in-C. Of course, these are illustrations only.

The real importance of our work was to be found in the legitimacy it gave our exiled government to be seen to be in continuous contact with our people in Holland, and to be effective by awaiting the first post-war cabinet. And just as important was the security our work gave to the Allies in knowing exactly what went on across the rivers to the flank of the Twenty-first Army Group, not to mention our detailed reporting on the V1 and the V2 launching sites. Daily liaison was exercised between SHAEF and BI in situations of urgency. When the First Canadian Army came to Holland, south of the Rhine, its intelligence office settled in the same building with BI and MI6 Dutch section and was informed, so to speak, every hour on the hour about developments north of the river. When the whole of the Netherlands had been liberated in May 1945 the leaders of the Canadian Army assembled agents and leaders of intelligence groups in The Hague, and formally thanked them in words that I quote: General Ffoulkes said: 'It is probably safe to say that never has there been so highly organized a system of espionage as that which existed in Holland over so long a period.' Considered in terms of lives saved to the Canadian Army, the following remark of a battalion officer may be quoted: 'In Italy we had to go out and get our information the hard way, but here in Holland, the Dutch presented it to us on a platter, and our casualties have been that much lighter in consequence.'

To end my presentation, I quote General Crerar, C-in-C, Canadian Army:

Since September 1944, I have been responsible for many operations in the Netherlands, and Canadian and Allied troops under my command have fought a number of notable battles leading to the final and complete defeat of the enemy in your country. In those operations I have been constantly assisted by the information furnished to me by you. I realize the great risks that you have run to gain this information, and the penalties which have been exacted from you and from your comrades who are no longer with us, but what I want you to know is that your devotion to our common cause was constantly in my mind, and that long before your country was free, I was relying on you to help devise the operations we carried out against the enemy. Your reports were accurate, prompt and an important factor in the final defeat of the enemy forces in the Netherlands.

DISCUSSION

Drs Wellenstein

May I comment on Mr Paape's remarkable overview of resistance during wartime in the Netherlands? I did not quite agree with what Mr Paape said about the railway strike in the Netherlands in 1944. From my recollection, the management of the Dutch railways was not taken by surprise; perhaps a few people in the management were, but certainly not the management as a whole. I remember very well that discussions with them had taken place for a year at least about a possible eventual strike at some opportune moment in the final phase of the war; and indeed it wouldn't have been possible to accommodate some 30,000 people, to provide them with food stamps, with money – they had to be paid – if that had not been very meticulously prepared; and all that worked excellently. So I think it is a bit exaggerated to say that you were totally taken by surprise when the London government for the Netherlands gave the order to start the strike. I think they were very well prepared.

Dr Andrew asked: 'Is it true that the fifth column had such an enormous influence, as the envoy Sir Neville Bland reported to London?' From my recollection, these stories were very much exaggerated. There was a Nazi fifth column, but I don't think it influenced in any significant way the outcome of the five days.

Drs Paape

About the railway strike, you're right, there had been contacts between Utrecht, where the central direction of the Netherlands railway was, and London, and there were some preparations made in Utrecht, but my term 'taken by surprise' doesn't mean more than taken by surprise *at that moment*, at the very moment of mid-September.

Professor de Jong

I would like to point out first of all that Sir Neville, when he reported the picture as it occurred to him during the days of fighting in The Hague, was completely trustworthy and authentic. He reported what had been officially said in the Army communiqué. I pointed out in my general book on the German fifth column in the Second World War, published in this country I think in 1956, 33 years ago, that with the exception of Poland and Yugoslavia, most of the stories dealing with the intervention of the German fifth column at the time of the German invasion, are merely a projection of the feelings of fear engendered among the nation. It was I think furthermore shown that any major war in recent history has started with what one might call a fifth column panic! It was very much apparent in the early stages of the First World War in Britain and France, but the same thing occurred in the Franco-Prussian war of 1870–71. The main point is of course that these exaggerated stories about a fifth column were disproved by events in the First World War, whilst in the Second World War there was no possibility of correction. People came out of the Netherlands with the firm conviction that the defeat of the Dutch Army had been caused by the intervention of a German-inspired fifth column, and later on, the actions of the Dutch Nazis, who politically gave support to the regime of Nazism, merely strengthened the belief in the intervention of a German fifth column in the invasion period. I think I may say that this belief was maintained until the publication of my own book in 1956.

Drs Schulten

I have a question for Mr Paape. On 10 May, the Dutch Army entered an alliance; the surrender was on the 14th and then the Army was largely intact. What makes me wonder always is that so much resistance has a military background, so has the fighting spirit of the Army disappeared at the moment of the defeat? When I think that Baron d'Aulnis was a far better officer than a student, that Mr Paape has also a military background, and that in a most famous novel on the resistance by Herman Friedhoff, there are so many people of a military background, I wonder what is the relation between the spirit of the Army, the mentality, and the first resistance?

Drs Paape

Well, I ask myself whether this is a question for an historian or a question for a psychologist. Of course you are quite right when you say that in the resistance, throughout the whole of the war and not only in the first period, the element of former Dutch military men was considerable. But what was the significance of having been in the Army, having fought in those five days in May 1940, or not having met any Germans in those five days, for the willingness and the capabilities of their later resistance? As far as I am aware, there have not been any serious studies in this direction. Perhaps that is something for a military historian?

Leen Pot

The problem was that there were quite a number of people who tried to do something against the Germans at that time, but the possibilities were very limited. We knew people from the Army, but at the time we were students or we were involved in sports. There were quite a number of people, but we could find nothing practical to do. It depended very largely on the position of all the people involved. If you were single, and you had some money, it helped: it is always somewhat easier to start to think about these things, than when you have a large family to support, and for most people in an occupied country, the first aim was how to survive. Next, when you could survive, you could think about doing something against the Germans. I don't see that there is a connection with people in military service who were particularly likely to do such work. So I can't give a clear answer to this.

Drs Paape

I think also there were circumstances which tell against the thesis of my friend Schulten. The first is the atmosphere at the end of the five days' war in May: the shock of this sudden defeat, in no more than five days, the way in which everybody thought to have to wait for the end of the German campaign without any confidence that even Belgium or France would have a resistance which would lead to a victory for these Allied countries. Second, if the military, the Dutch Army, had thought of a resistance of their own immediately after the defeat, why then did they surrender practically all the hand arms and weapons at the moment of capitulation? There was a great lack of small arms in the first years of the occupation and if these people had the idea of going into some activities of a resistance nature, they wouldn't have delivered their arms – they would have kept them.

Gervase Cowell

I would like to make some comments arising from Christopher Andrew's presentation. He ended with three questions and I would like to answer the cheekiest of them. Yes, there is still a close and valued collaboration between the intelligence services of our two countries, full-stop! I would also like to take up the point about rivalries between services, and say a few words on this – not for Christopher Andrew's sake, because I am sure he doesn't subscribe to the more extreme mythologies, but there is a concept that there was some kind of dire organizational antagonism between SIS and SOE. Now the explanation of this is quite simple. First of all, nobody in those two services was uniformly wise, uniformly brave, uniformly competent. There were some who were extremely so, there were many who were more so than we had any right to expect, and there were others who were as human as the rest of us. Now the ideal circumstance in which you obtain intelligence is a complacent enemy. Your enemy doesn't remain complacent for very long if he keeps getting blown up, and this was the discord which was at the origin of the conflict between SIS and SOE. Nobody, I think, certainly not the operators on the ground, certainly not the infuriated desk officers in London, could really decide whether any one SIS report was of more value than any one SOE bomb. So finally, I would like to try and defuse this idea that there was a great organizational antagonism between the two – there were many, many points of friction, there were many, many examples of the human condition under the stress of war.

To come to the present day, I would like also to dispel a delusion that there is any great secrecy about the SOE archives as they now exist. Some people are hesitant about coming and asking questions about SOE. My function is to supply any information about SOE and I would welcome any enquiries that people have about matters of fact, about the wartime records of SOE. The records are in a dreadful state. Michael Foot will testify as well as anybody how badly, how inadequately, they were kept, how ineptly they were weeded and how difficult it is to find answers as they now exist, but we are open. It is an open shop for anybody who wants to enquire.

Professor Janssen

We have heard several fine lectures, but all gave me, as a foot soldier in the war, simply a Dutch student, an impression of being seen from above by historians, and for my feeling, it's not exactly as it was when you lived through it. I know we need the qualities of a literary author to unravel how it was to live through it day by day. You can listen to stories about the secret service and they're absolutely correct, but how it was, to go as a courier on your bike, with wooden tyres, through the snow from one city to another to deliver a message, which you have never seen, which went somewhere you didn't know where, you didn't know what it contained, you didn't know what it was good for – that is an aspect which I missed today.

Sir John Hackett

Chairman, what I heard in those last remarks was music to my ears. Sitting through the last couple of very interesting days, hearing of the conferences, the statements, the to-ings and fro-ings of great men, at an enormous altitude, I felt as if I were in the stalls at Covent Garden watching a ballet of Olympic choreography. Right out of my own world. What Professor Janssen said just now reminds me of the world I lived in for four months in the winter of 1944–45, getting a worm's eye view, not even that of somebody in the engine room who is occasionally allowed a glimpse of the gracious life on the promenade deck, of which we've heard quite a lot in the last couple of days. No, a real worm's eye view was what I had, and living as a heavy 'under-diver' for four-and-a-half months 50 yards away from a German military police billet, looked after by brave Christian women, one was in the worm's burrow, with a vengeance, and a very interesting and amusing time it was.

And at one time, avid listeners as we were to BBC broadcasts and Radio Orange through the wireless set kept under the floor, which you always had to have screwed down to a whisper in case its voice carried to the military police billet down the road, we made up the news and put together a little underground paper which enjoyed the rather corny title of *Pro Patria*. I was our military correspondent, and I would write notes on the war in the west, which I would write in English and they would then be translated into Dutch by one of the ladies in the household, who had studied to be an English teacher, put on a wax by the young woman who was nursing me, and then typed out on that. All 200 copies of *Pro Patria* were distributed on a bicycle by brother John, and it went for three numbers before the *Sicherheitsdienst* began to take an interest in this little publication; and they had to close it down and I was moved to a somewhat safer residence under the wing of a retired colonel of artillery. All this while, of course (and I was enchanted to hear echoes of it this morning), I was in very close touch with an old friend and colleague of Baron d'Aulnis, who became a very good friend of mine ever since I was a client of his as an under-diver in the winter of 1944–45.

Coming away from that atmosphere, with my acquaintances there, none of whom really knew very much about the divine ballet being played upstairs, I carry with me several things: first of all, three copies, one of each edition of *Pro Patria*, which I preserve. I also carried away the false papers under which I lived, and if Tony Benn ever becomes Prime Minister in this country, I shall blow the dust off them and resume my Dutch citizenship as Mijnheer van Dalen, which is what I am on those papers; I have all the right documents to help me, including one excusing me from going to work in Germany, and so on, signed in various handwritings, mostly by the mother of the young man who was looking after me, now a retired Minister of the Reformed Church, who sent me these after the war and said, 'These, of course were not signed by the people whose names are on them – they were signed by my sainted mother, who developed a skill in forgery, almost unexampled, which was of the greatest service to us all.'

But the thing that I carried away with me most strongly, apart from these little relics, was an awareness among the people with whom I lived of their deep devotion to and confidence in the Queen. This was very, very marked, very widely spread and very deep and I carried away, with these trinkets that I brought out, a letter from these good people to Queen Wilhelmina to express what they could of this loyalty, trust and affection. And I am quite certain from my worm's eye view, that this was one of the very greatest elements in preserving the Dutch national spirit of resistance.

Jan Aart Scholte

Christopher Andrew – you asked yesterday about the Far East and the collaboration there. I don't know much about it and perhaps someone else can fill in and correct all my mistakes, let me just say the few things that I do know, or think I know. One was that there was no foreign intelligence service in the Netherlands Indies before the war. SOE did set up an oriental mission in Singapore in 1940, but Brooke-Popham, who was Commander-in-Chief Eastern Forces, was quite reluctant to let them make any contacts or do anything, so they had no connections with the Dutch and no agents were recruited, and nothing was really in place before the war, although they did have some informal contacts. In any case though, after the invasion, there were no stay behind parties. In the actual operations of 1941–42, there was no Dutch participation in the Malaya campaign, save one unit which came from Sumatra and went over; and the British commander says that they scored a 'considerable success' behind Japanese lines. As for British participation on the intelligence side in Java, there was none that I really know of. Between 1942 and 1945, SOE was in exile in India. The Dutch did have a contingent of 154 soldiers who had been sent out from England to go to Java, but they got stranded in Colombo halfway, because Java fell so quickly. Of those 154, about half were recruited into a Corps Insulinde, which was then brought in as an Anglo-Dutch country section in SOE. There were all sorts of Anglo-Dutch tensions there too, just as there were in most areas, and in fact they had about half-a-dozen missions to Sumatra but didn't really gather anything. The other part was, of course, the Australian branch which you mentioned.

There a Netherlands forces intelligence service was set up in 1943. They had some collaboration with the other Allies, although again tensions ran high and the Anglo-Dutch relations, in particular, were difficult. The head of the Netherlands Indies government in exile complained that the American and British Allies didn't give him any submarines, flying boats, etc. that he needed to carry out intelligence missions to Java and Sumatra. I don't know any more than that. I haven't seen documents beyond that. All in all, there was no intelligence known in the Netherlands at the end of the war, and so they confronted the territory in total ignorance.

Chairman

Part of the trouble, I believe, if we can believe Charles Cruickshank – and I don't see why we shouldn't on this point – is that the Dutch and SOE had different objects in mind when trying to run parties into the Dutch East Indies. The Dutch were anxious to mount commando-type raids to go in and blow something up and come out again, and SOE was toying with the idea of setting up semi-permanent circuits of the kind that it had running already in France and Belgium, or northern Italy, where there were whole bodies of natives co-operating with SOE prepared to take part in an eventual national rising, the prospects of which, we now know, were nil; so perhaps the Dutch were right to contemplate simply going in and blowing something up and coming out again. But there were these two completely conflicting ideas of what people ought to be sent into Java and Sumatra for, so no wonder the two forces got on rather badly.

Jhr Beelaerts

May I just enlighten you a little on some matters that I know about. First of all, there were contacts between the Netherlands Indies and Delhi. The late ambassador in Canada went there as chief of the Far Eastern part, and I don't think there were ever contacts between Java and either Sumatra or Ceylon where I was myself. The problem in Ceylon originated in the different points of view of two captains there. We were first asked in India, a whole troop of us, if we were ready for commando raids, and only volunteers were taken. All the officers stepped forward, a large number of NCOs, then some of the men reluctantly volunteered too. There was one man, a bookseller in Schevenigen, who was 40 years old. He stepped out first, and I always had great respect for that man. But then the other captain had more the SOE idea, and so there was within the Corps Insulinde a great cleavage, and that came to the knowledge of London, and they said there was a report of a revolt and then I had to explain to those in London what had really happened.

DISCUSSION

Mark Seaman

My question is addressed to the Baron. I was just curious to know what was the extent of the activities of Dutch agents, and what intelligence they managed to gather from outside the Netherlands itself, and if there were any instances of, say, the forced workers in Germany being used to acquire information from inside the Reich itself. And just as a second ancillary question, was there any evidence of any co-operation with the Dutch communist party and any form of Dutch intelligence service at all?

Baron d'Aulnis

When I was asked to come here and make a presentation, I had forgotten all about intelligence, and never thought about it, so I had to read a number of books and my own reports from the war, to warm up again. Now in all these books and reports I have not found anything about a systematic penetration into Germany. Of course, there was incidental information from men coming back from Germany, but nothing systematic, and the only man who could answer this question would perhaps be Charles Seymour. I know that in 1944 we were all instructed to go and try, but that was a bit late to set up something systematic.

Charles Seymour

I agree with what you say. We did get some information from you and others, but it was incidental and mostly came from your countrymen coming back from captivity in Germany.

Baron d'Aulnis

The second question is – was there any co-operation between Dutch intelligence and communists in Holland? The communists in Holland had some very ferocious underground activity and they were very good at it because they were far more ruthless than we were. In the underground groups that I mentioned, there was, for instance, a Raad van Verzet, and in this Raad van Verzet, a very good underground communist called Gerben Wagenaar was very active and co-operated in complete good faith with everyone else. During that period there was no conflict to speak of between communist underground workers and patriot workers in the intelligence community.

115

Leen Pot

I went to Eindhoven in September 1944 with a group consisting of OSS (American), MI6 and three Dutch officers, and we tried to send agents to Germany. The problem was we could only instruct these people, give them radio sets, etc. but little was known about the possibilities of getting these people established in Germany. We were asked especially to give information about the west of Germany, and transport movements in that area. The Americans had rather a different approach to such a problem. We said we must have a reasonable chance that the mission would be a success, while the Americans said, 'Yes, there are so many people dying, let them drop somewhere in Germany.' That created a problem as they were Dutch nationals. We said, 'No, we are only prepared to do that when we are certain that they have a chance to succeed.' Therefore it was long delayed and finally practically non-existent.

Anna Harvey-Simoni

I should like to add a footnote to Dr Andrew's remarks about the panic after the fall of Holland which led in England to the large number of internments of poor refugees who had left one country already, if not two. After the loss of the *Arandora Star*, which took internees to Canada and was torpedoed, Churchill didn't change his mind. He asked parliament to stand up in memory of the dead of the *Arandora Star*, which didn't bring them back, nor was internment lifted on the people interned, for example on the Isle of Man, which in the end gave us the Amadeus Quartet.

Colonel Cooper

Chairman, just a short observation on the resistance people whom we met when advancing on to Nijmegen. I was with the Guards Armoured Division in the armoured car squadron, Life Guards, doing a liaison job, and my task was to get through to the American airborne in Nijmegen. After Zon and Eindhoven, we were beginning to pick up resistance people all the time. They were absolutely invaluable, and when on this occasion I reached Nijmegen, the outskirts and suburbs, I picked one up purely by chance who guided me to the American forward troops on the right flank of the bridge, overlooking the bridge, where I stayed for about three days – I couldn't get out owing to heavy shelling. The Resistance were also most helpful to two of our troops, who eventually got through to the Polish airborne brigade near

116

Arnhem. The map-reading was difficult; they went through in the early morning mist, as you know, and by talking with the resistance people beforehand, they were able to take by-roads and so on. At that time, nearly every squadron and sometimes armoured car troops, and certainly our headquarters, had worked with resistance people. The organization must have been good for us to meet up all the time.

Chairman

This was largely, I believe, because there were some SOE Jedburgh teams in the neighbourhood who were assisting in providing that organization.

Tex Banwell

I was captured at Arnhem, and escaped with two others from the train that was taking us to Germany. We made contact with the underground, and being a platoon sergeant, I was thoroughly conversant with all weapons, explosives, and whatnot. After a day or so, contact was made with London by a Captain King who was liaison officer, and I was ordered to stay behind in Holland as an instructor. At this time, the Dutch underground were getting supplies of bren guns, sten guns, rifles and explosives, but they weren't used to handling, assembling, dismantling or firing them. So I was ordered to stay as an instructor.

After a week or so at the beginning of October, we had orders that a high-ranking German officer was coming through from Berlin to the front with a secret document and a secret piece of metal bearing on the V2 rocket. This officer was to be stopped at all costs. There was no transport on the roads after dark in Holland at that time, so I took ten of my underground men out and laid an ambush. We were told on the night after we had a rehearsal that this German officer was on his way. No other transport was on the roads, and about midnight, the car came into view. I had the bren gun, shot the German car out, killed the escort and the driver and badly wounded the officer. The officer was taken back to our headquarters and interrogated. He was badly wounded in the knee, and afterwards they were at a loss what to do with him. So I said, 'Well, the best thing is, I'll shoot him.' They said, 'Oh no, you can't do that.' So I said, 'Well, if one of you were to be captured, you would suffer severe torture.' So again I offered to shoot him. They said, 'No. We'll take him back to the old bridge [which was where we laid the ambush, just near Putten] and we'll leave him alongside the road.' I had already said, prior to leaving the area, that we should have pushed the German vehicle into the woods, picked up our empty rounds of ammunition, which could be identified as British, and left the place clear. But they wouldn't do this. So they took him back and laid him alongside the road. In the morning, of course, the first vehicle along had to be German.

So we only know what the Germans said about this – but we do know that the men in charge got the Burgermeister out of his accommodation and asked him what he knew about it. The poor man knew nothing about the ambush, so he was ordered to take every man between the ages of 16 and 60 and put them in the big church in Putten. They were all interrogated, but of course none of them knew anything about it.

In fact Putten is such a religious area that everything people do they believe is with God's will. These 600 poor people were taken away and eventually, to the best of my knowledge, and everybody else's knowledge, they were all shot. And as proof of this I have a book here, which was the first book printed and given to me by the Municipality of Putten, and in it are pictures of every one of the 600 men who were taken away. I would like to pass the book round, because I still believe that not so many people in Holland are aware of this unfortunate experience of the underground, but for all that they were a great bunch.

Chairman

Thank you. I saw one or two heads being shaken. Do you want to comment on that, Dr de Jong?

Dr de Jong

First of all I would like to point out that the people from Putten who were arrested and driven away were not shot, but that most of them died, in the months to come, in Neuengamme concentration camp. Second, I would like to reassure Mr Banwell that the tragedy of Putten is very well known in Holland, not only among the inhabitants of the unfortunate village itself, but nationwide. And I myself have given as many reliable details as possible in a minute description of what really happened during the incident on which Mr Banwell gave his personal recollections.

Chairman

I am also bound as an historian of the war to remark that though Putten is scandalously well known in the Netherlands, just as Oradour is scandalously well known in France, there were areas 100 miles across in Poland and the Ukraine where there was not a village left standing. You must remember that these few massacred villages in the west are symbols to us of a horror that was vastly more widespread on the eastern front and helps to explain the tension between east and west that survives to the present day. Dr Andrew, I believe that you wanted to make one or two comments on what has arisen this morning.

Dr Andrew

I can respond I think very easily to the various comments that have been made about areas I touched on in my presentation by saying that I agree, I think, with all of them. Let me just press a couple of points which still remain to be clarified, with which we may make some further progress. Twenty years ago the history of British intelligence during the Second World War was written exclusively in terms of human intelligence. Since the early 1970s nobody would dream of writing about the British intelligence effort in the Second World War without signals intelligence. Now, what I find difficult to understand in the Dutch case is that we know, and have known for some time – the evidence is there in the Congressional Enquiry on Pearl Harbour, for example – that the Dutch succeeded in breaking one of the more sophisticated cipher systems of the time, the Japanese Purple system. Can it really be the case that this highly sophisticated system was the only cipher system that was broken by the Dutch on the eve of, or at the beginning of, the Second World War? That would be really quite remarkable were it the case. So there seems to me an interesting area for further enquiry there.

Second, since the discussion has turned to some of the atrocities of the Second World War, there's one element in the Dutch experience which is perhaps worth mentioning briefly. I suppose one of those many remarkable and horrible things about the final solution is that almost no one ever dared to challenge Hitler face to face about the most appalling policy of the twentieth century. The one exception that we know about is one which derives from the Dutch experience. This was Henrietta von Schirach, who saw Jews being rounded up in Amsterdam and sent, as she correctly supposed, to their death and who, because she was the daughter of Hitler's photographer and had known Hitler since childhood, dared to go and confront the Führer with it. As she describes, accurately I believe in her memoirs, she was told not to be so sentimental.

CHAPTER FOUR

THE *ENGLANDSPIEL*

M.R.D. Foot

Right at the start I must make it clear that this is not a definitive account of the *Englandspiel*, not even an attempt at one. The *Englandspiel* was the German coup against the British secret services and against the Dutch regime in exile. This is simply an interim report based on those SOE archives I have seen and those books I have read, before I have attempted to plumb the riches of the archives in the Netherlands and before I have interrogated many of the survivors, two of whom are present today. I hope to open up a few fresh perspectives on that famous disaster by putting it into its historical context, and exploring a few of the personalities and oddities involved.

The *Englandspiel*, that is, the game against England, was the German name for the successful playing back over 18 months, from the spring of 1942 to the autumn of 1943, of far too many Dutch agents dispatched to the Netherlands by various British secret services: nine from MI6, the intelligence service; 51 from SOE, our Dirty Tricks department, founded (hardly before time) in July 1940 to use the Nazis' methods back against them; and one, the only woman in the whole lot, from MI9, the escape service. They not only fell into German hands but were most of them successfully played back, so that the services who sent them thought that they were still operating against the enemy. Their controllers in London, whether British or Dutch, were entirely deceived.

The manifest truth about this, as presented in a BBC television programme five years ago, was that it was all a ghastly mistake on the part of N section in SOE, which alone bears all the blame. The truth, so far as I can make out, was not really anything like so simple.

Let us begin by considering the myth, still widespread in the Netherlands, that the whole business was all part of some deep English deceptive ploy. So strong is Continental faith in the omniscient and omnipotent British secret service that it is taken for granted that such a service cannot make catastrophic mistakes: a total fallacy. Had this been a deceptive ploy, what possible British interest could it have served? It may be that Hitler got worried by the amount of effort the British appeared to be pouring into the Netherlands; he took a keen personal interest in the *Englandspiel*, as in many other aspects of SOE's activities, which served to waste a certain amount of his time. He may even have moved a very few divisions from the eastern front to the west, as a form of safeguard. What did half a dozen divisions weigh in the strategic scales on the eastern front, where each side had over 200 engaged? At the same time as the first agents involved in the *Englandspiel* were dropped, in the winter of 1941–42, there was not much else going on that the Russians could appreciate as likely to take even a feather's weight off their own burdens; so the distraction of a division or two may have counted for a trifle – not for more.

Consider, moreover, how a deceptive ploy is actually worked by experts. We have an excellent text on this: J. C. Masterman's *The Double-Cross System in the War of 1939 to 1945*. Masterman was the number two in a branch of MI5 (the security service) called B 1 a which, all through the war, successfully played back to the Germans all the agents the Germans thought they had on this island. This was correctly referred to this morning by Christopher Andrew as one of the greatest intelligence coups on record. Those who want to understand how to do this sort of work should read it up in Masterman, who explains the minute attention to detail that is needed in order to do it correctly. None of the accounts that have come out about the sort of people whom N section of SOE dropped into Holland suggest for a moment that they were of a calibre to take part in this kind of deceptive ploy.

There is no point in trying to defend the indefensible; N section was indeed indefensibly stupid; but it was not alone, or even wholly, to blame. Why did it stumble as it did?

Various explanations – not excuses, but explanations – for what happened deserve more weight than they have habitually been given by historians. The first point to consider, so simple that it is often overlooked, is terrain. Is the terrain of the Netherlands really suitable for undercover or sabotage operations? At that time, back in the early 1940s, only the Irish had shown any aptitude for urban guerrilla. In Dublin, under the matchless Michael Collins, who was killed in the Irish civil war in 1922, they had brought off a number of coups against the British intelligence services, and had indeed seen the backs of their occupying army when the British gave up the struggle in December 1921. At this moment we have the IRA around our ears, seeking to prove that they are still competent to carry on this kind of campaign, at a strength reliably reported to be about 200, when some of them are not away at school. But SOE did not have much in the way of capacity for urban guerrilla; in a largely urbanized Dutch society, there was nowhere they were likely to work with much success. And in the Netherlands countryside, as every Dutchman knows, movement is very easy, but also very easily controlled. Bridges abound; on any bridge police can set up snap controls to check who is moving to and fro. Nor is it easy country to cross, even on horseback, or by motor-cycle. Motor-cycles cannot swim; horses can, but no horse can dive in and out of dykes too wide to jump, over and over again, and remain fresh.

There is also a fundamental difficulty of timing, which needs to be considered. The *Englandspiel* began, as far as SOE was concerned, with its second pair of agents, who parachuted in in November 1941. Those were very early days for starting up this kind of thing from scratch. First steps are always the hardest in this field. It may be that there was undue pressure on Laming, the first head of N section, by Dr Dalton (no relation to SIS's man who killed himself), the loud-voiced and thrusting first minister in charge of SOE, who was determined to get results, and kept bullying his staff to produce them. Possibly he bullied Laming into starting off before he was really ready.

There were also dreadful difficulties about communications, always the central point for SOE. Of all the occupied countries, the Netherlands – though only just across the North Sea – was one of the most remote from Great Britain. The early experiments in moving people to and fro by boat had mostly to be closed down by the spring of 1942, because the guards along the coast had become too alert for parties to slip between them. Two men present, Mr Jorissen and Sir Brooks Richards, will recall that a few weeks ago they and I attended a ceremony at Wassenaar in memory of six Frenchmen killed in February 1944 in an attempt to find out whether a single brave man could pick his way through the guard belt: none of them could. If you went to the Netherlands at all, you had to go there by parachute, or take a very long journey round by land. There was, it is true, a courier line run by MI6 for a while by boat between Delfzijl in north Holland and Sweden, until the Germans took it over.

When SOE was founded, in July 1940, MI6 explained that clandestine communications, especially by wireless, were a difficult and esoteric business, best left to the professionals. So until 1 June 1942 SOE was compelled to use MI6's wireless sets and MI6's codes. In the presence of Leo Marks I don't want to say much about this, but I will observe that Colonel 'Passy', General de Gaulle's head of secret services, remarks in an acrid footnote in his memoirs that by 1943 it was a blissful change for him to be able to deal with an efficient signals section in SOE, instead of the bumblers in SIS with whom he had had to put up before. MI6's agents and methods were by no means infallible. One of their agents was arrested in the Netherlands in February 1942, broke at once under interrogation, and explained in the minutest detail what MI6's coding systems were; he had been elaborately trained. So Sergeant May, the Germans' decoding expert, was fully informed about them when, a month later, the first of the SOE agents fell into his hands.

The cardinal factor in starting up the *Englandspiel*, so far as I can make out, was the prevalence in the Netherlands of a few efficient Dutch criminals who thought their bread was buttered on the German rather than on the Dutch side. When it was all over and the Germans had been defeated, the Allied services picked up the two Germans who had been running the *Englandspiel*, Lieutenant-Colonel Giskes of the *Abwehr* and *Hauptsturmführer* Schreieder of the *Sicherheitsdienst*, who oddly enough – in the light of what was said this morning about secret service rivalries – worked absolutely hand in glove in running the captured agents. They both, on being captured, sang like tame canaries. One of the numerous reports of Schreieder's interrogations runs to 78 single-spaced foolscap pages of typescript. In it he produces a list of over 50 Dutch double agents, men and women, who were working for him.

It was through one of them, when for once one of the SOE agents let his guard down a little, that the SD made its first break-in. Thijs Taconis, saboteur, dropped in November 1941, lived in Arnhem and worked pretty strictly as he had been trained to do by SOE at Beaulieu, keeping up a stiff run of security precautions, until he got a signal from England saying he had a supply drop coming shortly. He could not think how he was going to get his supplies away from the dropping zone; he badly needed someone with a lorry. By accident he bumped into someone who happened to run a small transport firm. A perfectionist would have made inquiries; he had no time. He did not know that the man who had the transport firm was one of Schreieder's favourite informants, who passed word on to another.

Sergeant Willy Kup of the *Abwehr* heard about it, and went to tell Giskes that he was in touch with a man who was going to get a drop of parachuted stores from England. Giskes replied, *Gehen Sie zum Nordpol mit diesem Geschichte*, tell that one to the marines; hence the *Abwehr* codename for their coup, North Pole. Giskes, much doubting, staked out the site Kup indicated, and saw parachutes falling, with containers on their ends; saw men emerge from the hedge, pick up the containers, and load them into one of the double agent's lorries.

After this, it became easy. The Germans knew from their wireless direction-finding service that there was a clandestine operator somewhere in a downtown suburb of The Hague. They had not yet pinpointed the precise spot, but soon did so. Through the lorry driver they planted on Taconis a message about the *Prinz Eugen*, a German cruiser, which they reckoned Taconis was sure to report to his control. For, although it was not SOE's job to collect intelligence, whenever a gobbet of intelligence came their way, of course agents passed it back.

A parenthesis is needed here about the relations between SOE and SIS. At the very beginning of SOE's career the chiefs of staff laid down that any intelligence SOE got, from whatever source, was under no circumstances to be distributed by SOE. It was to go instead to Colonel Dansey of SIS, who would do with it what he saw fit. Dansey had a desk in SOE's headquarters in Baker Street, certainly till 1942, perhaps all through the war. Every telegram that SOE sent, down at least to 1 June 1942, crossed Dansey's desk. SIS was much more fully informed about SOE than SOE was about SIS.

As expected Taconis passed on to Lauwers, his wireless operator, news that *Prinz Eugen* was currently in Schiedam. In March 1942 Lauwers was just standing by to open up a transmission to home station when his watchman, who owned the flat from which he was operating, came in and said that three cars had just drawn up outside; he thought the Gestapo was on to them. Whereupon Lauwers unscrewed his set, tossed it out of the window, and strolled off down the street. He had only made one mistake: he still had in his pocket the ciphered texts he had been about to transmit, which he had not had time to burn. He had walked two or three hundred yards down the street when one of the black cars pulled up beside him, a group of gentlemen tumbled out and arrested him. He produced his false papers and explained he was going out for a walk. They were not interested in where he was going; he was being arrested after having been watched for weeks.

He was convinced he had never been followed; he may have been badly trained, the Germans may have been bluffing. Either way, they had him. A first search revealed the ciphered messages, which could not be explained away. Moreover the set he had thrown out of the window had stuck on the washing line instead of falling into the rosebed, and was covered in his fingerprints; he could not deny that he was a clandestine wireless operator.

Sergeant May took the messages away for a few minutes, came back, and said 'Ah, I see the *Prinz Eugen* is in Schiedam.' This completely shattered Lauwers: would it not shatter anybody? When the Germans said, 'There are your messages, you were going to send them anyhow, when's your next sked?' he told them, and he sent the messages. He was astounded when N section's next message told him to send a ground onto which another operator could drop; the Germans were leaning hard on him by now, and he did so.

A well-known aspect of this problem, that has received a lot of attention from journalists and broadcasters, must now be tackled: the business of security checks. I lift from a paper Leo Marks wrote at the time a splendid phrase about MI6's security checks: 'This was simply a device to give the agents confidence.' It was of no earthly use; it was purely mechanical. Lauwers' orders were to make a mistake in every 16th letter, for his real check. The Germans recorded all the secret traffic they heard, as a matter of routine; it was easy to work back over past traffic and unravel checks. A much safer system lies in the prearranged question with an utterly irrelevant answer. Home station sends 'Would you like more cigarettes?' Any reply but 'How is Aunt Angela?' means the agent is in the wrong hands. This system is all right until you have an agent who goes over heart and soul to the enemy; but in that case you are lost anyhow.

There was a famous case in Malaya. SOE put in a local agent with a wireless operator, who were within three hours of their arrival delated to the Japanese by the villagers near by, who did not like the look of them. The wireless operator was caught with his set, and his codes, on the back of which he had scribbled down the test question and answer, which in his case was, 'Have you met Miriam?' 'Yes, I would like some whisky.' Underneath he had also written, 'Yes I saw her yesterday morning,' which was what he was to say if everything had gone wrong. At his interrogation the organizer – not the operator – was asked what these questions meant. 'Clever fellow,' he replied, 'He's transposed the right answer with the wrong.' Ceylon inquired, 'Have you met Miriam?' The Japanese replied 'Yes I saw her yesterday morning', so that for the rest of the war Peter Fleming had this channel available for deception messages. Leo Marks may be able to tell us more.

One point does tell in Lauwers' favour about security checks. Up to the moment of his arrest, he had been meticulous in his use of them; thereafter he was much more erratic. One of the messages he was caught carrying had a deliberate mistake in the vowel of the word 'stop', and he pretended that this was his proper check – to say stap or stip or step or stup instead. Nobody in Baker Street appeared to notice or to care. N section may have said that the checks were part of some trumpery fuss made by MI6, about which SOE did not need to bother.

Similarly, Marriot and Buckmaster's highly successful F section of SOE did not bother about security checks at all. Harry Peulevé, one of their best operators, never for example troubled to insert them; they all said what a reliable man he was.

Lauwers tried also, as did one or two of the other captured operators, a very simple device. It is a routine piece of clandestine security to begin every message with a jumble of letters before getting on to the real text. He took to beginning CAUCAU and ending GHTGHT. He did not know the office drill: by the time messages got onto staff officers' desks for action, all the surplus letters from before and after the message had been shorn off in the signals office. Bad luck – or bad management.

Two other technical points are worth a brief mention; Mr Marks may expand on either. One is what is called 'fingerprinting'. My sister spent half the war in the Y service, listening to Japanese submarines, and could soon tell which submarine she was listening to, because she knew the operator's style, his personal touch on the key. A lot of SOE's operators at home station were supposed to be familiar with the touch of the man who was working to them. The trouble about this is that touch is as easily imitable as handwriting; moreover, SOE does not seem to have recorded all its outgoing operators properly before 1943, by which time the *Englandspiel* was well under way. Again, direction-finding might have revealed that all the operators the Germans were working back were broadcasting from a single point.

It was also somewhat odd that no use was made of the S-phone. The S-phone, invented by SOE, was a device of which it was proud. A portable, secure, early walky-talky telephone, it was thought up by Tommy Davies in SOE's earliest days, and was available from late 1941. Several S-phones were dropped to 'North Pole' agents who we now know to have been in enemy hands. It may be that our airmen found the S-phone unusable: any pilot might be excused for asking not to have to circle round for several minutes over the Kammhuber Line, the most heavily defended anti-aircraft belt in the world outside Berlin. But if the S-phone could not be used, for RAF reasons, why send it at all? As it turned out, it made a pretty present for the enemy's signals intelligence staff.

A word is also needed about the individual agents who were victims of the *Englandspiel*. SOE's experiences in recruiting them were not altogether happy. Anybody who succeeded in escaping from the Netherlands made a point of going to see the Queen; Wilhelmina in turn made a point of seeing each one personally, so that she could tell them how proud she was that they had come out to join her. Any who showed the slightest inclination for secret work she referred to Mr van't Sant, who was running her secret service for her early in the war. By bad luck for SOE, van't Sant and Laming, the first head of N section, had had a slap-up row in Rotterdam over an espionage case in 1916 and had never spoken to each other since. So van't Sant made quite sure that anybody who was any good did not go anywhere near SOE, and Laming had to put up with the leavings. To put it bluntly, not all the agents sent to the Netherlands by SOE were absolutely the best that the Netherlands had to offer in the way of potential clandestines. Moreover, they were almost all privates or NCOs in the Netherlands forces; hardly any were officer types. As so often happens with other ranks when confronted with officer types in beautifully turned out Gestapo uniforms, they felt it their duty to answer questions put to them. Now no prisoner is on oath under interrogation; and we ought to try to sympathize with these unfortunates.

General Hackett spoke this morning about the importance of trying to look at the war from inside the wormhole, instead of from the peaks of Olympus. To manage a successful parachute jump in the dark, onto a strange field, which is an achievement in itself, brings a great surge of joy; to do it secretly and then be greeted by the correct codename in one's own language by one's reception committee brings another great surge of joy; anybody with an ounce of patriotic feeling is delighted to be back in the homeland; further surge of joy. Then, just as he is about to set out on the work of liberation, someone on the reception committee says that there's a rather awkward control near by, and it would be as well for the newcomer to hand his pistol over, so that it can be smuggled past by those who already know how. So one holds one's pistol out by the muzzle – and is thereupon handcuffed. In a moment, one is surrounded by men in Wehrmacht helmets and being questioned by an elegant officer in Gestapo uniform. The shock is bound to overwhelm anyone.

Moreover, the questioning goes on and on and on, all through the night and all through the next day and all through the night after that, if need be. One of the items Schreieder produced during his own interrogation was a list of a hundred principal questions put to every arriving agent during the *Englandspiel*. Not only the routine questions about date and place of birth, but the minutest details about one's companions on every course, one's fellow travellers in the aircraft coming over, who else was with one in training, which schools, which classrooms in which schools, everything down to the colour of the wallpaper. The Germans in 1942 were not yet aware how soon the sun of the Thousand Year Reich was going to set. They thought they had all the time in the world; they thought the captured agents were putty in their hands, and that every conceivable fragment of information would be squeezed out of them.

Moreover, according to one captured agent – Dourlein, one of the five who got away – if the captive started to get difficult, the Germans would simply say, look, we admire the way you are trying to keep things from us, but if you don't answer this question we shall simply prop you up against the nearest wall, and send a message to London that the Germans have captured you. That way, most agents unravelled quite fast. And with all their faults, which were legion, the agents who went into Holland on this extraordinary series of ventures were neverthe-less extremely brave men, who deserve our respect as well as our compassion. With that awful condescension with which history looks back on the past, we can hardly help, in retrospect, putting some blame on them for having talked at all.

One cannot help wondering why sometimes they did not try, more often than they did, to feed the Germans with false information. A man dropped in the spring of 1944 – after 'North Pole' had been closed down – was captured, and asked what his security checks were; he gave entirely false ones, and Marks noticed immediately. It is easy to wonder why the operators captured during North Pole had not adopted so simple a device: give really startling security checks, and somebody is almost bound to notice in Baker Street.

When eventually two of the agents, Dourlein and Ubbink, did a very good Sunday night escape from the prison at Haaren, where most of them were kept, they cast up months later in London – and were promptly put back in prison. This has always been a puzzle, but one that can now be explained, even if – again – it cannot be excused. They were locked up for security reasons that seem wholly intelligible in retrospect.

They escaped in August 1943; cast up in Berne in the third week in November; and did not get to England till February 1944, coming round through southern France and Spain. When they got back they went first to MI9's interrogators, who by this time were thoroughly skilled in talking to men who had done escapes. There were several sorts of question they always asked. You went over a wire fence? What sort of wire – barbed or plain? Did you get over at the posts, or between them? Was the wire straight at the top, or bent over? Dourlein's and Ubbink's answers contradicted each other on a couple of dozen of these trumpery details: each contradiction trivial in itself, the cumulative effect damning. It looked very much as if at least one of them was a Gestapo plant.

SOE was eventually able to clear their names with MI9; other troubles supervened. During their Odyssey, they had brooded on their troubles; and had become convinced – quite wrongly, but the conviction was firm – that an officer on N section's staff must have been a German agent, because the Germans had hardly mentioned him, while they had talked in detail about all the rest. Having been trained in unarmed combat, they were determined to seek him out and kill him. What was to be done with them?

Lord Selborne, who had succeeded Dalton as the minister in charge of SOE, wrote to Herbert Morrison, the Home Secretary, to explain that SOE could not maintain a concentration camp, but could hardly let these wild men loose. Morrison replied that he could not keep a concentration camp either, but had a perfectly secure flat in Brixton prison; would that do? It would; Dourlein and Ubbink were shut up in that flat till a fortnight after Normandy D day, that is, till late June 1944.

This was not a very warm welcome for two men who had brought back firm news that for 18 months all SOE's efforts in the Netherlands had been counter-productive. On the other hand the invasion of Normandy was a cardinal operation of war, and strong measures were needed to make sure that its secrecy was preserved.

In conclusion, how much did the Germans gain from the *Englandspiel*? On the intelligence front, where they hoped to make their main gain, they made none. In France the Gestapo, by a neatly-managed wireless game, got 18 agents dropped slap into their arms in the spring of 1944, in the hope that they would discover from them the date at least, if not the place, of the impending invasion. They discovered nothing. Similarly the Gestapo in the Netherlands plied their captives with questions about the forthcoming invasion and got nothing out of them; for the excellent reason that they knew nothing. On the secret army front, however, the *Englandspiel* did impose important, even significant delays.

The Dutch government in exile in London had to put up with SOE behaving in much the way that MI6 behaved over clandestine communications – we are handling an esoteric subject, you amateurs must not interfere with the experts. It was through the channels of SOE, which were not under Dutch control, that the Dutch government in exile tried to conduct much of its business with the Orde Dienst, that large and not very successful resistance movement, not very successful because the Germans read so large a proportion of the correspondence. Now, compare the *Englandspiel* with Operation 'Fortitude'. Through 'Fortitude', a colossal deception operation mounted by the British deception service with the help of B 1 a controlled agents, a major twist was inflicted on German strategy. The

'Overlord' landings could thus be made with success on the left bank of the Seine while crack divisions of the German Army were pinned on the

right bank by General Patton's notional forces in Kent and Essex. The Germans did not bring off anything like this.

Nevertheless they did impose severe delays, to which there will be only too many witnesses present, to the organization of armed resistance in the Netherlands. Nobody could foresee in 1943 that the course of combat was largely going to sweep past the Netherlands, so that opportunities for armed action would have turned out fairly limited. On the other hand, after the *Englandspiel* was wound up in the late autumn of 1943, as we heard this morning 56 more agents were sent in, of whom it is true 19 did not come back; but none of these 19 was arrested on his landing ground. Most of the dead were killed in action, or died because of further depredations by the only too prevalent Dutch double agents, who had wormed their way into their circuits.

Thanks to the rest, there were a number of highly successful Dutch resistance actions, many in conjunction with SAS, during the last few weeks of the war, in the north-eastern Netherlands.

The worst problem that arose from the *Englandspiel* was that it helped to implant deep suspicion of Dutch resistance in the minds of the highest British commanders, who had been shaken already by the troubles at Venlo which Christopher Andrew described this morning. The idea got about that it was not going to be safe to trust the Dutch, with some distressing consequences at Arnhem, about which we shall no doubt hear tomorrow. Yet though the course of the main battle gave Dutch subversive activity little chance to show what it was made of, it was far from useless, and deserves its place on the battle honours of successful resistance against Nazism.

*   *   *

Dr Andrew, Chairman

The best introduction to our next speaker is provided by Professor Foot on page 122 of his book *SOE*: 'Night duty officers in Baker Street found Leo Marks ready to defend or attack any philosophical position at any hour.'

Leo Marks

I have the greatest respect for Michael Foot as a person and as an historian; he has one outstanding quality, he is always prepared to admit when he is wrong. He has had a certain amount of practice in this since he first wrote *SOE in France* and I regret to say he is going to have considerably more because he is not in sight of the truth of the *Englandspiel* and I have warned him again and again that he would not be. There were just two minor points of his, and remember this is a major historian and an honest man who does admit when he is wrong, and if Michael can be misled, there are very few people who cannot. So there are just two minor things I would like to correct. One is that N Section was stupid. Well, it wasn't, it was average. If N Section were here today, N Section would ask your average type questions, but the answers must not be in Dutch, because only one member of the Directorate spoke it.

The other thing that Michael said is very dangerous, immensely dangerous. He said the only safe system of security checks is pre-arranged questions and answers. When an agent goes into the field you ask him a question, 'How is your Aunt Julie?', and if he doesn't reply 'She has got diabetes' the agent is caught. Well that happens to be quite the most dangerous system of the lot: for one elementary reason. The enemy are reading your traffic, because you are using something called a poem-code, so they have got the questions and answers already. If they capture you they will torture your code out of you, so they will read your code out of you, so they will read your answers anyway, and unless you take in at least as many questions and answers as there are messages, that means hundreds of questions and answers, then it's no bloody good. We had to change the face of agents' coding. Now Michael was kind enough to quote from a report I wrote, and again this is the danger of historians looking at records and quoting extracts. He is kind enough to say I used a phrase that agents' security checks were devised to give them confidence.

There was a time in the war when SOE believed its poem-codes worked, because C had given them to them. It took me nine months to convince them the system was no good and was losing a great many agents. I briefed during the war such characters as Yeo-Thomas, the White Rabbit, Knut Haukelid who dropped onto the Barren Mountain to deny the Germans an atomic bomb, and Violette Szabo, for whom I wrote a poem-code. And to get my girls interested in agents, and aware of what they suffered if they were caught, I would show them a telegram, which was always in my pocket, about an agent whose eyes were taken out with a fork.

I was 22 years old when I joined SOE, and I decided I had better brief an agent. This was the first agent I had ever briefed, and I was terrified of briefing him. He was about 23. He was more terrified of going into the field than I was of briefing him. And he had this ghastly poem system. So I said, 'Come on, let's go through your poem.' He was terrified, so was I. And he looked at me and he spoke his poem and it was:

> Be near me when my light is low,
> When the pulse beats fast, and the nerves prick
> And tingle, and the heart is sick,
> Be near me.
> Be near me when I fade away,
> To point the term of human strife,
> And on the low dark verge of night,
> The twilight of eternal day,
> Be near me.

Well, I tried to be near that boy, when he went in and made a mistake in his coding and it took me 23,000 times before I could break it, so he did not have to come on the air and repeat it. I tried to be near him when he was executed six months later and I tried to get SOE to be near him when a lot of our senior members thought it was time they went into the field. This was after the invasion. And they were all senior members of the SOE. And I was obliged to lecture these gentlemen. Now when an agent was in terror – and my God he had reason to be in terror, he had no electric light to do his coding by, he had no squared paper, he was not even as comfortable as you are – he would make a mistake in his coding. So I instituted a rule, 'There shall be no such thing as an indecipherable message.' Now I had 400 girls to help me. We would break these messages against the clock. But in some country sections, if they had an agent on the air at 4 o'clock and we had not broken it by then, he would have to repeat it, whether or not he was surrounded by direction-finding cars. Sometimes we failed. But we broke 94 per cent of all agents' indecipherables without their having to repeat them and suddenly I was faced with all the people who would not give us the extra time we needed to break messages. So I wrote an indecipherable on the blackboard, and showed them how to break it, and made them try it for themselves. And I kept them there for four hours. I really gave those bastards a taste of what it is like to have to break a message against the clock; and read them 'Be near me when my light is low'.

I have been asked by all kinds of agents of other sections, what went wrong with the *Englandspiel*. I have never been asked by any Dutchman anything else about SOE. And it really is time you recognized that to begin to understand the *Englandspiel* you have got to understand the rest of SOE. It is time you asked questions about what happened elsewhere. Now, Professor Foot has started with a major mistake and because he more than makes up for them, it is most encouraging. Before coming to that major mistake, I ought to tell you that, for certain reasons he has not even touched upon, I was so concerned about Holland that I dropped all other duties (and there were one or two), and shut myself away for three days and the best part of three nights, with every single message that had been exchanged between London and Holland both ways: every single message that any Dutch agent had used in training and certain other material which again has not yet been referred to by Michael Foot. Now that was three days with Holland, and at the end of those three days I had a total conviction, as to whether or not the Dutch agents were caught. Yet I have only 20 minutes to talk to you about something that has been on my mind for 40 years, and of which I have been writing for the last five. I want just to read to you, though I have no right to whatever, the briefest extract from my book, because when I had spent those three days I had to write a report about Dutch agents and this is what I said of it: 'I could have confined my report to four words, "God help these agents." Instead I wrote 12 pages and then drained them of feeling and reduced them to four.' I then go on to say what is in those four pages, which I cannot yet tell you because of the Official Secrets Act. But I will tell you the conclusion that those four pages taught, and it was this. The question was not, how many Dutch agents were caught, but how many were free? I then ended by saying, 'After three days of total immersion in Holland, I renounced my Dutch citizenship and resumed my normal duties.'

Well, I take up that Dutch citizenship again today, to tell you first that no agent in my experience – and I think I met almost all of them – tried harder than Ebenezer [Lauwers] to let us know that he was caught. Poor devil, Lauwers did his best, and if ever you see him, because I never met Lauwers, I wish you would shake his hand for me. He did his damnedest. Now, that being said, sometimes historians, however honourable their intention, get totally out of their depth. The Code Spiel is essentially a coding matter, a coding battle, and very little has ever been written about SOE's codes; I am trying to remedy this, but I ought to tell you that every single signals record of the slightest value has been destroyed. We will come to that later. But to those present who might think – and I don't believe Professor Foot is in this category – that the code department did not take its responsibilities seriously, it took me nine months to get rid of the poem-code. It was replaced by this little toy [silk code displayed] and with this little toy [another], and every time you use a message you cut it away from the silk and burn it and it can't be tortured out of you, because you cannot remember it.

Now SOE did not know if this new concept of codes was a good idea at all. And my Brigadier, who was a brilliant man, newly appointed, was a great expert on wireless; he knew nothing of codes, but he had an instinct for people and that made him a good signals officer. So, to see if this new code was any good, they took what they thought was the best advice in the land on codes: is this a good idea for agents instead of poems? And the answer came back emphatically, 'Yes'.

SOE was delighted with the new code, but I wasn't yet satisfied, because for security reasons the agent had to transmit at least 100 letters in it, which was a vast improvement on the 200 letters he had to transmit in the poem-code but still not good enough. So this was introduced [silk code displayed], so safe that the agent can come up and send only five letters in it and get off the air. That is called a one-time pad, and these had never been used by the agents of any other organization. We were ultimately paid the supreme compliment of being copied by SIS and the Germans, I don't know in which order, because there was not much difference. And in answer to one particular person here who said that the SOE–SIS relationship was not as bad as was alleged, I can assure you that at my level we used to talk to each other, but officially SOE and SIS hardly spoke.

Now, for those who may think we were an unproductive code department, here's something that might interest you. Michael talks a little academically about deception. This [silk code displayed] is a code, a rather special one, and it took me over three months' research to get it going. I had to be especially careful with this one for one particular reason: it was designed for the exclusive purpose of being caught by the Germans to convince them that there was a large resistance movement at work in an area where there was none. And to make the deception work we had to devise others like it which we dropped into other territories just in case the Germans wondered why we were using the system in one area only. I could also show you codes invisibly printed on handkerchiefs and 100 letters on the end of a matchstick. Now I am not talking in the first person, I talk on behalf of 400 girls and a brilliant

Brigadier who just did not have a feel for codes. So when I say I, I mean we. Do you really think that a code department that can come up with this [silk code displayed] and more that I cannot tell you about is going to ignore the Dutch traffic? Do you think we didn't notice anything? And having noticed it, do you think we did nothing about it?

When I wrote that report, SOE for various reasons was reluctant to credit it. I then took certain steps to prove to SOE that the Dutch agents were caught. I was convinced that the proof that I obtained as a result of these steps was wholly conclusive. I cannot tell you today what those steps were because of the Official Secrets Act but I can say this about them. They are nowhere on record because most of our signals records have been shredded. But I put this to you. The Germans also made mistakes. The code department gave them a chance to make one in Holland and my God they took it. But there is an aspect of *Englandspiel* that has never been touched on by anyone in this room however sophisticated. They are not in sight of it and it is not on record.

At the end of the war, I was asked by Colin Gubbins to write three reports, one about codes used by SOE everywhere, including places we had no right to be. I must tell you that by the end of the war our codes had been seen by the Prime Minister and they were called 'the toys', and the 400 girls who worked for me were called by Baroness Hornsby-Smith 'Marks's harem', which I regret to say was a gross overstatement. Anyway, I had to write an account for Gubbins of the code department's work and it took me three months to do it. I didn't write this report or any others with Michael Foot in mind. I wrote them for the time which I hoped would never come when someone might be faced with the kind of job I had, and I would like that poor devil to know what mistakes I made, how difficult it was, what girls to look for, not just what codes, and the mentality of the agents. It was 300 pages long.

I was also ordered by Gubbins to write a report on Holland, not just about *Englandspiel* – do not just think about the *Englandspiel*, that may be box-office but it is not the whole of the Dutch story which deserves to be told. Now I wrote a 15-page report on the *Englandspiel* and was allowed to take only one copy of it which I had to deliver personally to Gubbins. To be totally accurate – as one must be in the presence of distinguished historians who are the only ones allowed to make major mistakes – there was appended to that 15-page report a three-page supplement which I would give a great deal to be able to tell you about. So these were delivered to Gubbins. I then had to stay on after SOE was allegedly disbanded, for certain other jobs, and I thought it would be proper to have on the SOE archive a suitable selection of agents' traffic in every theatre in which we operated, which took six weeks to prepare. I also had a little extra work to do and that took six months.

Now, when I started to write my book I asked the then Foreign Office archivist if I could have access to my reports. He informed me that my 300-page report was missing, nor could they find the Dutch report anywhere at all. There was, however, a third report, and for you to understand its significance I should tell you that at the age of 22 I thought I knew everything, especially about Freudian dogma. I was particularly interested in why agents failed to bury their parachutes and in why the young ladies who handled their traffic who were normally so reliable, made astonishing mistakes at apparently regular intervals. We discovered what is now known as pre-menstrual tension during the war. I thought at the time that periods meant moon-periods but by the end of the war I knew better.

I wrote a paper for Gubbins on why all of us in SOE made mistakes for unconscious reasons with particular reference to the code department, and I called it 'Cipher, Signals and Sex.' I wrote it partly out of devilment, it had been a tiring war, but many years later when I had forgotten all about this paper (undoubtedly for unconscious reasons) I received a letter from the Foreign Office Archivist saying that 'Although we cannot find your two main reports we know you'll be pleased that we have a copy of a paper that you wrote called "Cipher, Signals and Sex" and someone has put a label on this report saying "To be preserved as a document of historical importance"; someone else has cross out "historical" and put "hysterical".'

Now it is very important that you are absolutely clear what has been holding up the story of Holland. In the 1970s the chief [secret] archivist of the Foreign Office was well into his eighties. Now he was a former member of SOE and during the war I used to think he was eighty. And in peacetime this fanatic would be reluctant to tell you what the initials SOE stood for, assuming that he knew. He was ultimately replaced by Christopher Woods. Now everything changed when Christopher Woods arrived. He is a man with a feeling for SOE who would go out of his way to be helpful, put himself at risk, if he possibly could. He's now been replaced by someone who is here today. This newcomer seems to be a very promising boy, we think he is going to be all right. What he is up against and what Christopher Woods was up against is their terms of reference. I had more than 40 million code groups across my desk and find it a little difficult to remember all of them off hand, so that when I want specific information the archivist usually gives it me if he can find it. What he cannot do because of his terms of reference is allow me access to the few reports which they have retained. Sight of these reports would remind me of many things which I have forgotten to ask and one particularly annoying example of this is a 31-page report I wrote called 'Be near me when my light is low.' I wrote the damn thing but am not allowed to read it.* But Michael Foot has been allowed to read it as he is the official historian and if anyone reads it, I am glad that it is he. He is a first-class historian and what is almost as rare, a brave one. Michael and I are in no way rivals because we are seeking to tell different aspects of the same truth.

I am going to tell the facts as I know them, not just about the *Englandspiel* but about certain other matters concerning SOE. So is Michael and we may well be faced with problems under the Official Secrets Act. Now if there is anything I have written which in any way impinges upon national security I like to think that by reflex I couldn't have written it in the first place. If I am satisfied that it is not in the national interest for me to make certain disclosures I shall be the first to expunge them, but in fairness to the authorities, they have a problem too. Because of *Spycatcher* there could be a question from some other authors: 'If Foot and Marks are allowed to write like this, why can't we?' And the others might well have worked at Bletchley. That is a problem we are going to fight at the highest level, to get clearance for our books, and I am convinced that the new archivist is as anxious as we are that we should win it. As far as *Englandspiel* is concerned I am going to point Michael in a certain direction when my book is cleared. I think the truth of *Englandspiel* will surprise some, anger many, and sadden all. It is an unexpected truth. Just what its damage was, and who authorized certain decisions which neatly contributed to that damage, is for historians like Michael to establish.

I joined SOE in June 1942 and became head of agents' codes in February 1943, having fought throughout most of this time to rid SOE of the poem-codes. In 1943 I introduced these [displays silk codes] in their place. I stayed in Baker Street throughout the *entire Englandspiel*. The only time I ever left that desk and that code office, where the truth of the *Englandspiel* lies, was to make a brief visit to a foreign code room. Now, I'll make you a promise, and it is this. It was a fight getting these passed [silks again displayed]. Michael and I will have a fight getting our books passed. Between us we will give you not just my truth of Holland, but with Michael's ability to stick at it he will produce truths which are not within my compass. We *will* do this and in the battle that is ahead of

---

*Since the conference, Mr Marks has been allowed to read his own report.

us to tell the truth that has to be told, all I would ask of you is – 'Be near us'.

* * *

Dr Andrew, Chairman

We are privileged to have as our final speaker today Leen Pot, leader of the Group Kees in the Dutch resistance, holder of the Dutch Resistance Cross.

Leen Pot

Ladies and Gentlemen, to my astonishment, I find on the agenda of this conference the *Englandspiel* as one of the important subjects. In my opinion this very tragic affair had no effect at all on the outcome of hostilities in Holland, as all SOE actions were based on plans which had lost any validity at the time of execution. It can only be regarded as a serious incident which completely fitted into the pattern of the ancient Greek tragedy: a fantastic plan, supported by brave people with a fatal end. I will now try to relate essential points which are relevant to the history of the *Englandspiel* without mentioning until the end all the details that surround this affair.

In July 1940, when the situation in England was considered desperate by many, the British government came up with a bold plan. A new organization named Special Operations Executive was to turn the tide of war by utilizing unorthodox ways of waging war. No long confrontation of troops, but fighting Germany from within. Minister Dalton, in whose department this large organization belonged, stated at the start that he was highly confident that it could end Nazism within a year. Widespread sabotage, serious shortages of important materials and food, and propaganda would cause political unrest. This would result in a general uprising of the social democrat masses in the occupied countries and Germany itself, making the continuation of the war impossible for Germany.

With enormous enthusiasm, the organization was started and within a few weeks the SOE Dutch section was founded. This section made a beginning with this new method of conducting the war in the Netherlands. The head of the section was Mr Laming, who had worked for many years as consul in Amsterdam. He succeeded in sending out as early as August 1940 his first agent, Mr van Driel, recruited with the assistance of the Dutch Secretary of the International Labour Union in London. He had to make contact with social democrat organizations in the Netherlands. This seaman had a wireless set, but very little training. Unfortunately the operation failed as van Driel was picked up by the German Navy even before reaching Dutch shores. It would take considerable time before better trained agents could be sent out to occupied Holland as most of the facilities for more thorough preparation, such as recruitment, training, equipment, transport facilities and communication were not directly available.

As practically no useful information had reached England since May 1940, the next two agents, Homburg and Sporre, got a reconnaissance mission to prepare the arrival of future agents. Their task was to study these possibilities and then return to England. They were parachuted in in September 1941. After a short time in Holland, Homburg succeeded in returning to England, but he reported that they saw no possibility of getting sabotage and political unrest off the ground. He had no confidence in the SOE approach, left it, and went on to fly with the RAF.

By October 1941 several agents were trained; the problem was to get them into action. On 7 November 1941 the next two agents were dispatched: Taconis as organizer and Lauwers as radio operator. Their first task was also a reconnaissance mission as well, as SOE lacked any detailed information on how to form a basis for sabotage activities. On top of all their problems getting settled, their transmitter did not work. It took them till January 1942 before they were able to contact London by radio. This long silence of two months ought to have warned SOE Dutch to treat this delayed contact with the utmost care, or even better to ignore the radio contact completely. But SOE reacted quite differently. It was their first and only contact which was necessary for the further development of the SOE plan. Also SOE Dutch was in a hurry as their progress was behind that of other countries such as France, Belgium and Norway. Even though Taconis and Lauwers could not achieve very much sabotage or intelligence they were running a big risk. They had no idea of the activities of their opponents, the *Abwehr* and the SD. Taconis, the organizer, had made contact with a group which had been infiltrated by a provocateur, while Lauwers the radio operator did not take the necessary precautions against a well organized German direction finder. It always took Lauwers a long time to make contact. He was then transmitting too long from the same building, on the same wavelength at regular and predictable intervals. While London considered their agents as having got off to a good start, they were in reality sitting ducks for the Germans.

The task of SOE Dutch now was to get 12 agents, who were trained on the knowledge and plans of December 1940, off to occupied Holland to start their mission. As we thought, the best chances would be to contact as quickly as possible the leader of the pre-war Social Democrat party in Holland, who could be instrumental in getting those 12 agents settled in Holland. The British Labour party had found a way, with assistance of a Dutch journalist, Mr Slager, to contact Koos Vorrink, the pre-war leader of S.D.A.P. On 27 February 1942, the agent, Dessing, was parachuted into Holland with this task. Later on a radio operator would follow to report about the proceedings.

At that time a thorough re-organization of SOE took place. Dr Dalton was replaced by Lord Selborne, which resulted in adapting the SOE principles of 1940 to the changed conditions of 1942. But also the Head of SOE Dutch was replaced. Mr Laming left and was succeeded by Major Blizzard, a professional soldier without experience in SOE work. He also lacked any personal acquaintance with the agents in Holland and had not been present at their briefing before they left. In March as well Dessing contacted Vorrink and explained the assistance the S.D.A.P. could give to the development of the big SOE drive in Holland. But unfortunately Vorrink and his friends refused to co-operate with these agents who were going to conduct a big sabotage drive in Holland. Dessing had no possibility of reporting this refusal to London. On 6 March the same year, the Germans arrested Taconis and Lauwers and SOE Dutch had no idea that anything was wrong. After a week of silence, Lauwers came back on the air. The Germans promised to spare his life if he was prepared to work for them. He agreed to do so hoping to be able to warn SOE by omitting the security checks. But as we know, this effort was not understood by SOE.

Even though SOE Dutch had not received an answer from Dessing, it was decided to send out the waiting agents. In March five other agents were sent to Holland; one was killed landing, another was arrested after landing, and three arrived safely. In April another three agents were sent. One was arrested, so at the beginning of May five agents who had survived the pitfalls of arrival were ready to start operations. But they found themselves faced with the same problems as their predecessors.

None of them had been provided with clear instructions and proper contacts to make a start. They asked London for guidance and London could do nothing better than refer them to Taconis and Lauwers. This resulted in the arrest of all five agents with their codes and equipment. In these conditions SOE Dutch decided that new agents could be best introduced to their task in Holland by linking them up with agents previously dispatched. All agents sent out by SOE Dutch from April 1942 onwards were sent out on such a basis. The result was that all those agents dispatched between April 1942 and May 1943 were arrested on arrival. Quite a number of agents should have followed as a new type of agent was required. Their task should have been the formation and training of a secret army which would come into action when Allied command gave the order.

Maybe such an operation was possible in other countries, but in Holland in 1942–43 it was not feasible for an army of more than 1,500 men to be trained and equipped without their coming to the attention of the Germans. Here again lack of information and experience coupled with haste were the deciding factors of failure, and as these 35 agents of so-called Plan Holland were linked up with earlier arrivals, not even a beginning was made for this military formation. With these agents SOE sent thousands of guns, tonnes of explosive, ammunition and other equipment. It all fell into German hands.

In the opinion of many people, it was a blessing in disguise. How was it possible that during 13 months all agents dispatched fell into the hands of the Germans? The main reason was that information other than SOE communications was practically non-existent. Between August 1942 and March 1943 very few reports about the situation in Holland were received in London. Only in spring 1943 a little more information reached London which could give some indication that doubts existed on the activities of SOE agents. But naturally the more critically information was received, the more SOE started to defend themselves. As SOE was at that time a very big and powerful organization, with support in the highest circles of government, it was unwilling to listen to advice, and described all critics as jealous, incompetent, mendacious.

The decline of SOE Dutch from May 1943 to the final collapse in April 1944 was therefore a long drawn out process. In May 1943 the last agents of Plan Holland were parachuted. Two months later, the so-called control agent was sent; in October 1943 the last material was sent, and from that time on, until April 1944, only a more and more unrealistic telegram exchange continued.

The main reasons for these operations failing were the following: the basic principles of SOE were not realistic; the information necessary to support such an operation was not available; the staff of SOE Dutch were amateurs and no match for their German counterparts; all operations were carried out with urgency and clouded in secrecy. The Dutch advisers, Colonel de Bruyne and his staff, had no influence at all on these operations so none of the agents ever had a chance to make a success of their mission. From the moment that more doubts were raised, vigorous efforts were developed by SOE to keep everything secret. No discussion was possible and emotions that spoke strongly of treason and deceit were aroused. After the war these uneasy feelings could grow as no acceptable information was provided to make the whole story understandable. The statement issued by the British government in 1948, that error in judgement was the basis of the accident, could not dispel the serious doubts raised in the previous years. The very thorough investigation of all these allegations of treason and deceit, which was never published, made the story of the

142

Englandspiel into a history far out of all proportion. And in the standard work of Professor Hinsley, *British Intelligence in the Second World War*, the *Englandspiel* is not even mentioned in its 3,000 pages. [But see its Vol.iii, Part i, pp.462–3 – Ed.] In the Netherlands, however, it would grow to be one of the most tragic episodes of the war. In this résumé I hope I have given you a better understanding of the development of the drama.

DISCUSSION

Sir Robin Brook

My reason for speaking is that most of this fell within my orbit of authority at that period. I think it only appropriate that I say something about the division into two halves of the Dutch Resistance contribution. You appreciate that I am involved strictly from the point of view of military co-operation, very little from other points of view, except perhaps political psychology overall. The point made by Dr Andrew, and supported to some extent by Baron d'Aulnis, is that after all the debris was cleared away from the *Englandspiel*, which was only one aspect of resistance anyway, the Dutch resistance really came to a second life and a second value. As at that time I had ceased to be what I was in England, the Director for resistance for Western Europe, and had become the liaison officer in a rather more co-operative operation than some of those referred to earlier representing both General Menzies and General Gubbins on the Supreme Command, all this was very pertinent to me and very significant to the High Command, and I had to write the report for General Eisenhower about the contribution of SOE. This contribution stood high not only in my view but in the view of General Bedell Smith, the Chief of Staff, supported by numerous commanders' reports and commendations.

And it was a great grief to me that the BBC programme, good though it was as a show, as an historical record concentrated so much on 'North Pole' that they more or less omitted the rest. We had originally hoped that a further programme would evolve and I think Dominic Flessati, the overall producer, hoped the same. After it was done, we still had reasons for thinking a further programme would be made, and Douglas Dodds-Parker and Brooks Richards both supported me in appealing for this and there is still talk of what you might call a remedial or just programme; I no longer have any hope of it actually taking place. But this discussion, I think, has taken the place of the programme, in bringing to light more history, more knowledge in the light of intelligence and more illumination altogether about what happened, and the value of what happened.

So I have nothing to add to all that: the elaborate set-up made before I left England, for working arrangements in the case of field operations with resistance groups, enabling them to be recognized, dealt with and properly supplied and also for the provision of direct communications with London on their account, all worked marvellously and especially so in Holland, and I feel that a comparable programme for what happened at Eindhoven – communication through the German lines, that has been mentioned, the passage of bodies, but particularly messages – is just as dramatic a story and perhaps a more pleasing one and I would still like to see that take place.

There still remains, of course, and has to remain, great dissatisfaction about the lack of skill in allowing North Pole to take place. A comparable situation developed in Belgium early in my time of office. I took over in November 1942 when my predecessor went to North Africa; in Belgium it was checked right at the start and never got going, never lasted in German control to the same extent. It's a great sadness that it was allowed to flourish so in the case of Holland.

When our Chairman was talking of the problems of Holland, he mentioned the territory. But the aspect of territory that was most difficult for us was not so much the ground, which only mattered immensely in certain particular respects, urban sabotage and later guerrilla warfare possibly, but all the time as a matter of remoteness. Holland was at the end of the line. And we heard earlier of the communication of documents coming down to Geneva and then getting back to London via maybe Lisbon, maybe even Sweden, and that's a purely secondary indication of how difficult it was to contact Holland in any direct sense. And the passage of agents was precarious when escapers did set out; in one case the escapers were German, in another case they got arrested at Miranda, and so on, and it was a process of several months to get a person in, perhaps almost impossible to get a person out, which was not quite so unusual but took months and involved a great deal of suffering. And the treatment in Miranda could compare with a minor arrest in, say, France.

That difficulty was complemented of course, by the fact that in other places we could provide resources occasionally en masse by ship, by submarine, by other means and eventually by immense Liberator loads. None of that took effect in the case of Holland.

I must make a last comment specifically on the coding, etc. We have heard a brilliant exposition by Leo Marks on the coding and how it took place, how it was developed. But beyond that there is an insoluble problem, of how the breach of signal security continued and was tolerated. When I arrived one operator had the field name Ebenezer [Lauwers], and his telegrams came in all the time with the comment by signal security 'One or other safety check omitted.' But for some reason this had been accepted early on and when I arrived it was familiar that Ebenezer's telegrams would come across my desk as though valid – and remember that the volume of traffic by then was simply tremendous. By D-Day, I've been told, the traffic we were conveying behind the enemy lines was the equivalent of the entire commercial traffic of the Imperial Cables and Wireless. A substantial proportion of this of course related to France, but also from all over the world. And that is inexplicable; what caused it to be accepted and how did it continue so long?

And there's one other clue that has not been mentioned, and it is definitely a question of hindsight that if any of you were involved in this sort of activity again, I hope you would bear in mind, that it is possible for too good a ground reception to be in itself sinister. And we were constantly getting returns from the aircraft, 'Splendid reception, all lights in order,' etc, etc. I think that I can justly claim that it is hindsight to say that that was a clue; but it is the sort of clue we picked up in Belgium and failed to pick up in Holland and I think it was a tragedy for Holland and for the RAF. I think perhaps those are comments rather than points for further debate. I thought I knew most of it already, but I have learnt a lot today, and I hope you have too.

Professor de Jong

I would like to raise one point mentioned by Michael Foot and address myself to Leo Marks. Michael Foot has drawn our attention to the case of Ubbink and Dourlein who, having escaped courageously from the prison of Haaren, were put into prison here after their arrival in Britain. And he refers to the contradictions in the statements they made after their arrival either in Spain or in Gibraltar or here in Britain. And I would like to add one important point because one of the questions – one of the most important questions – put to them was: Who was the man who helped you escape from Holland? They gave his name and it was the name of a Dutch police officer, van Bilsen. Now keep in mind that in the Autumn of 1943, two separate warnings in underground publications were printed in Holland, one by the Orde Dienst and one by a different group, listing the names of the police officers who had to be considered as Gestapo agents. One of them – the accusation was wrong, but that is immaterial in this respect – was the same Mr van Bilsen. And these numbers of the underground publications arrived through Geneva in London at about the same time as Ubbink and Dourlein arrived in Gibraltar. So I think this was an important factor in determining the way these two agents who had escaped were being dealt with after their arrival.

Professor Foot

There was a tragic sequel to this. They had indeed stayed with him in a suburb of Tilburg; he had done marvels for them. Later in the war on the strength of that denunciation in a clandestine newspaper he was assassinated by the resistance.

Professor de Jong

I know, but I try to limit myself. Now as regards the *Englandspiel* I have drawn only one conclusion from the magnificent performance, histrionic perhaps, given to us by Leo Marks. And that conclusion is that I am willing to believe that in January 1943, when you drew up your first written report, you came to the right conclusion. Of course I have an open mind, and I'm keenly looking forward to the publication of your book, but you have so far utterly failed to convince me that there is another explanation for the tragedy of the *Englandspiel* than the ghastly blunders committed by some of the officers of SOE Dutch. You have constantly hinted at a darker explanation, about things that have not been revealed so far. I do feel that in addressing an audience like the one that has been assembled today, you should have been more specific. And I blame you for not doing so.

Furthermore, I am of the opinion that Bingham, the officer who was longest in charge of SOE Dutch during all the long and weary and tragic months when the *Englandspiel* took place, after his transfer to Australia, committed in his contact with the resistance group on the island of Timor exactly the same ghastly blunders he committed in London. I am of the opinion that this fact alone blows sky high all your innuendos so far, that there might be another and more sinister explanation for the *Englandspiel*.

I do feel that I should have to pay some attention to the positions in which officers like Blizard and Bingham were put. They had extremely skilled and dangerous opponents. They wanted to believe that they were gaining tremendous successes in our occupied country, and this belief was constantly being fed by German manoeuvres of high character. Take the fact that one of the agents was asked to blow up the transmitting masts of Kootwijk, which were being used by the Germans in their contact with their U-boats on the Atlantic. It was reported back by Schreieder and Giskes that the agent in question had tried the operation, but that he was unable to approach the transmitting mast because of the minefields laid by the Germans. And the Germans went so far as to make an official announcement, by the Commander in Chief

147

of the German armed forces in Holland, General Christiansen, and published in all Dutch papers in August 1942, testifying to the fact that an attempt had indeed been made to blow up the transmitting masts of Kootwijk. If you take into account that in some cases railway lines were blown up in Holland by the Germans, that in one case in August 1943 a ship full of fairly important war material was sunk in the harbour of Rotterdam by the Germans themselves, merely to create the impression in London that indeed important acts of sabotage were being carried out by the agents sent out by SOE, I think if you put yourself into the minds of the officers conducting the operations it is, if not excusable at least understandable, that they were confirmed in their false and frankly optimistic view of the operations going on in Holland.

I would like to add that having said all this there isn't a single line in the books written by me which I am not willing to change and if necessary change drastically in view of new convincing evidence, when it is put before me. And I would like to say that my attitude with regard to the *Englandspiel*, although I have published at great length my own conclusions, is exactly the same. I am entirely willing to be convinced by you that my view and the view of Michael Foot on the *Englandspiel* is wrong. But I want to stress with all the strength that is in me that this afternoon Mr Marks has utterly failed to convince me.

Dr Andrew, Chairman

Before asking Mr Marks to respond to that perhaps I could also ask him to answer the question, if he feels able: Who else in SOE at the time knew of your suspicions?

Leo Marks

I'm delighted to have failed to convince Professor de Jong. I suspect if I had I would have convinced nobody else and – at the risk of increasing histrionics, because those people who may be names to you were men and women to me – I don't know quite what Professor Foot's view of *Englandspiel* is, with which you agree – I didn't hear him express one. So I'd like to ask you a question, Professor de Jong. You've written extensively, you are an authority, you are a most honourable historian, could you please tell me what KK or KAR or HH mean to you?

Professor de Jong

Nothing.

Leo Marks

No. Well may I say with respect before you express your convictions about the *Englandspiel* and your opinion of what I cannot say to you here – much as I want to – I can't tell you. So keep your mind an extra inch ajar. Do you, Professor Foot, know what those letters mean?

Michael Foot

I do not.

Leo Marks

You do not. So we have two senior historians not yet aware of a fact so elementary that if a junior FANY didn't know it, we'd dismiss her. So ... no no, I am speaking, I will not stop it ...

Professor de Jong

Stop that nonsense. I can give you 20 quotations of German abbreviations which are unknown and which if I omitted would not make me irresponsible.

Leo Marks

I'm not suggesting you're irresponsible. I'm merely suggesting you are not open-minded. However, let's accept that you are. In terms of HH and nonsense like that, which you call histrionic, we were rather suspicious and we cared about the Dutch, and I suspect you want the truth. I can't help, I can't tell you, I am dying to. I have wanted to for 40 years. So if I put it on record and give it to the Foreign Office it's the same thing. So in terms of HH, a little minuscule piece of drama: We were worried about the operating of a certain key Dutch agent. Nobody else was worried except Signals. It wasn't right. Now 'fingerprinting' is highly unreliable because of weather conditions. I took on under my own aegis a girl, super little kid, who was pioneering 'fingerprinting' and it was certainly useful sometimes, but it was not a staple diet. Now we were worried about a certain agent, operator, and if this man was wrong, Dutch Section was in great trouble. So, at the end of the transmission, without authority, we sent to the operator in question the classic German signing off HH (Heil Hitler) in morse code. Back came the answer HH, Heil Hitler, by reflex. Now that little thing, that is the least thing we were suspicious about. When you get an operator in the field and he is frightened when he is not caught suddenly knowing how to reply in the German way, that is to us total proof and that is the least of the proof. It is grossly unfair to you and to this audience that I can't tell you what was done about this proof and what the resistance was and the extraordinary discovery that came out of it. Entirely by accident. I wish I could. If you, sir, professor, can change the Official Secrets Act before you go back to Holland please do and I'll tell you on the plane going back. But, do remember that when an operator replies 'Heil Hitler' the Signals Directorate has troubles. In reply to your question, Dr Andrew, which was?

Dr Andrew, Chairman

Who else in SOE knew of your suspicions?

Leo Marks

It's hard to quantify something called gut feeling. If you get it in a girl, you've got a master coder. It's hard to find it. I had a gut feeling about Holland with absolutely no proof to go on. There was something that wasn't quite right. It's a feeling. You had it sometimes about agents going into the field. I had it about Violette Szabo. I didn't think she was coming back. Well, that's by the way. I just had a feeling about Holland. And talking to the most important single man in SOE, the Director of Finance, trying to cadge new girls, I suddenly thought of something about the Dutch traffic. And what was a gut feeling became a conscious and a total anxiety. That was November of 1942. I expressed these anxieties then to an awfully bright man, Brigadier Nicholls, whom we've discussed before, brilliant man who had no feel for codes but a marvellous feel for people and a great peace-time intelligence signals man. And he said, 'Get me proof.' Well, that is the most terrible thing in the middle of it all with everything else to do. How do I get proof? But, suddenly, on the 3rd or 4th of February, standing in my father's shop which was at 84 Charing Cross Road, to escape the nightmare of getting proof, looking at an original Gutenberg Bible, I found the way to get the proof. I got that proof to my total satisfaction in February. In answer to your question, who knew? I first told a man called Heffer whom very little is known about. I don't suppose he saved more than a hundred lives so his contribution was minor by the standards of SOE. Well, the other person who knew was Brigadier Nicholls. He was still a colonel, fighting for his position, fighting to get out a man called Ozanne whom I've been asked about. And I was taken straight, instantly, by my Brigadier to Colin Gubbins who was in charge of all operations, Deputy CD, and I showed him what I considered total proof. He then reacted in a certain way. And the only other person in the whole of SOE who knew this was not that marvellous man who has just left us, Robin Brook. He wasn't told, nor to my knowledge was the executive council. It was between CD, who was then Sir Charles Hambro, Colin Gubbins, Brigadier Nicholls and myself. So four people knew and at the end of the war there was one copy of what they knew; and our friend up there and his predecessor. They have tried and tried and they can't find it. I think I know who shredded it. And I may conjecture about that in the book. Four people in SOE knew. And that means probably a few more because they all had secretaries.

Dr Andrew, Chairman

Are there any further questions?

Jhr Beelaerts

George Dessing has been named. Well, he was a man of my platoon just as some of the others who were among the first people to be dropped. You don't tell what the end was. I do know that they tried to get out the chief of the Socialist party. But later, when I came back from India to England, I heard that George Dessing had gone away disgusted, left the service and went to South Africa back where he came from. Could you tell me what is the real story about Dessing?

Professor Foot

I could if my bear leader doesn't jump to his feet and cry, 'Silence that man!' He was sent to Holland with two missions. One, to Vorrink the Socialist leader. The other, which was regarded by SOE as the more important of the two, to reconnoitre from the landward side a sea route to England via the islands (which were still then islands) between Walcheren and Rotterdam. He couldn't get anywhere near the sea coast because the patrols and the restrictions on movement anywhere near the sea coast were so strict. So he gave up that part of his job. He got hold of Vorrink who entrusted him with large quantities of material for the Queen's eye and he then set off to try and find his way back to England, which took him seven months. And by the time he got back he gave the impression to the people who cross-questioned him that he was ashamed of having done so little when he'd been in the Netherlands. He was clearly holding something back, but they couldn't quite make out what. They supposed that he was anxious to cover up for his own incompetencies and he was allowed to go back to South Africa.

There was one moment when alarm bells might have started ringing quite loudly on the operational front, quite apart from what Leo Marks was discovering on the operational signals front. Dessing had a rendez-vous address at which he could make contact with another agent who

151

had gone in already. They made contact as prescribed at Beaulieu in a bar in which they both met pretending not to know each other, though in fact they had trained together and knew each other quite well by sight. Making contact through code messages tossed into the bar conversation, he noticed that the friend whom he was meeting had someone with him whom he didn't know, who stuck to him like the proverbial leech. So, remembering what he had heard at Beaulieu, he slipped off to the gents; then his friend slipped off to the gents with him, still accompanied by his proverbial leech. So there was no chance to exchange a word there and after about an hour of desultory conversation he gave it up, and went out onto the pavement. His fellow agent came out onto the pavement with him and momentarily they were separated by passers-by between the leech and the agent. A momentary gap opened and the agent hissed the one word, 'Gestapo!' Dessing reported this immediately by a message which he sent off to a wireless operator who was, of course, under German control and never transmitted it. And when finally he got through into Switzerland on his way home, he also went and called on the Dutch Legation in Bern. One of the things that I have been hunting round for, in complete ignorance of what was going on on the signals front, about the moment when N Section really ought to have realized something was going wrong, I can date with confidence. Early in the morning of 5 April 1943 SIS passed to SOE a message they got from their man in Bern that Dessing had reported that the friend he'd met was in contact with the Gestapo. Nobody in N Section appears to have taken the slightest notice.

Dr Andrew, Chairman

Next question.

Baron d'Aulnis

I don't have a question. I have a communication. In the first place I think that Louis de Jong is quite right in saying that Leo Marks hasn't given us anything specific, but he has done something which has pleased me no end. And I would give him credit for that. And that is that he has defended Lauwers. And he has said that in his opinion Lauwers had done his very best to make known in England that he had been caught. That pleases me very much. Then you talk, Mr Marks, a few times about agents being frightened, especially while they were manipulating their wireless sets. Now a soldier in the field under fire may be frightened so long as he doesn't have anything to do. But according to my small experience under fire as soon as you do have something to do you have no time to be frightened. And agents, cabling, working their wireless sets, were so concentrated on trying to get this connection right because it was damned difficult that they weren't really all that frightened. In any case, I wasn't and I know a lot who weren't. Now another thing is that when we were trained in England to be agents we were taught the operation of wireless telegraphy. And at first we did this in Hans Place and we learnt the code, the technique of sending out letters. And later, before we were sent out something very curious happened because we were then dispatched with a set to the suburbs and told to communicate with Central. But this could not be done voluntarily; it had to be done after the counter-espionage people had been warned otherwise we might immediately be arrested. Nobody had ever told us anything about direction-finding and when we went off to Holland, in any case in 1943 and up to the summer of 1944 we knew nothing about the danger awaiting us in direction-finding by the Germans. But we did know that we couldn't go out of Hans Place even once with a set without running a terrific risk that the British police would come and arrest us. That was really rather funny. In 1944 we ourselves in Holland came to realize that little cars were approaching our W/T location, clearly manned by German D/F personnel. Eventually we evolved a routine to defend ourselves against direction-finding consequences by placing little girls in the street, with eye contact to people in the operator's window. Then we even had radio schemes which would provoke this phenomenon, so that we could train more watchers.

Leo Marks

You, sir, were one of the first Dutch agents to go into the field with a one-time pad. I'm sure you were not frightened. Your predecessors went in not with a one-time pad, and not with a silk code, they went in with a poem and with that poem they had to send a message at least 200 letters long in a highly complex double transposition which would take a girl 40 minutes to do and here's an agent in the field having to code against a time element without making a mistake. Now you didn't have this because we gave you a one-time pad. So as far as anxiety is concerned which is a paraphrase of fear, a lot of agents knew the risk of plugging in their W/T sets and using electricity. They knew damn well how many operators were being scooped up and if they weren't frightened overall they were no damn good to themselves or us. Fear, caution, anxiety is why we broke so many indecipherables. And it is an indispensable part of the brave. Now the bravest single agent of the war in our opinion, mine and a lot of other people's, was Yeo-Thomas, the White Rabbit; he was an agent's agent. He was a great agent. A

Molyneux dress designer. And when we wanted to film his life, I introduced him to one of the great English film directors whose name was Roy Boulton, and Yeo-Thomas was a legend. He was the birth of the French resistance. I knew him well, we had many a midnight together. Roy Boulton said to Tommy, 'Tommy if I'm to film your life, your story, there's something I've got to understand.' This man, I tell you one thing about him, he was sent to Buchenwald, due to be gassed, and walked into the office of the CO of Buchenwald and said, 'I am Wing Commander Thomas, your superior in rank, stand to attention when I'm talking to you.' This was our cream agent. So Roy said to him, 'Tommy, forgive me asking you this, I ask you with all humility, were you never scared?' 'Oh Roy,' he said, 'I was shit scared every minute of the time but I couldn't let the Germans see it.' That was SOE courage. As for not being specific I set out to be non-specific, so thank you for helping me succeed.

Leen Pot

I must draw your attention to one special fact. Two agents of SOE returned to England. The first was Homburg and the second Dessing. Both had fortunately nothing to do with codes. They were without radio sets, without codes. When they came back, they were not too well received. Then they did not talk the same language as their bosses and I know that when Dessing came back they were not talking about the failure of a mission but the mission of a failure. But he did a remarkable job for more than a year, and he was a long time in Holland.

Dominic Flessati

Could I ask, Dr Andrew, whether the history of games like the *Englandspiel* shows any previous experience of that type of operation whatsoever anywhere before?

Dr Andrew

I think that would take another session, but perhaps I can give a brief reply by saying yes and no. Every successful deception has to start from the possibilities of the moment and therefore cannot repeat exactly any previous deception. But nonetheless, if one looks for example at the Double Cross system and the *Englandspiel* I think one can see that there are common elements. But because each has to take a different starting point, there are distinctive elements as well. That's a highly unsatisfactory answer, and I don't propose to enlarge upon it.

DISCUSSION

Robbert de Bruin

As the Chairman knows, I do visit the records office at Kew. There are quite a few SOE documents there and a couple of years ago, I went through the SOE documents that are freely available to everybody and I found a document raised by the Chiefs of Staff, the combined Chiefs of Staff here in England, and quite a long document, quite a long meeting and minute No.16 was called 'Penetrations of SOE in Netherlands.' I thought, ah here we are, at last we've found something. This, ladies and gentlemen, was not the case. Because there was a little note attached to the official document saying that this minute had been removed. The date of the removal was 25 May 1980. Furthermore, attached to the combined Chiefs of Staff's meeting minutes was a JIC report (Joint Intelligence Committee) and I believe that the JIC was charged by the combined Chiefs of Staff to go into this problem of penetration. This particular JIC document was also removed in 1980 and was destroyed. To come back to the combined Chiefs of Staff's document, this particular document will be available on 1 January 1995, so we must have a few years' patience, but based on the 30-year rule, this particular COS document must have been available to us, to researchers, to historians, between 1974 and 1980. My question is this, Mr Chairman, am I correct?

Professor Foot

The 30-year rule does not apply to the documents of the secret services, which under the Public Records Act have been resolved by the Lord Chancellor and the various ministers as unavailable, period. As a former intelligence officer, I applaud this decision, as an historian I deplore it. I'm pulled both ways. This particular document I have actually read. It's part of a long and highly involved story which there isn't time to go into, but a side effect of the appearance of Dourlein and Ubbink at Bern was that it provided C, the head of SIS, and Sir Arthur Harris, the head of Bomber Command, with an excuse for combining together to persuade the JIC that the proper thing to do with SOE was to close it down. The JIC held a series of meetings at which the SOE was not represented and decided the whole thing had better be handed over to SIS. Selborne thereupon had to call upon his long-standing relation with Churchill, with whom he had voted solid on the India bill in 1935, and was therefore regarded as reliable. He telegraphed to Churchill saying, 'Look, they are trying to close down my secret service, stop it.' And Churchill telegraphed back, 'We will certainly go into all this when

155

I return' (he was abroad at the time). When he came back, he said to the others, 'You can't shut SOE down now with the invasion about to take place, it's important to the invasion, let it go on.' So it was saved from being killed by the *Englandspiel* after all.

CHAPTER FIVE

OPERATION MARKET GARDEN

Chairman

Heroic and unforgettable were the words Queen Wilhelmina used about the fighting at Arnhem, as early as 8 October 1944 – in a broadcast in English on the BBC – when the smoke had hardly drifted away from the battlefield. We are particularly fortunate to have today a witness who was present: General Sir John Hackett.

Sir John Hackett

Operation Market Garden was the Allied airborne operation, with ground forces following up, which in late 1944 was planned as a lethal thrust into the industrial heartland of Germany to bring the Second World War to an early end. Two possible courses of action had lain before General Eisenhower: to press forward towards the Rhine along the whole front, exploiting success where it occurred, or to develop one strong, single narrow thrust in depth. The Americans, with Bradley commanding the 12th Army group in which Patton's Third Army had been making the running, favoured the first. The British, with Montgomery commanding the 21st Army group, favoured the second. The Supreme Allied Commander, against strong representations from his American commanders, opted for the latter.

The sketch maps on the following pages may help to make what follows more readily comprehensible.

Market was an airborne operation to capture and hold crossings over the water obstacles between Eindhoven and Arnhem, to lay what was called the airborne carpet. The canal crossings from Eindhoven up to the Waal were to be secured by the 101st U.S. Airborne Division. The

U.S. 82nd would take and hold the Waal and Maas crossings at Grave and Nijmegen. The British 1st Airborne Division would secure the most important bridge of all, over the lower Rhine – the Lek – at Arnhem. Garden was to be the follow-up operation of the XXX British Corps (under General Horrocks) to advance 64 miles from the Meuse–Escaut canal to Arnhem, to link up there with the 1st British Airborne Division. Garden was to be completed in two days and would be followed by an advance to the Zuider Zee and a right wheel into the Ruhr.

It is argued that the great resources put into Market Garden would have been better employed in first consolidating a hold on Antwerp and re-opening the estuary of the Scheldt. The logistical support of Allied forces operating in continental Europe still depended on points of entry hundreds of miles to the rear, and Antwerp, as you can hear from those who moved freely around in it from as early as 4 September, was there for the asking. It would not now be open as a supply port till 28 November, more than two costly months later. Opinion is still divided here.

Although Eisenhower did his best to support Market Garden, even at the cost of some disappointment to Bradley and Patton, the resources available, particularly in aircraft, were insufficient to meet the vital requirement upon which the success of the whole operation depended. This was the utmost exploitation of surprise. The deployment of the entire airborne force in one day could have transformed the operation, particularly at its furthest point – the all important road bridge at Arnhem. Of the two American airborne divisions one, the 101st, was flown in pretty well complete on the first day, 17 September 1944. The 82nd was completed in a second lift next day. It took three days to fly in the British 1st Airborne, with its two parachute brigades under command. The bulk of the airlift, of course, came from the American IX Troop Carrier Command, but this was not the main reason for the allocation of the major part of it to the delivery of the two American divisions. Unless the approach to Arnhem could be secured for the link-up by XXX Corps there was no point in sending the 1st British Airborne in there at all. The so-called airborne carpet had to be laid from the southern end upwards, and priorities in allocation of resources were determined accordingly. When the 1st British Parachute Brigade and the 1st Airlanding Brigade with some Divisional troops, including General Urquhart and his tactical headquarters, arrived in the vicinity of Wolfheze in the afternoon of Sunday 17 September, surprise was complete and Dutch civilians exploded in rapture. German response, however, was swift. Over-optimism at

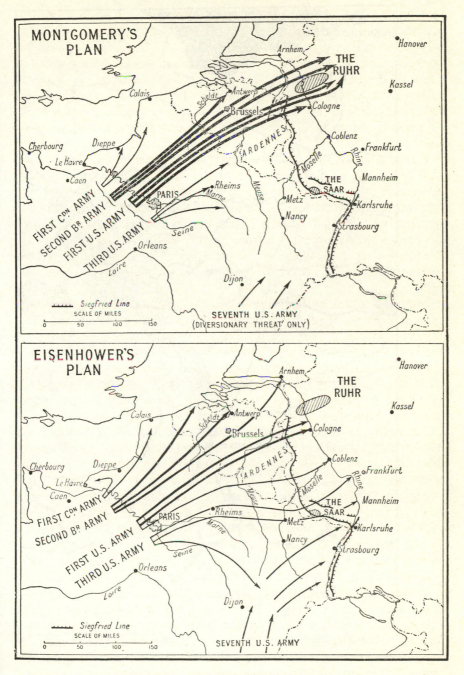

MONTGOMERY'S PLAN

EISENHOWER'S PLAN

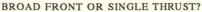

BROAD FRONT OR SINGLE THRUST?

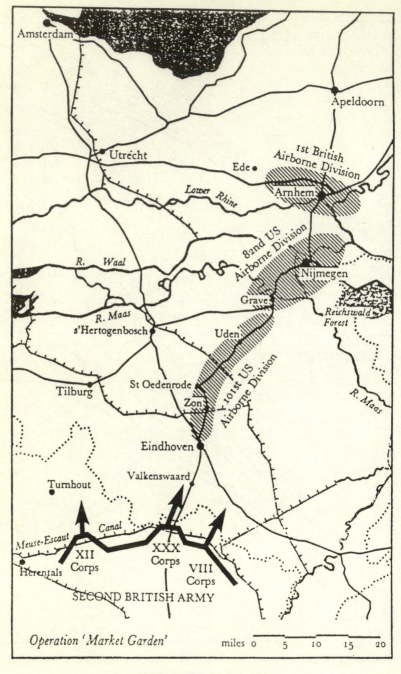

Operation 'Market Garden'

miles 0   5   10   15   20

APPROACHES TO ARNHEM

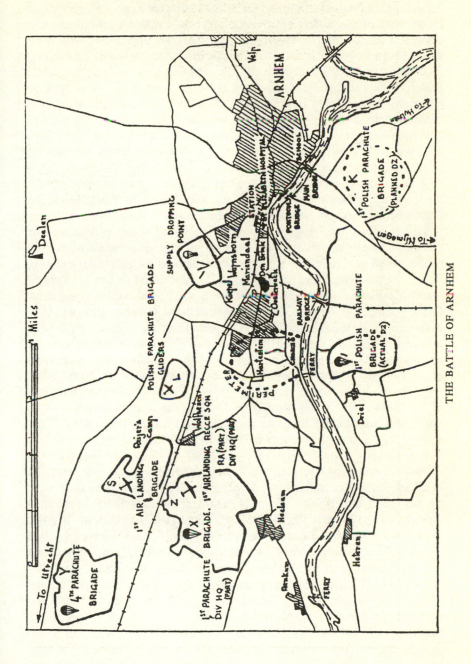

THE BATTLE OF ARNHEM

some levels of Allied command (at XXX Corps for example), generated by the astonishing speed of advance after the break-out in Normandy, invited a harsh rebuff. Assurance that German opposition would be slight, from troops of low calibre, weak in armour, were ill-based, and evidence that the 9th and 10th SS Panzer Divisions, with a few tanks, effective as structural cadres, were moving through the area back to Germany to refit, was largely ignored. British airborne planning was admirable up to the point of delivery of an airborne force on the ground but rather less effective for the conduct of the battle thereafter. Failure to make use of sound Dutch information and advice was a prime source of weakness in Market Garden. After the exhilarating dash, harrying a defeated enemy across western Europe, Allied commanders and staff tended to think they knew it all and were also less inclined to listen to the Dutch because of unfortunate experiences with the partisans in Italy.

Those of us who had some experiences of fighting against the German Army, which was to the end of the war the most highly professional of any in the field, knew that however light their existing strength at any one point on the ground, a real threat to an objective of vital importance would be met with a swift and violent response. Greatly aided by surprise, but with some hard fighting, the two U.S. divisions firmly established their positions along the corridor leading to Nijmegen, though the crossing over the Waal here would not be secured till 20 September. The first lift of the British 1st Division west of Arnhem on 17 September also came in successfully and Frost's 2nd Para Battalion, in about company strength, secured the northern end of the bridge which they were going to hold in an epic defence for $3\frac{1}{2}$ days, 36 hours longer than the time allowed for the link up by XXX Corps. This approached not two days after the first landing, but seven.

Immediately after the first happy landfall on 17 September, with the exhaustion of surprise, and with an unfortunate failure to land the vehicles of the Reconnaissance Squadron which was expected to seize the bridge in a swift *coup de main*, a strong German reaction set in. I brought in the second lift of the 1st Airborne Division, with my 4th Parachute Brigade Group, on the second day, further delayed by bad weather, in the afternoon of Monday 18 September, jumping on to a dropping zone even then being cleared by a bayonet attack from the King's Own Scottish Borderers, one of the three glider-borne battalions brought in the day before. Our task was to move in and occupy the northern perimeter of Arnhem town but we were never to get there. Rapid action by the two skeleton Panzer Divisions, with some re-equipment, set up a defence impossible for lightly armed airborne troops to penetrate. When 2 Para's stout defence of the northern end of the Arnhem bridge was finally overwhelmed on 20 September, Urquhart concentrated the very considerable remaining strength of his division around Oosterbeek, to hold a bridgehead there in the hope that XXX Corps could come up in sufficient strength before it too was driven in. The hope was vain. The remnants of the 1st British Airborne Division were withdrawn on the night of 25 September, nine days after the first landing, when some 2,400 men were brought back across the Rhine out of over 10,000 flown in.

It is not my purpose here to set out the course and conduct of the battle of Arnhem–Oosterbeek as a military experience, with its strategical, tactical, logistical and other military aspects. This has already been done quite often enough. I shall choose instead to say some things which seem to be of particular significance and end by offering my own view on what makes this battle unusually important in the history of the Second World War and something of high and enduring value in the relationship of our two countries.

The most important first question to ask is: Why did Market Garden fail? If it had succeeded the war could have ended at least six months earlier, with the saving of thousands of lives and the prevention of much grievous destruction. Why did it not succeed?

First of all there were insufficient aircraft available from the combined strengths of the U.S. IX Troop Carrier Command and 38 and 46 Group RAF to put the whole force of three airborne divisions down in one lift. Some invaluable air transport was wasted. There was no need at all, for example, for General Browning's Corps H.Q. to be flown in on the first day using 38 gliders, which was the exact requirement for two much needed anti-tank batteries brought in on the second day. Whether there was ever a requirement for an Airborne Corps H.Q. at all, with the H.Q. of XXX Corps expected to link up within three days, is open to argument. It should certainly not have been put in on the first day as a top priority.

There was an over-optimism in XXX Corps, particularly in regard to the likely strength of the opposition, which those of us with experience of fighting against Germans, with their great powers of reaction to real threats, viewed with misgiving. The presence of powerful cadres of two Panzer Divisions in the area, not initially strong in armour but easily reinforced to a level against which lightly armed airborne attack was doomed, was sheer misfortune but what was already known of the location of the 9th and 10th Panzer Divisions was taken too little into account.

I had myself already been disquieted by what seemed to me a combination of light-heartedness and inexperience in our airborne planners. They seemed inclined to work out on the map an acceptable airborne deployment (which they did very well) and only then add in a probable enemy response, like cooks adding salt and pepper to a dish already prepared. The last operation planned (and happily cancelled) before Market Garden – Operation Comet – the last of the 16 planned for the 1st Airborne Division and all cancelled, was intended to achieve with *one* Division, the British, pretty well exactly what (in the event) we failed to do with three. I shall always remember being briefed on my brigade's task for Comet, while General Sosabowski learned what was expected of the Polish brigade, in a little conference on Cottesmore Airfield, and the expostulations of my friend and ally, that brave and highly experienced Pole, as he rasped in his deep voice, 'But the Germans, General, the *Germans*!'

With hindsight, and having in later years come to know that part of the world rather well, I am surprised at the XXX Corps plan for the link-up. It involved the use, as a main axis for advancing armour, for some 60 miles, of one road over open country, sometimes raised above the level of surrounding polder and easily denied to armour by well-placed 88 millimetre anti-tank guns at no more than a few points. Standing on the high ground at Westerbouwing for the first time a few years ago, moreover, and looking south, I could not help thinking that, with observation from there, well-placed artillery on the north bank of the Rhine could totally control movement along that road for many miles. The Guards Armoured Division was here set an impossible task. Why was this road used as the main axis anyway? I was told that on Dutch Staff College exercises based on Groesbeek, between the wars, when the task set was an advance on Arnhem from Nijmegen, a solution involving the use of that road as a main thrust line got no marks at all. The preferred solution was an advance in a north-westerly direction to force a crossing over the Lek lower down and then to move in on Arnhem from the west. We, the British, should certainly here, as in other respects, have paid much more attention to Dutch advice.

I hope it will be understood that apportionment of praise or blame is no part of my task here, which is simply to enquire in retrospect what went wrong in an enterprise of such very high importance, and I pay principal attention to the operation of the 1st British Airborne Division because it fell to me to play a major part in it. Our own lack of success, though it did not lessen the very great value of the gains by those two great American divisions, the 82nd and the 101st, meant the failure of the master plan.

A further main difficulty, and perhaps the most serious, lay in the delivery of troops on the ground so far from their objectives. The polder country south of the Arnhem bridge and the built-up area north of it were both thought unsuitable for airborne delivery, and their use likely to cause heavy casualties, though some have argued that this would have been preferable to what happened in the event. The Air Forces were unwilling to run serious risks from the flak defences of Deelen airfield, which were later found to have been over-estimated, or to land us closer to the objectives, because the air column would then have to withdraw over Deelen, or move into airspace designated for follow-on flights. In the event the Division was put down on dropping and landing zones between five and eight miles from its objectives, the furthest away being my own, where the 4th Para Brigade was delivered, on the second day, with surprise lost, eight miles from our designated defensive positions north of Arnhem city, between which and ourselves was swiftly growing German opposition.

There were other factors contributing to our lack of success. The weather was bad, which gravely hampered air operations, and for this and various other reasons we saw little or none of the powerful fighter and ground attack forces now available to the Allies. Resupply by air, most gallantly brought in by the RAF, was ill-directed and mostly fell into German hands. Signal communications were inadequate, though more has been made of this than is quite fair to our signal personnel. The Division had long been pressing, in vain, for the replacement of unsatisfactory radio equipment by something better. Moreover, we had never operated in that area before and had no means of knowing that the environment was for technical reasons a difficult one for radio communications. I have myself been surprised to discover on later enquiry how good they were, even if far from perfect. In criticizing the handling of the Division and its communications it is as well to remember the very special difficulties attending the deployment of an airborne division in battle. An armoured or infantry division moves up with its command and staff structure intact and its communications all deployed and working. An airborne division is dismantled before departure and stowed in aircraft in little packets, to be reassembled into a working whole on arrival, with some parts of it not arriving at all.

General Urquhart's unavoidable absence from his H.Q., incommunicado, on the first and second nights, left him with little choice when he got back but to accept the deployment more or less forced on him by circumstances, with his H.Q. at the Hartenstein Hotel in Oosterbeek. Again with hindsight it is possible to say that the bridgehead, whose defence he then organized, was not in the best place. We can say now that it ought to have included the high ground at Westerbouwing and the heavy ferry, still in working order and invaluable for the tanks of the Guards Armoured Division, at Heveadorp. Both could have been ours at little or no cost. Neither was secured. When Urquhart got back on 19 September and took charge of the battle it was really too late to uproot the Division from where it had settled and make major changes. It was also too late to do then, on the morning of D+2, what should have been done after the second lift's arrival, late in the afternoon of 18 September – to get co-ordinated reinforcements up to Frost at the bridge.

Should the operation ever have been launched? There were indeed bad omens from the start, but there had already been 16 missions of various sorts planned for the Division, every one cancelled, several when we had already emplaned, and we all knew that cynicism and declining morale would set in if these first-rate, deeply motivated and highly trained troops were not soon put into action.

The very last thing to be assumed from what I have said is that there was anything in the 1st Airborne Division but total commitment and high enthusiasm. We were really grateful to be going at last. Somewhere there is a letter I wrote to General Urquhart from St Elizabeth's Hospital, where I lay later rather seriously hurt, a letter carried out when a large group of airborne survivors made their way out with Brigadier Lathbury. I say in it, 'Thank you for the party. It did not go quite as we hoped and got a bit rough but, speaking for myself, I would go on it again any time and so would everyone else.' I meant every syllable of that and still do.

But of course, when we did go in, the eyes of some of us were wide open. When my book *I Was a Stranger* was published, with its simple tribute to the monumental heroism of Dutch civilians, I was asked, at a conference, when it was that I first came to realize that disaster loomed. 'Before we left' I replied. I then spoke of my last brigade conference for all officers and other key personnel, which went into minute detail of the plan for our defence of the northern perimeter in Arnhem town. When that conference was over I sent away the hundred or so participants and kept behind only the three battalion commanders with a small group of others. 'You can forget all that,' I said. 'Your hardest fighting and worst casualties will not be in defending the northern sector of the Arnhem perimeter, but in trying to get there.' And we never did.

But though our battle was a failure from the point of view of the course of the Second World War, and with its failure died the hope of an early end to the war, there were often things born in those few days which will never die. One is the record of the fine performance of officers and men who fought in this battle, their inexhaustible courage and good humour. A young American liaison officer at First Airborne divisional headquarters has testified to this, in a previously unpublished report:

> I learned this from the Arnhem operation: that men, born and bred as freemen, have a great strength and will power which they distrust until they need it. I saw men who were hungry, exhausted, hopelessly outnumbered, men who by all the rules of warfare should have gladly surrendered to have it all over with, who were shelled until they were helpless psychopathics; and through it all they laughed, sang, and died, and kept fighting ... The greatest tribute that I think could be paid to the 1st Airborne Division was paid by a German prisoner, a major; the old Prussian type of officer, who saw service in the last war and in this one. The prisoners were in a cage about 200 yards from divisional headquarters. They were complaining that they were not getting enough food. At that, they were getting more than we were, and they could sleep. The major called them together and dressed them down severely, concluding with something like this: 'These men have stood up under the most tremendous artillery bombardment I have ever seen. They have fought on without food or sleep for several days. Even though they are our enemies, I never saw braver men. When you complain you make me ashamed of our being German. I suggest you be quiet and follow their example.'*

I think I ought also to mention a weakness in XXX Corps which attracted, with some justification, adverse American comment. There seemed to be too little awareness in the follow-up troops of the real urgency of the situation, and the need to push on with maximum pressure. This was probably another result of the swiftness of the dash out of France into Belgium and Holland.

In this country the whole operation Market Garden tends to be seen as a mainly British affair. What is often overlooked in Britain is the splendid battle fought by two of the very finest divisions ever formed, the U.S. 82nd Airborne under Jim Gavin and the U.S. 101st under Maxwell Taylor. Their successes on 17 September and the two days following, in securing the route northwards from the XXX Corps start line on the Meuse–Escaut canal up to the Waal crossing at Nijmegen, not only made XXX Corps' operation possible but secured ground later to prove vital for the Reichswald battle and the Rhine crossing that would follow. It is also sometimes overlooked that whereas the

---

*Lieutenant Bruce E. Davis, narrative of the battle of Arnhem.

battered remnants of the 1st British Airborne Division were with-drawn after nine days of admittedly desperate action, the two U.S. Airborne Divisions stayed on in the line, where they had been put down, for another two months. General Dempsey, Commanding Second Army, said to Jim Gavin of 82nd Airborne, soon after the battle, 'I am proud to meet the commander of the greatest division in the world today.' There is nothing I can add to that.

My own task today, however, has been to look at Market Garden not just from a ringside seat but from within the ring itself, and I come now to what is to me the most important outcome of this battle, as indeed it is to very many others. The two figures I personally find of truly heroic proportions on this scene in the battle at and near Oosterbeek fought by the 1st British Airborne Division are General Roy Urquhart, that great, brave, imperturbable fighting Scot, the best battlefield commander I fought under in all the war years, and a Dutch lady called Kate Ter Horst. Mrs Ter Horst's story is, I think, well known. Her house by the old church in Oosterbeek became a refuge for British wounded. At one time she was harbouring more than 200, as well as a family of small children in the cellar. When there was no more that could be done to relieve pain, to feed and to comfort, she read them the 91st psalm. I mention this dear friend of so many of us as a shining example of what the battle brought out on the Dutch side – the courage and compassion, the hope and conviction, the confidence that with God's help and that of their friends the good and right would conquer. This was a lesson more important than any in the military sphere, a lesson in a spiritual dimension of high and lasting importance. Go to the British Air-borne cemetery in Oosterbeek, immaculate and beautiful with its two thousand and more carefully tended graves. Watch at the service held on the annual pilgrimage, so strongly attended. See the Dutch children, now nearly half a century after the event, sometimes up to a thousand strong, each laying a bunch of flowers on a grave, and reach deeply down into what is a spiritual experience. Not only were none of these children born when the battle raged, almost none of their parents were born either. We did our best to free the Dutch from a harsh and intolerable burden. We failed, but the warmth of our reception brought upon courageous men and women in Gelderland a cruel retribution. It is a sign of greatness of spirit that these people have long forgiven us our failure and the bitter tribulations that ensued, and because we did our best remain our friends. The bond between our two countries tied by this battle will prove, in the words of Horace, *aere perennius* – more enduring than bronze. It is a bond which in today's world is of the highest importance. It is in recognition of this that I am grateful to be allowed – flanked and defended by my Dutch friend here* – to say what I have put before you today.

*The speaker pointed to an eighteen-inch bronze figurine of a Dutch soldier, which stood on the lectern beside him. It was inscribed: 'To General Sir John Hackett from the Royal Netherlands Army. In gratitude to a great friend in times of War and Peace.'

CAUGHT BETWEEN HOPE AND FEAR

Operation Market Garden and its Effects on the Civilian Population in the Netherlands

Piet Kamphuis

If it is true that 'fools rush in where angels fear to tread', I cannot help but wonder why I accepted your invitation to broach the subject of the effects of Operation Market Garden on the civilian population in the Netherlands. The subject is, at the same time, as daunting as a minefield, and, as Keats might have put it, 'it is an endless fountain of never ending speculation'. I should now like to elucidate this statement and in doing so, I shall also attempt to mark the boundaries of my contribution here today.

The Second World War is among one of the most extensively chronicled periods of Dutch history. Within this historiography, Operation Market Garden occupies a unique position, and even a leading one, when it comes to the number of publications.

Most of the authors focus their attention on the struggle for the 'bridge that was too far', and not on the 'road that was too long'. This is hardly surprising: The battle for Arnhem contains all the ingredients of a classical tragedy, both from a civilian and military point of view.

Indeed, although I am certainly impressed by the dedication, courage, and even the suffering of the American Airbornes and the civilian population along Hell's Highway, the special fascination of the battle for Arnhem could not fail to influence the contents of my presentation. My first remarks have particular bearing on the fortunes of the civilian population in the area of operations: How did they react to the airborne landings, to what extent did they share the success and suffering of the paratroopers, what were the consequences of the

German victory and how did the people cope with this disappointment? Although I have necessarily had to restrict myself to a survey of the literature, the large number of publications on the subject makes it possible to portray rather accurately the prevailing mood during these historical events in September 1944; this aspect of the war is one which up to now has received little attention in Dutch historical works.

Following this, I shall note the effects that this operation had on the population elsewhere in the Netherlands, paying particular attention to the part of the country that was still occupied. What did the people there know about events in Arnhem, and how did they obtain this information? What price did they subsequently have to pay? It is not possible to answer this last question without discussing the railway strike, which was called by the Dutch government in exile in London, as a means of supporting Operation Market Garden. The effects of this strike were widespread, for many people far-reaching, and made themselves felt until after the Netherlands had been liberated.

In his fascinating work *The Face of Battle*, John Keegan remarks that, in times of severe personal danger, the soldier's perspective is often reduced to one major issue: How can I survive? This is, if anything, even more true in the case of civilians. The choices one makes in combat situations and the way in which one experiences reality at that particular moment in time, differ greatly from individual to individual. Generalizations, including my own, are therefore bound to be an inadequate reflection of subjective experience.

CIVILIANS IN THE FRONT LINE

For most people living in the Arnhem area, the start of the airborne operation was a dream come true. Sunday 17 September was a splendid late summer day, sunny and warm. Although the RAF had rather rudely disturbed regular attendance at church that morning, the ensuing sight of the giant armada and descending paratroopers created a feeling of excitement and joy. The people turned out enthusiastically to welcome their liberators.

Four facts are worthy of mention at this point. First of all, the unshakeable belief that everybody held in a successful outcome: flags were put out, members of the resistance could be seen in public, and persons in hiding appeared in the streets.

Second, there was a great admiration for the English and their equipment; the jeep especially, described by some sources as a 'toy vehicle', or as a 'dodgem car for the fair', caught the public eye.

Next, there was a general willingness to assist the liberating forces in every way possible: guides were provided, transport and telephone connections were put at their disposal, and some people even took up arms against the Germans. Finally, there was a great deal of curiosity, which at first led to scenes reminiscent of those at the time of the *Ancien Régime*, namely battlefield tourism.

The terrible awareness that occupation had given way to war, to a battlefield filled with destruction, fear, and bloodshed, began to dawn on the people as a result of increasing German resistance. For some, the dream of liberation had been shattered by Sunday evening, others were able to cherish it for somewhat longer. During the battle, solidarity with the fighting men grew and where possible assistance was rendered: the wounded were tended, and food shared. The material conditions worsened rapidly. There was no gas, no electricity, and in some cases, no water. Hidden in cellars, the civilian population awaited determinedly the outcome of the fierce, often man-to-man, fighting. As well as the concern for their day-to-day survival, the uncertainty about the future began to trouble them even more. How would the Germans react on their return?

Members of the resistance, people in hiding, in fact everybody who helped the Allies in some way or another, had every reason to be afraid: the penalty for assisting the Germans' enemy was execution, and this everyone knew. Many tried to escape this hell of fear and mortal danger, but not all succeeded. Although the German military authorities generally acted in accordance with the Geneva Convention, several civilians were, nevertheless, summarily executed.

In the wake of the battle, the mood was one governed by a sense of disappointment and disillusionment, and not least by the physical circumstances in which people found themselves, as well as immeasurable suffering and anxiety.

In this respect, Arnhem did not differ from other such situations elsewhere.

To this description, I should like to add three notes. First of all, the Allied soldiers behaved extremely well towards the local population, indeed, they took as much account as possible of the civilian population. An example will serve to illustrate the point. As early as 17 September, an English company commander warned the population against premature celebrations; this same warning was also spread by Radio Oranje, the Free Dutch Radio, on 23 September. Another example: on the night of 25 September, despite being in a state of near exhaustion, the English military doctors did their very best to disguise Dutch combatants as civilian casualties, and so were able to save their

172

lives. The fact that people still speak with affection of those former warriors, is, I think you will agree, hardly surprising.

The second remark concerns the local resistance. For them, the battle did not end on 26 September. Their concern was to find safe shelter and food for the many Allied evaders, and this meant relying on the services of scores of trustworthy Dutch men and women. In addition, the numbers of Allied servicemen in hiding continued to swell, as a result of the many escapes from prisoner-of-war camps. At the end of October, MI9 and the resistance succeeded in accomplishing a spectacular mission: 130 servicemen were returned safely behind their own lines. A month later, however, a similar operation was a complete failure. From February onwards, stranded servicemen reached safety by way of the Biesbosch or the Alblasserwaard; one of these men was the previous speaker, General Sir John Hackett.

Civilians had to pay a price for this help as well, in the form of human life and trauma.

Last but not least, the occupying forces left the population little time to overcome their disappointment. As early as 24 September, the inhabitants of Arnhem received instructions to leave the city, to be followed some time later by their fellow countrymen from the area along the edge of the Veluwe. A total of 180,000 persons had to find another abode. The fight for daily survival now occupied all their energies. Taking only a number of essential belongings with them – the evacuation had been announced as being a temporary measure – they were obliged to comply with the rules and customs of their hosts where they were staying. It goes without saying that this often created a certain tension among the evacuees and the host families themselves. Added to this was the evacuees' increasing concern about the possessions that they had left behind, as the news gradually reached them of the systematic looting of Arnhem – subtly referred to in German as 'räumen'. Most of the inhabitants returned to the city after the liberation to find their houses damaged and most, if not all, their possessions gone.

The occupied areas of the Netherlands also had to pay the price. In the remaining part of the country that was still under occupation, Operation Market Garden raised hopes and expectations of an approaching liberation. For a long time, the population outside the area of operations remained in uncertainty about the scale and actual progress of the military actions. Only by means of comparing the information issued by the censored press and Radio Hilversum with the broadcast by Radio Oranje and the BBC and with the aid of an atlas, was it possible to obtain a fairly reliable representation of reality. The different emphasis in the broadcasts is understandable. In the censored press, which released information on the main Allied axis of advance as early as 18 September, the German successes were the focus of attention and consequently, the operations in and near Arnhem received extensive coverage.

The German message directed at the population was quite clear. A liberation operation leads only to catastrophe and not to Oranje festivities. The London source, by contrast, focused on the advance in the south. Pessimism about the situation in Arnhem did, however, creep into the transmissions by Radio Oranje from 22 September onwards. After a delay of one day, during the evening broadcast on 27 September, the dramatic announcement was made that the airborne troops had been withdrawn.

Not everyone was pleased with the manner in which the facts were presented. Queen Wilhelmina, for example, was angered by the – I quote – 'stupid, defeatist tone' of the announcement. The disappointment about how events had gone was, however, widespread.

The boundless optimism of Dolle Dinsdag (Mad Tuesday) 5 September had given way, after Arnhem, to the realization that liberation was still a long way off. The German occupying forces, witnesses of the true mood of the people in the first half of September, reacted in a more unrestrained fashion than had been the case in the past. The daily struggle for survival became increasingly grim, due not least to the railway strike, which had been called by the Dutch government in exile in London.

Dutch Railways, which up to that time had continued to operate fairly normally, played an important role in society. Not only were they responsible for the transport of passengers, they were also entrusted with the transport of fuel and winter supplies of food for the west of the Netherlands. This always took place in the autumn months.

The decision-making process which led to the call for the railways to stop work certainly does not deserve any marks for merit. It was a decision personally authorized by Prime Minister Gerbrandy who had only consulted the Minister of War and not the responsible member of government for Transport and Public Works. It was with good reason that the parliamentary Committee of Enquiry expressed criticism of this course of action later, in the nineteen-fifties.

The militant and impetuous Gerbrandy was convinced of the military value of a railway strike and appears moreover to have been somewhat carried away by his conviction that total liberation of the Netherlands would only take a matter of weeks. After the call for a

5. A day's adult ration in Holland, April 1945

6. The Queen and Churchill in Amsterdam, May 1946

strike had been broadcast during the evening transmission of Radio Oranje on 17 September, the Premier reassured L. de Jong: 'Cheer up, we shall be in Amsterdam on Friday.' For him too, it was clearly a case of 'Don't worry, be happy!'

The railway strike was an unmitigated success. Railway personnel, totalling some 30,000 men, stayed absent from work and large numbers of them went into hiding. All railway traffic came to a standstill. From a military point of view, it dealt the German armed forces a severe blow and all this during such a vital week! However, by bringing in German railway personnel, the occupying forces were able to resume their own transport of goods and personnel after approximately ten days. They never succeeded in breaking the strike, however, and thus it can be claimed that in that respect, Gerbrandy and the Dutch resistance achieved a moral victory.

The negative effects of the strike, and thus also indirectly of Market Garden, cannot be termed as slight, at least as far as the civilian population was concerned in the occupied part of the country. It will suffice here to mention three of the most important effects.

First of all, there was the problem of caring for the railway personnel and their families. They had to have money, food, and other essentials. Yet another category of citizens had been added to the list of those having special cause to fear the occupying forces. Being able to provide a sufficient number of safe addresses became an additional burden for the resistance. Second, a process of compartmentalization had been set in motion. The loss of public transport, on which postal traffic relied heavily, combined with the disconnection of all telephone lines, meant that communication with friends and acquaintances outside one's own town or village became increasingly difficult and necessitated more and more effort. As a result, people became more isolated, especially in the large cities in the west of the country where the struggle for the basic necessities of life became more arduous every day. This brings me to the last aspect: the Hunger Winter of 1944–45.

Thanks in part to an efficient system of distribution, the Dutch population had not gone hungry up to September 1944. On 18 September, which was the first day of the railway strike the occupying authorities issued the following message to the censored press: 'A railway standstill means a standstill in the supply of provisions.' As a retaliatory measure against the strike, the Germans prohibited the transport of all goods by barge on the rivers and canals. Supplies of food accumulated in the east of the country, while the situation in the west became desperate. German military reports even warned of hunger revolts.

When, at the beginning of November, the occupying authorities went back on their previous decision, organizational problems and early winter weather prevented the laying in of sufficient supplies for the winter. The results were disastrous: thousands of people in the west of the country suffered from hunger and cold, and although the extent of the disaster has been placed in another perspective in a recent study – the researcher arrives at 'only' 16,000 fatal victims in the cities by 1945, these being mainly old men, the very poor and people who had been placed in institutions – this does not alter the fact that for hundreds of thousands of people, their very existence was reduced to two existential questions: how can I obtain food, and how can I obtain fuel?

The consequences of Operation Market Garden were therefore certainly not restricted to the population in the area of operations; in the entire occupied part of the country, a price had to be paid for this daring operation.

German propaganda, which blamed all the personal suffering on the English actions, fell on deaf ears. Indeed, it even aroused a feeling of contempt. In the opinion of the Dutch people, Operation Market Garden and the accompanying railway strike were necessary to put an end to German oppression in the entire country. Dutch citizens were united in attributing the negative effects of the unsuccessful offensive to the occupying forces and not to their potential liberators. For the people of the Netherlands, Arnhem was and is the symbol of Anglo-Dutch solidarity. A deep sense of involvement with these events in the past still remains today. The annual commemorations, the number of visitors to Hartenstein, the unveiling of new memorials and monuments and the continuous stream of publications would seem to provide sufficient evidence of this. Furthermore, this is the one military operation that from time to time still succeeds in captivating the Dutch media, often with 'King Kong' Lindemans being brought to life once again as the evil genius.

Even when the last veteran and last Dutch witness of these events has passed away, the drama of Arnhem will not be forgotten, but will instead remain imprinted in the historical consciousness, just like Chatham, William and Mary and Waterloo before them.

The first evidence of this is already becoming apparent and it is on this note that I should like to end. An anecdote serves to illustrate the point nicely. Only two months ago students in the Netherlands who were about to qualify for a teacher's degree in English were given a piece of prose in which the words 'market garden' featured. The Board of Examiners were astonished by the various ways in which this combination of words was translated into Dutch. Their theory was that many of the candidates could only have been confused by the 'Market Garden' of 1944. I hope that today's discussions will be less confusing, but that they will turn out to be as fruitful as the many market gardens this country has to offer.

DISCUSSION

Professor Janssen was present in Arnhem during the battle, as a student in hiding.

Let me tell you how as a simple civilian I experienced the events of those days. I possessed a permit to stay but it was so false that it could not deceive any German who looked at it. I also have a false identity card, in my own name, which is so common in Holland, but written in a slightly different way. However, one cannot disguise one's age, and my age (22) meant that I had to be at work in Germany and not any more in Holland at that time. Therefore, I could not go out on the street, and was in hiding for over a year in a flower shop on the Steenstraat.

On the Sunday morning of the attack one of the ladies with whom I was staying went to church. She returned late, since during the service an air alarm had sounded – it was never ended by an all-clear. Early during the afternoon we heard some bombing, supposedly in the area of the railway station, and soon planes came over very low. We dived into the cellar, and a series of bombs fell just a street further on. After a quarter of an hour we came out of the cellar – fairly shocked, for you should remember that it was the first time we felt bombs falling around us. We were not yet used to it, as people became in London during the Blitz. Ascending the stairs, we found that a row of houses on which I had looked for more than a year of hiding in the attic was completely destroyed, the remains burning. Soon we began to take our most valued possessions across the street into the shops of acquaintances, afraid that the fire would also reach our house.

Outside in the street people stood looking, till suddenly an approximately 16-year-old German soldier appeared, who started to shoot in the air when a plane passed over. It seemed to me fairly senseless since the planes were some hundreds of metres high, but tense as he was he shouted at me as I went in. There was no chance at that moment that a fighting soldier would arrest a civilian who was the wrong age to still be in Holland, but in his nervousness he might easily have shot me.

Later that afternoon the ladies in whose house I lived sent me in the direction of Oosterbeek in order to inquire whether all was well with some friends of theirs. I passed through back streets, seeing no soldiers, until I reached the main road to the west. There, some troops were evidently putting up a road block. Having reached the house where I had to be, I was admitted and soon looked out of the window on the first

178

floor at the back of the house. I suddenly saw a soldier in a, for me, foreign uniform, clearly a 'Tommy' – he must have been a Canadian – crossing the gardens between houses along the main road and those of a parallel street lower down, nearer to the Rhine. He soon went through another house on the latter street, and would have joined the troops who went along it in the direction of the bridge. As we again came down, a German before the door shouted: 'Der Brit, der Brit?' This was all we understood, and nothing more happened. It was my first and only experience of the fighting during those days.

Safely returned to the Steenstraat, I went towards twilight with my girlfriend of that time to the house of her parents, in the north-eastern quarter of the city, where I stayed for the next week. During the night – we did not go to bed being too tense to sleep – we heard strange, frightening bangs, at a distance. You must realize that we had no idea of what exactly was going on. Clearly there was fighting somewhere in the city. In the middle of the night we heard tanks or armoured cars, and people talking – were they Allied troops or Germans? They turned out to be German, unfortunately; possibly the few tanks that succeeded in crossing the bridge.

During the next days hardly anything happened. Monday afternoon we saw in the far distance to the west a cloud of parachutes coming down: evidently the second dropping. For the rest, there was only tension. No traffic, no news, no organization. The shops were closed, everyone stayed in or near his house, endlessly talking with neighbours. The only persons we saw from other streets were doctors; all other special organizations, founded for emergency, failed to show up in this area of the town. Apart from incidental walks to the Steenstraat, we were virtually confined to our immediate surroundings. A sad incident was the death of a neighbour opposite. While crossing the street, he was killed by a German car which came racing around the corner. He was buried by his neighbours in his front garden – the only solution at that moment.

At the end of the week – the fighting was already over – a car with a loudspeaker came through the street ordering everyone to leave Arnhem on Monday. With our bikes we went north-east, to the next village, called Velp. Passing along the road, we saw a group of captive Allied soldiers with red caps standing before a villa and loudly singing, 'It's a long way to Tipperary' – well, it was indeed a long way for them.

In Velp the people from Arnhem were billeted all over the village. Here we stayed a week, until the Germans started to round up young men for work on the defences of the Veluwe. Evidently, I would do better to leave. Early on Sunday morning my girlfriend and I started with our bikes in the direction of Utrecht where my parents lived. The main road was absolutely deserted. Where we passed through the woods, not far from the city – cycling with difficulty, afraid because of the deadly silence – at a moment we heard a cry: 'Feuer!', immediately followed by a blast of gunfire no more than fifty yards away, at the other side of the road. I nearly fell from my bike, as you can imagine.

Further on, not far from Ede, we passed the heather that had been the landing spot of the paratroopers, the place where General Hackett came down. I must admit that I did not see anything, although the remains of several of the gliders must still have been lying around. We were far too intent on the road, looking out for the Germans who would certainly have arrested us. It nowhere happened, and about six o'clock we safely reached my parents' home.

That is all my experience of the battle of Arnhem, which in its unimportance is similar to that of thousands of civilians who lived through those historic days.

Colonel Powell

I think too many people have made too much of the handling and the intelligence of Market Garden, and amongst those who have not studied the battle carefully there is a general impression that the main reason why matters went wrong was the bad handling of the intelligence. Now this story of the two panzer divisions is just the sort of thing the media likes – secret intelligence, a grim battle, and so-called incompetence in high places. In actual fact the information about the enemy which was passed down to the troops or the Headquarters involved in the action was reasonably accurate. For 'Comet', which as General Hackett has mentioned, was the operation by the 1st Airborne Division alone to do what the Airborne Corps eventually tried to do, we were told that there was one broken panzer division resting and refitting. Now for Market Garden, the information was that there were 50 to 100 tanks in the whole of Holland, and General Browning told General Urquhart he could probably expect about a brigade group and a few tanks. Well, of these two skeleton panzer divisions, the 9th and the 10th, which were refitting, the 10th was involved largely in the early part of the battle, in the fighting against the 82nd Airborne Division at Nijmegen, which left the skeleton of the 9th available for the fighting against the 1st Airborne Division. This, you see, was reasonably accurate. It was about a brigade group and a few tanks.

On the Thursday, five days after the battle started, the 106th Heavy Tank battalion was sent down by train from Germany equipped with 50 King Tigers, and then things got more serious. But, by and large, the fighting around Arnhem took two forms: there was the open fighting and there was the defensive fighting round the bridge and on the perimeter. Now most of the casualties were taken in the open fighting and if we had come in in one lift, and been put down near our objectives – exactly the same error was made by the 82nd, they were not put down near their objectives, and that's why they were so long in taking the Nijmegen bridge – we'd have been fighting a defensive battle well dug in amongst houses and we could have competed with the armour as we did do – we competed very well in the houses of Oosterbeek against these King Tigers. They never broke through; we put them out of action with our hand-held weapons. That's really what I wanted to say – beware of the media stories about the intelligence, which I think we managed to bolster when we came back slightly 'cock-a-hoop'. The press had told us we had held off two panzer divisions. At that time we had no idea at all what the strength of them was. We went home and told our friends we'd fought for a week against two panzer divisions. I remember I was asked to go and speak at Cambridge in the November after the battle, and I made a wonderful story about how a few survivors had held off two panzer divisions. But we didn't – it wasn't two panzer divisions.

Chairman

I might add from the Commander of one of them, whom I met subsequently, an SS General, that they had just finished – the week before – a fortnight's exercise on how to repel an airborne landing. That was bad luck.

Sir Roger Cary

When Operation Market Garden was planned, it appeared to be a bold and imaginative thrust, quite different from the natural style of Mont-gomery, who, like Wellington, was master of the defensive battle. Had it succeeded, it would have been regarded as a master stroke. Of course it was heart-breaking for all involved to see Allied soldiers day by day being apparently slaughtered unnecessarily at Arnhem whilst XXX Corps seemed unable to reach them. This is what Brian Horrocks, and indeed all in XXX Corps, like Colonel Roddy Hill and Pat Winnington here, felt so keenly. However, I am not sure, with hindsight, that the whole operation ever had much real chance of absolute success. The popular film may have been wrong on some detailed points, but it was at least right in its use of 'Boy' Browning's phrase 'A Bridge Too Far' for its title. For the operation of XXX Corps contained some of the best elements of the British Army, particularly the Guards Armoured

Division and the 43rd. Throughout the operation the troops of XXX Corps had their backs exposed and any departure from their main axis would have risked their iron horses becoming bogged down in low-lying marshland.

Moreover throughout September, flying weather was quite unusually bad, as Shan Hackett has said. This adversely affected all Allied transport in attack. In this sense, Holland was a very different country from Belgium where the advance had been so swift. The fact that Arnhem was all along an ultimate aiming point ensured, in my view, that Nijmegen and several parts of Holland behind it were in fact overrun by the Allies by September 1944, they might not have been liberated until early in 1945.

Leaving aside strategy, there are still a large number of tactical questions about the Arnhem operation which I don't think have been quite resolved. Could XXX Corps have in fact done more, if the Army command had originally given it two axes for advancing on instead of one? Was the actual Arnhem operation vitiated from the start by dropping zone procedures which, I think all would agree now, were somewhat too scattered? Was the success of the operation also vitiated from the start by a quite inadequate emphasis on good communications? Surely in an operation of such importance, the ability of different parts of the operational group to communicate quickly with each other, with their home base, with the Air Force and with XXX Corps, should never have been in question.

Alternatively, were the airborne units imperfectly prepared to be cut off from one another? In 1805 Nelson's sea captains could never expect to communicate during a battle, yet each knew in advance exactly what action to take in almost any circumstances. Further, was 21st Army Group to blame for having so got into the way of advancing successfully that it no longer made the very careful assessment of Enigma information that in June and July would have been commonplace? In fact, for instance, detailed Enigma information backed up by air reconnaissance had specifically revealed the presence of elements of 9th and 10th SS divisions in the Arnhem area, albeit resting and recuperating, but no one seemed to be paying attention. Was something of a blind eye also turned to operational risks by both 21st Army Group and 1st Airborne because of a desperate feeling that after so many postponements and false starts, crack airborne troops *must* be used this time and dropped *somewhere*?

Colonel Cooper

I would like to emphasize the feeling of frustration and despair that we all had at that time. I was still doing my reconnaissance and liaison job with the American Airborne at Nijmegen and was up on the high ground on the 20th September. On the 19th there had been very severe fighting by the Grenadiers and the Americans in Nijmegen all day, and the same on the 20th. Rather to my amazement on the morning of the 20th I was in a fox-hole with the Americans keeping our heads down, when General Horrocks and General Allan Adair both came up. Later on that day, the fighting got more and more severe and as we all know now, at about 6.45, I think it was, in the evening when it was getting dusk, the Grenadier tanks got across the bridge – the Americans had already gone across in rubber boats near the railway bridge, 504 Combat Team I think it was – and cut the road. I could see the whole thing from where we were except for the mist and smoke and firing and so on, and I could see the two first tanks which were knocked out on the bridge and the third one which, as we now know, got across. Well, the next day I was recalled to my headquarters; I was with the Armoured Car Regiment, Guards Armoured Division, and I had to take D Squadron with Major Jackie Ward across the bridge, because I knew the route. They fanned out and all that day was spent with all four troops of armoured cars, with what they called a blitz troop, a detachment of infantry, trying to get through on the left flank *and* the right flank. They were held up, they had casualties, and they didn't succeed, and as most of us know, that day was really a wasted day. The Irish Guards had passed through the Grenadier Guards and we got held up since we couldn't get off the road; if we did we were shot up or got bogged down. But on the 22nd, a very determined effort was made, and we had orders to try again to get through to the river or to link up with the Poles at Driel. C Squadron, which was my squadron under Peter Herbert, sent out Captain Wrottesley with his armoured car troop in the very early morning, and he got through by motoring along the north side of the river, and then cutting north again and coming into Driel where he contacted the Poles and was there for the next two or three days until the disaster caught up with us. Having succeeded, Herbert sent another troop, Arthur Young, who also got through. The mist lifted behind him; he just made it, he could see on each side of the road, Germans brewing up, but he moved so fast that he got through. We now had two troops with the Poles at Driel on the 22nd. Arthur Young then went down under orders to try and do a recce, and he got as far as the Arnhem railway bridge. He was under fire the whole time and was held up; it was difficult. By then the 43rd Infantry Division still hadn't got through, but there was no back-up, the Poles were only armed with light weapons, and they were already running out of ammunition.

Wrottesley stayed with the Poles, and they were attacked all day on the 22nd and the 23rd. Finally, Wrottesley was asked to withdraw and he brought out GSO 1 Arnhem, Mackenzie, and also an engineer, Myers, but not before having very severe trouble on the way; indeed, the armoured car was turned over in the ditch and they were hit. Young had some casualties and was told to withdraw soon after that. Well, by then the 43rd Infantry Division were getting through and the DUKWs were coming up but they were having casualties as well; shortly after that I was recalled again across the bridge and brought across Brigadier Norman Gwatkin. After that I was withdrawn to the rear, and about that time, the road had been cut in two places behind us. So that episode more or less ended for me then.

Drs Margry

I want to ask a question about the first day of the XXX Corps advance. I don't want to sound too critical, or look like an armchair historian. But it is a question that's been on my mind for so many years that I would like to ask it because there are so many Guards Armoured Division people present here. We may recall that on the first day after a stiff fight, the Irish Guards broke through the German defence screen and got some way along the road to Eindhoven, and then stopped over-night, not advancing until next morning, 6 a.m.; this loss of 10 hours in the first 16 hours of the operation has always been a mystery to me. Various explanations have been given for this delay.

Brigadier Gwatkin, who has just been mentioned, said in Cornelius Ryan's book that it was no use advancing because they had got news that the bridge at Zon, 10 miles out, had been blown, and the 101st Airborne Division had not captured it, and there was no use advancing because a new bridge had to be built first. But this sounds rather odd to me because the ones who were to carry the bridging material to Zon were XXX Corps themselves, so this should have speeded up the advance. That explanation also sounds odd because according to my information, Guards Armoured did not know, at the moment when they decided to stop, that this bridge had been lost. Another explanation that has been put forward is that the troops after this stiff fight needed rest, the tanks needed maintenance, but as far as I know only the Irish Guards group had been in the action, and it always puzzled me why the three other groups, Grenadier Guards, Coldstream Guards, Welsh Guards, who had passed through them, did not continue the advance; they were fresh, they had not seen any recent fighting.

General Hackett has said that his explanation of why XXX Corps' advance was slower than expected was partly over-optimism and partly the one road they had. Now I know from the operational orders of XXX Corps that there was a second axis. XXX Corps axis was not just a single road, there was also a hard route which was a few miles further east and C Squadron, of which Mr Cooper formed a part with the Household Cavalry, was given specific orders to reconnoitre this second route on the second day. They found Germans there, so they limited the advance to the one other axis. I would like to call on the Guards Armoured people present here whether they could shed any light on these points.

Colonel Hill

I can answer the last speaker in regard to one of the groups. He wonders what it was doing. The Coldstream battalion that I was commanding was placed under command of General Gavin of the 82nd American Airborne division immediately we reached Nijmegen. That division – I agree with everything that has been said about it and its commander – was holding a line eight miles long, facing the Reichswald, which is a rather frowning black forest on ground slightly higher than Nijmegen itself, and it took my battalion all it could do to back up that amazing American division holding an eight-mile front. In the middle of doing that, we were called away to open the centre line which had been cut twice. I can't answer why the whole of XXX Corps was on one road; better qualified officers I am sure can, but you've only got to imagine that road, just the width of that table that our Chairman is sitting at, something in the nature of 50 miles long. The amazing thing to me was it was only cut twice. The Grenadiers were sent once to open it, and I was sent the next time. So that accounts for what the Coldstream were doing while they were not able to go and relieve the Irish Guards on the other side of the bridge, until it was safe for them to do so.

CHAPTER SIX

PRINCIPLES OF DUTCH FOREIGN AND DEFENCE POLICY

Frits Bolkestein

INTRODUCTION

This conference was set up as part of the William and Mary Tercentenary Celebrations, marking 300 years of friendship between our two countries. But was it really friendship which made William III accept the invitation of the Tories and Whigs to intervene in British politics? I am afraid the answer is no. William III was a king who, in the words of Winston Churchill, 'was never fond of England, nor interested in her domestic affairs'. The reason why he and his Army landed on the beach at Torbay was that he wished to enlist the aid of England. He needed her power and wealth in order to meet the overshadowing menace of France's drive for hegemony in Europe.

Apart from this it would be an overstatement to say that we enjoyed only friendship during the 300 years which have passed since the Glorious Revolution. After all, we had our quarrels, especially at sea. In the present century the British, for quite understandable reasons, did not appreciate our neutral stance when in 1939 the winds of war began to blow over Europe.

What cannot be disputed, however, is the fact that during the Second World War the bonds of friendship between Britain and the Netherlands were tightened in such a way that it would have a lasting effect on our post-war relationship. We in the Netherlands shall never forget what Britain meant to us in those difficult days. That is why I regard it as a privilege to speak at this conference. Many of those present here today played an important role in the war and on many occasions displayed great personal courage.

As a leitmotiv for my speech I should like to take the Anglo-Dutch tradition of joining forces against expansionist powers on the Continent. In so doing I cannot, however, overlook the fact that the Netherlands broke with this tradition in the nineteenth century. After that I shall go into the reasons why, in 1948, both Britain and the Netherlands decided to press for the Atlantic Alliance. Finally, I shall point out that today there is still a dominant power in Europe to be opposed, even if that power is showing signs of change.

PAX BRITANNICA

I began my speech by saying that during the last 300 years Anglo-Dutch relations were not always characterized by friendship. The Netherlands became a great power during the seventeenth century. Maritime trade became our national strength – and a source of Anglo-Dutch friction. Britain fought Dutch supremacy over the seas with protectionist measures. After three Anglo-Dutch naval wars we had to yield our first place to England and gradually we lost interest in European power politics.

It is interesting to note that although our two countries were opposed in their quest for maritime trade, more often than not they needed each other to maintain the balance of power on the Continent. From a purely economic point of view Britain and the Netherlands had reason to be enemies. But our mutual political interest in containing the most dangerous Continental power limited all our confrontations to short struggles.

NEUTRALITY

Continental powers which became too dominant through the centuries were Spain, France and, of course, Germany. But when Germany had to be opposed twice in our century, the Netherlands wished to remain strictly neutral. This stance was the result of a historical process which had begun well before the twentieth century. Historians mark the secession of Belgium in 1839 as the beginning of a new phase in Dutch diplomatic history. Our country was reduced to the rank of a small power. Non-participation and strict political neutrality became firm principles of Dutch foreign policy. Unable to have any significant influence on world affairs we avoided power politics, especially the volatile power politics in Europe. It was no surprise that when the First World War broke out in 1914 we decided to remain neutral and mobilized our Army to defend ourselves against any invader, be it

Germany or Britain. In retrospect it may be said that it was good fortune plus the balance of power between Britain and Germany which saved us. We gave in a little to the demands of all sides and managed to stay out of trouble. It was more a question of good luck than good management. Dutch politicians at that time thought otherwise, however. This obsession for neutrality and non-involvement continued to blind us after the First World War. We did not want to think about what was happening elsewhere, especially east of our border. Something dreadfully wrong was going on there, yet we did not dare wake up. Dutch leaders were convinced that neutrality was the right attitude and they took to the moral high ground. 'Dutch neutrality is a beacon of light in a dark world', said prime minister De Geer in 1935. The Netherlands was viewed 'as a steady island of peace in the midst of the infatuation of the nations'.

Great faith was placed in the League of Nations' system of collective security. And if ever war should break out again in Europe the belligerent countries would surely leave us alone, as they did in the First World War. The upsurge of pacifism and idealism in our country in the 1920s had a devastating effect on our defence, as was explained in detail by Rear-Admiral den Boeft on the first conference day. Of course, many people in the Netherlands detested Hitler, but the thought that our country would be involved in war was even more detested. Shortly after the outbreak of the war in 1939 Menno Ter Braak, a well-known Dutch writer, wrote in his diary: 'I don't know if one ever gets used to wars, but one certainly gets used quickly to the thought that war is being conducted elsewhere.' Ter Braak warned against the danger of Nazi Germany but few people took any notice.

The Dutch policy of strict neutrality was not abandoned after Germany attacked Poland. This, of course, was not conducive to British efforts to fight the enemy. In a radio speech of 20 January, 1940, Winston Churchill spoke of the neutral countries which hoped 'that the storm will pass before their turn comes to be devoured'. 'The storm will not pass', he said, 'it will rage and it will roar, even more loudly, even more widely.' Nevertheless, he got a cool response as far as the Netherlands was concerned. Foreign Minister van Kleffens denied the moral and legal duty of the Netherlands to take part in the war and he was supported by the Dutch parliament and public opinion. Just a few people expressed a different opinion and made it clear that something more was going on than just another war between imperialist European powers. The early hours of 10 May 1940 proved that they were right.

ATLANTIC ALLIANCE

What happened between Britain and the Netherlands during the war has been dealt with by previous speakers at this conference. I shall therefore move on to 1945 when the enemy was defeated and Europe had to be rebuilt – physically, economically and politically. Although our wartime co-operation had been magnificent, this did not mean that our two countries had a common view of the future of Europe. Britain, of course, was a direct participant at Yalta and Potsdam and had seen that dealing with Stalin's Russia was becoming difficult. It became clear that the Soviet Union would not tolerate freely elected governments in Eastern Europe because most of these, if not all, would have been anti-Soviet. No wonder that in Britain the threat of the Soviet Union as the post-war dominant Continental power was pretty soon understood, while other European countries were more preoccupied with Germany itself at that time.

For the Netherlands it was not simply a question of how to prevent Germany from becoming dominant again in Europe. We were aware of the fact that reconstruction of our economy very much depended upon the revival of the German economy. Perhaps more than any other European country, we set our hopes on the four-power talks about the future of Germany.

Although there was some scepticism about the ability of the new UN organization to take effective action if needed, the Netherlands believed that the four great powers would sort out their differences. 'Preventing renewed German aggression', Foreign Minister van Boetzelaer said in 1946, 'is of such importance that I refuse to believe that the differences between the members of the Alliance cannot be settled.' Therefore, the government in The Hague was not inclined to conclude an agreement with France and Britain similar to the British–French Dunkirk Treaty of March 1947. This idea, put forward by Paul-Henri Spaak, was described in a telegram to our embassy in Washington as 'pactomania'.

On 22 January 1948, Bevin made his famous speech in the House of Commons calling for the creation of a Western European Union. The Dutch response was positive. Now, after so many years of disengagement, our country was suddenly willing to join a political and military alliance. What had made us change our minds in the nine months since we rejected a Dunkirk type agreement? First of all, it was very important to us that Britain, our closest wartime ally and friend, was not only prepared to participate in European co-operation but had also taken the initiative. Second, East–West relations deteriorated sharply. The London four-power talks on the future of Germany had broken down. In February 1948, a *coup d'état* brought the Communists to power in Prague.

Bevin's speech was a masterstroke. In May 1946 he had already warned the British cabinet that the Soviet threat was 'certainly as great, perhaps even greater than that of a revived Germany'. He took the initiative of concluding the Dunkirk Treaty with France to take away French fears of Germany and allow them to concentrate on the Soviet threat. Yet at the same time he opposed Jean Monnet's ideas on European unity. His goal was to get the United States committed to the defence of Europe. This had to be done carefully. Some proof of European self-help was needed, in order to overcome the last vestiges of traditional American isolationism. But creating an integrated European Union was, in Bevin's view, a bridge too far. He succeeded. After the signing of the Brussels Treaty of 1948, President Truman could state that he 'was sure that the determination of the free countries of Europe to protect themselves will be matched by an equal determination on our part to help them do so'.

General Marshall told the signatories that the Brussels Treaty was 'an essential prerequisite to any wider agreement in which other countries including the United States might play a part'. That wider agreement was signed the following year in Washington. It created NATO, an alliance which was to have unprecedented success. Confusion about which country would be the greatest threat to peace and security in post-war Europe had ended. Swift action to meet this threat had been taken.

POST-INF ERA

This year we celebrate NATO's 40th anniversary. In those 40 years we have had our differences of opinion but at the end of the day we were always able to close ranks. The main reason was, of course, the attitude of the Soviet Union. For a long time it left no doubt about the necessity of joining forces in order to prevent this power from becoming too dominant in Europe. Especially after the Cuban missile crisis the Soviet Union's first priority was to achieve parity with the United States, and it succeeded.

The period of *détente* did not prevent Moscow from modernizing and expanding its conventional forces as well. Under President Brezhnev the influence and power of the Soviet military increased significantly. Its requests for resources rarely seemed to be challenged. In a period when the Soviet economy began to show the first signs of stagnation, the military share of Soviet gross national product increased to between 15 and 17 per cent, almost three times the US share. For a long time the Soviet Union spent enough money to outproduce NATO in most categories of weapons, thereby creating a serious conventional imbalance in Europe.

On top of this, the Soviet leaders took a political gamble by deciding to develop and deploy a new intermediate range nuclear missile. This gamble did not pay off. The European NATO governments which were to deploy INF weapons were able to overcome considerable domestic opposition. They could point to the unrelenting build-up of the SS-20 force, which convinced many Europeans that something had to be done. Now, with the INF Treaty a fact, we should be able to convince our citizens that the Harmel approach, adhered to by NATO, is still relevant. We were not afraid to negotiate but at the same time took measures to ensure that our strategy of flexible response would not be undermined, should negotiations fail.

At present there is some confusion about the way in which NATO should face the future. People wonder whether the Soviet Union will remain a dominant power in the years to come. Sometimes NATO is accused of displaying the same sceptical attitude as Prince Metternich at the Congress of Vienna. He was woken up in the middle of the night by his valet who said: 'Sir, the Russian ambassador died in his sleep.' Metternich pondered for a moment and said: 'I wonder what his motive was for doing that!' It cannot be denied that a remarkable change of Soviet policies has been brought about by President Gorbachev. Apart from the INF Treaty we have witnessed the withdrawal of Soviet troops from Afghanistan. Recently we heard Mr Gorbachev announce major unilateral reductions in Soviet conventional forces.

There are significant internal changes as well: a new constitution, reforms within the party, a change of the judicial system and a new law with regard to state enterprises by which, if implemented, the Stalinist economic structure would be abandoned. I could go on mentioning many more examples of *perestroika* and *glasnost*. These reforms, together with the change in the foreign policy of the Soviet Union, exert a strong influence on public opinion in the West, especially in the Federal Republic of Germany. Its people have been threatened by Soviet missiles and protected by NATO tanks for a long time. But it seems that a growing number of Germans increasingly regard the threat as friendly and the protection as threatening.

We must, however, bear in mind that although the internal changes taking place in the Soviet Union are radical and significant, they do not constitute an end to the undemocratic one-party communist state system. Moreover, these changes have not yet reached the point of no return. Mr Gorbachev still has to win the hearts and minds of his own people. No wonder they are a bit sceptical about a president who, while talking about more democracy, at the same time creates a presidential system which gives himself considerable personal power. What is more important, the Russians' daily struggle for survival is getting no easier. With regard to Soviet foreign and defence policy, there is reason to be more positive. Mr Gorbachev spoke in his UN speech of 'a turning away from the principle of superarmament to the principle of reasonable sufficiency'. He announced significant unilateral reductions in Soviet forces both in Eastern Europe and in the Soviet Union. We hope that in the Vienna negotiations an agreement on parity in Europe can be achieved. The long-existing conventional imbalance must be done away with. This must be accompanied by a sharp reduction in Soviet weapon production.

Let us suppose this happens in the next decade. We are then faced with a Soviet Union which poses much less of a threat than it does today. But still an essentially undemocratic Soviet Union, in which ordinary citizens are hardly able to influence policy. A Soviet Union in which any change of leadership will continue to be as mysterious and unpredictable as it has been since the Russian Revolution.

In other words, we cannot afford to let our guard down and simply hope that the Soviet Union will never again embark upon a course of confrontation. Whatever changes take place in the USSR, that country will for a long time to come remain much poorer than Western Europe, but it will retain the ability to be militarily stronger even if it cuts defence expenditures. There will always be the temptation to make use of this military advantage, especially when, after 1992, Western Europe will have even more to offer in terms of economic performance and technological resources. The instability caused by these disparities can only be checked by a continued presence of nuclear weapons. After all, the five years of history that are being discussed at this conference prove that conventional weapons alone are enough to deter aggression.

FINAL REMARK

That brings me to my final remark which is about the transatlantic partnership. The Atlantic Alliance is vital to Western Europe. It is the expression of common political, cultural and economic values. It is above all the expression of our will to defend these values. Professor Hans Morgenthau once wrote that 'the distribution of benefits within an alliance should ideally be one of complete mutuality'. This ideal is seldom attained, but the principle is important.

In the United States a renewed discussion about the distribution of those benefits is taking place, against the background of the American budget deficit. Or rather, it is a discussion about burden-sharing which we should not underestimate if we are to maintain the cohesion of the Alliance. The new U.S. secretary of defence, Dick Cheney, predicted in his confirmation hearings that budget pressures will soon force his country to reduce its forces world-wide. He called upon the Allies to offset those anticipated cutbacks. Most of the European countries, even the United Kingdom, are unable substantially to increase defence expenditures under the present circumstances. Therefore, the answer must be increased European defence co-operation, especially within the Western European Union. The adoption, last year in The Hague, of the Platform of European Security Interests by member states was a great step forward. However, it is not enough. The Platform has to be implemented by specific measures in the field of European defence co-operation.

In my view, increased European defence co-operation is absolutely necessary to maintain Alliance cohesion as we cross the threshold of the next decade. I have made clear in my speech that in the coming decade the Alliance will be as vital to our security as it has been in the past 40 years. The Second World War will always serve as a reminder to Europeans of what is at stake. To use the words of General Eisenhower when he revisited Normandy a few years after D-day: 'Never again must there be a campaign of liberation fought on these shores'.

DISCUSSION

Sir John Barnes

May I tell a story by way of commentary on the Minister's remarks, with which I entirely agree and wholeheartedly support? Some years ago I found myself sitting next to Harold Macmillan, and had no idea what to talk to the old man about. I remembered that I had been reading a book by Isaiah Berlin in which he said that Winston Churchill was one of the two greatest men of action the British nation has ever produced. So I said to Macmillan, 'Who do you think the other one was?' 'Marlborough', he said. Trying to make conversation, I said 'What about Cromwell?' He said, 'Well, I'll tell you a story. I was in Cairo with Winston during the conference with Roosevelt, and Ibn Saud and all the rest of them, and coming back from one of the sessions in the car, Winston said to me, "Of course, Cromwell was so obsessed by the power of Spain, that he didn't realize that the power of France was coming up behind."' And Macmillan said, 'Of course, I realized at once what Churchill was saying; he was saying that these Roosevelts and people were still so fussed about Germany that they didn't realize that the future threat was coming from Russia. So Berlin can't have meant Cromwell, he must have meant Marlborough.' I have to add that a week later I met Isaiah Berlin and asked him whom he meant, and he said, 'Cromwell, of course.' But that's neither here nor there. The moral of the story is that, for the last 40 years at any rate, the British and Dutch governments have both recognized where the main threat is coming from. We have joined NATO to resist that threat, and I hope very strongly that when a warmer wind blows from Moscow, even if we want to welcome it and to encourage it, we will still not succumb to 'Gorby-mania' but we will keep NATO in being, with its nuclear weapons and all, as the Minister has advised us to do today.

Dominic Flessati

The Minister referred to the state of Dutch public opinion in the 1930s at some length, and he referred very briefly to the state of German public opinion at the moment. Could he say something about the state of Dutch public opinion at the moment?

Dr Bolkestein

It is always hard to discuss something that may be changing as quickly as

194

public opinion, and certainly we seem to be getting into a period in which public opinion has become ever more volatile, so I hope that you will take my reply to your question as being of relative value and certainly not as a firm prediction. When I look at Dutch public opinion at the present time and compare it with what it was 10 or 15 years ago, I cannot escape the impression that we have moved a long way away from the climate of opinion that based itself on a generalized sense of goodwill among nations and was founded on a belief in the fundamental goodness of man itself. We have moved away from that, and I think that a greater realization of the part that power, as such, plays in international relations, a greater realization of the hard facts of international co-existence and international relations, has now come about. If one looks at public opinion as it is manifested in the Netherlands by the activities of the peace movement one sees that these activities are a shadow of their former self. We did have considerable public manifestations in the Netherlands. One in Amsterdam attracted 4–500,000 people. There was a similar demonstration in The Hague in which comparable numbers participated. These manifestations and the concomitant activities of the so-called Inter-church Peace Council were of some importance in determining the policy of the government of the day. We do not see, at the moment, anything that resembles that kind of activity; and also, in parliament, the main opposition party – the Dutch socialist party   is chary of re-engaging similar debates. They have not been in power since 1977, apart for one short period of approximately one year, and I know that they attribute their exclusion from these various governments to the fact that in the strategic debate, if I may call it that, they took the line they did: one of total opposition to any deployment and introduction of cruise missiles. I have the feeling that the Dutch socialist party is anxious to avoid a repetition of that debate, in order not to prejudice its chances of participating in government when the elections of May next year are held.

At the moment Dutch public opinion is, I would say, much more realistic in matters appertaining to international affairs and East–West relations than is German public opinion. In Germany, things are different. In Holland, I have spoken in parliament in debates on shorter-range nuclear weapons in Europe, and of course, I ran into opposition from the socialist party and the smaller parties to the left, but it was overcome. I could overcome it by pointing out that this whole modernization issue really was a case of having fewer weapons, but better ones. The logic of this is apparent. It's the way ahead to a reduction of these weapons, in particular nuclear artillery, and the governing coalition felt itself able to support the government line without too many difficulties. Now in Germany, that is a different story, and indeed the German ministers and other politicians, members of the Bundestag, tell me about German public opinion and how difficult it makes it for them to carry out a similar policy as is advocated by the Dutch and the British governments. I must say that I respect the problems they encounter, but should like to add, nonetheless, that politicians ought to be chary of praying in aid public opinion, as more often than not they themselves are instrumental in creating it.

Sir Douglas Dodds-Parker

May I ask the minister − after first of all thanking him for a very good speech − what his view is of the French? I was Under-Secretary at the Foreign Office when the Western European Union was formed 35 years ago after the collapse of the European Defence Community and, ever since, a group of us have tried to build up the WEU as the counterpart to the Atlantic Alliance. It seems to us even more apposite today that this should be done when France is playing an important but not co-ordinated role. Does he think that more might be done to encourage the French? Not to encourage the French to come into WEU − they're there − but to build it up with other countries in Europe which some of them are aspiring to join.

Dr Bolkestein

I very much value and appreciate the considerable French efforts in the area of defence. Their defence expenditure as a percentage of GNP may not be as high as that of this country, but it is nonetheless substantially bigger than that of my own country and has resulted in a mix of conventional and nuclear forces which is an important element in the deterrence of any potential aggressor. So I should like to begin with this important positive note. The strong effort made by France in the field of defence is carried by a virtual consensus in French society. There is indeed a striking difference between the north-western Protestant part of Europe and the southern Catholic part of Europe in the area of defence; to explore that further would require a discussion of the sociological differences between our two countries and the differences between the Protestant and the Catholic church when it comes to the matter of power as such. But let us leave that aside.

Your question is whether or not we should do more to associate France more closely with European defence. I have been led to believe that on a practical level co-operation between the French general staff and their allies, including the Dutch armed forces, is much more intense than it was 10 or 20 years ago, and of course I consider that to be an extremely positive thing. If we continue patiently to work with our French friends along those lines, much more can be achieved in future. Certainly my French colleague is one of the foremost promoters of co-operation among the European NATO countries in the field of armament procurement, since evidently the cost of new systems is now getting fast into orbit. So that is the second point that I want to make. The third point is about the famous 'European pillar' in defence matters. The argument is strong that any group of countries that aspires to an independent position in world politics should be able to look after its own defence. Therefore European countries should really pool their resources and manage their own affairs without having to rely to the same extent as they do today on American support. While recognizing the strength of the arguments in a theoretical discussion, I cannot help but point out that hitherto we have not been able to create much unity amongst ourselves in the matter of defence except within NATO. Some people maintain that a greater European defence identity need not conflict with the interest that our American friends have in that same area. In other words, that we can build up a European defence identity while at the same time cherishing and strengthening our relations with Washington.

Before I was in my present position, I was Minister for Foreign Trade, and there we have the 'European pillar' and also the transatlantic dialogue. Now my experience in trade makes me wonder whether it is conducive to a good transatlantic dialogue for a European position to be arrived at prior to that dialogue beginning. In the area of trade we meet in Brussels, and after many meetings we hammer out a common European position. That then is our starting point for engaging in a transatlantic dialogue. But it is very difficult to change that position precisely because it has been hammered out as a compromise among the 12 member states of the European Community. If we were to transpose that model to the area of defence, if we got together amongst ourselves before entering the NATO discussion and hammered out some kind of compromise, assuming that that were at all possible, it would make the dialogue within NATO very difficult. Therefore I am inclined to think that our very understandable desire for a greater European defence identity might not be to the detriment of our relations with Washington.

The French are not part of the NATO integrated command. What view do we take of that? It goes without saying that the steps taken by the French in the middle of the 1960s to withdraw from an integrated command is something I regret. However, it would be counter-productive to belabour Paris over this fact, and I don't consider that we should do so. We should accept the situation as it is; we should strive for a greater degree of co-operation at the practical level. We should also aim for more co-operation in the field of procurement. We should take part in the meetings of the WEU, such as the ones which took place two days ago in London. But let us not pretend that the WEU is the nucleus of a common European defence position in preference to NATO.

Chairman

Might I revert for a moment to yesterday afternoon's dispute between Mr Marks and myself, which has been going on for many years? Had I run into Sir Douglas Dodds-Parker on the way out, I would have congratulated him on his masterly silence. To his great annoyance, I revealed in my book on SOE in France that he had been a considerable personage in SOE, a fact that when he joined it he had been assured would never come out at all. He now wishes to say one thing about something that cropped up yesterday.

Sir Douglas Dodds-Parker

Very briefly if I may – following something that Leo Marks said about his report, that it only went to about four people. I think that's unlikely to have been so. It's impossible to add up who contributed what to SOE in those far-off days, but my personal opinion is that nobody contributed more than Leo Marks did, and the air transport, coding and telecommunications were the basis of all our work. There definitely was security, but security was rather loose at the top, because they didn't suffer the penalties of people at the bottom if they didn't carry out all the rules and regulations that Leo Marks and others set out.

I served under Colin Gubbins from March 1940 till the end of the war, directly and indirectly, and on more than one occasion we were sent for by No. 10 and asked to do things. In 1941–42 I was then in charge, from Baker Street, of air and sea transport in and out of Europe, for certain operations on condition that nobody was ever to know about them except Colin Gubbins and myself. On one occasion, that ferret, Bickham Sweet Escott, whom some of you may remember, let slip that he knew about one of them – he was then Charles Hambro's personal assistant. That alerted me to the fact that you had to be careful of things going upwards, and when by chance, later, at the beginning of 1943, I found myself as a very junior officer in charge in the Mediterranean, I decided not to refer anything successful to London, particularly the clandestine as opposed to the paramilitary. If things went wrong, Brigadier Dudley Clarke, in charge of deception, would always turn them to our benefit, and I didn't mind referring those back, because they had to be known to the enemy anyway.

Now I'll give one example: we carried out the Italian armistice in my villa in Algiers under Leo Marks's supervision at a distance: the negotiations went on for seven weeks. The day before the landings were due to take place at Salerno, Marshal Badoglio sent a message saying, 'The whole thing's off – the Germans have rumbled it', and I had
to get in touch with the High Command. General Eisenhower himself came on the telephone from Carthage 700 miles away, and asked 'Are you sure your communications are secure?' Possibly the most important quick answer I ever had to give, I said 'Yes sir, I'm confident they are.' The next morning, 70,000 people were going to land at Salerno, and I kept everything crossed until I heard they were safely ashore.

Ten years ago, Herr von Plehwe was at Western European Union headquarters here in London, and he was on General Student's staff in Rome trying to find out what was happening – they knew there was something going on. They found out nothing, because our security communication was secure. In 1945, he told me incidentally, that they were listening to the Roosevelt/Churchill transatlantic telephone conversations until December 1943, and when we got to Berlin in 1945, there was a complete record of these telecommunications. A ten-year-old child could have known that Mr Churchill was talking about the king of Italy and Mussolini. It seemed to me that the professional code people spent more time trying to break each others' codes than they did protecting their own. But that was always an example of how the communications should be kept secure, not just in the way that Leo Marks describes so brilliantly, but on the top level at the same time.

Chairman

Among the papers we captured in Berlin was a complete transcript of all of the Churchill/Roosevelt conversations; at the bottom were the words *Von keiner Interesse* and Ribbentrop's initials.

CHAPTER SEVEN

THE WAR, THE NETHERLANDS AND THE DEVELOPMENT OF THE EUROPEAN ECONOMIC COMMUNITY

Alan S. Milward

It is a popular simplification of history to argue that the experience of war, of occupation, and of exile during the Second World War converted men's minds and hearts so as to turn them away from belief in the nation state as a basic organizing principle of their lives and towards the idea of European unity as an alternative organizing principle. It is a simplification which has been supported by the history of the resistance movement in the Netherlands as well as in other occupied countries. There is, certainly, much truth in the perception that the small western European nation states had really come to the end of the road in June 1940, but the experiences of their governments in exile were more positive than the present histories relate. This can be seen from a brief comparison of what these experiences really bequeathed to the postwar world, particularly in the case of the Netherlands but by analogy in the case of almost every other western European country.

Virtually all the theoretical and historical explanations of the process of European integration start either from the assumption that the nation state must eventually wither away because it has been proved inadequate as a basic organizing principle, or from the assumption that the events of the war had demonstrated the inadequacy of the nation state and that something else must take its place: a united Europe, an integrated Europe, a federal Europe, a confederation, or some other arrangement of this kind. In all the theoretical studies of this question, there is a basic opposition between the idea of the nation state and the idea of integration – they are seen as absolute alternatives. The difficulty about this kind of argument is of course that we are left with the paradox that over the last 40 years of our own lifetime the nation state has successfully been restored as the major fundamental organizing principle of our societies. Not only that, in most respects its ambitions have become much greater than they ever were in the 1930s. This was particularly true for the first 20 years after 1945 when national governments laid claim to a whole range of powers and capacities which they would certainly have disclaimed as being improper or not feasible in the 1930s.

This paradox seems to have existed simply because of a misinterpretation by historians and economists of what the impact of the war actually was on the post-war world. What we have to explain is the co-existence of European integration, which was an evident constitutional and juridical process in the 1950s, and the growth of the power of the nation state from 1945 onwards. From the moment that any of the exiled governments returned to power they all pursued policies of state aggrandizement in domestic policies, particularly in domestic economic policies, which they would never have thought of doing in the inter-war period, while at the same time actively considering the merging or surrender of aspects of their national sovereignty.

How can we explain these parallel trends? My argument is that we should think in a much more complicated way about the impact of the war on the post-war world. I would argue that the war gave rise to three historical processes which have dominated the post-war world, although now their force gets weaker all the time, particularly in the Netherlands and Britain. Those three historical processes I would define as, first, the process of national re-assertion – the re-assertion of the power of the nation state; second, a further extension of the process of governing by political consensus; third, the process of integration. These three processes are as well observed in the Netherlands as anywhere else, but the argument is valid for the whole of Western Europe. The Netherlands is very much a part of the West European experience, and perhaps one of the best exemplars of that experience.

The process of re-assertion could be seen in the Netherlands first of all in the re-assertion of the concept of a Dutch nation and a Dutch national state as something which would continue to exist, or be restored if you prefer, after 1945. About this we have heard a great deal in this conference, albeit sometimes unconsciously. That process of re-assertion of the Dutch national state finds its expression in, for example, the tendency in 1944 and 1945 to suppose that it would be possible to annex regions of Germany, and even to populate them with Dutch citizens. It found its expression in the attempts to re-assert imperial authority in Indonesia and elsewhere. And it found its expression in the post-war so-called industrialization plans and in the actual micro-economic policies pursued after 1945, the extension of capacity in the Dutch steel industry to take but one example.

The process of furthering and deepening the political consensus arose from the belief, particularly strong during the Second World War in exile, that democracy had in some way failed in the inter-war period – failed because it had not really met the economic and social aspirations of a large enough sector of the population. Agricultural incomes, for example, after 1925 fell seemingly inexorably behind incomes in other areas of the economy. Agricultural interest groups in the Netherlands sustained those corporatist and nationalistic aspirations of patriotic movements which sometimes saw National Socialism as not absolutely and entirely bad. Perhaps this is the moment to bring the conference back to the sad historical truth that there were such sentiments everywhere, not just in the Netherlands. Unemployment in the 1930s, too, was seen during the war as a profound cause of alienation of voters from the existing political system. Devaluation and the inability to stay on the gold standard were seen as having been a crippling blow to the standard of living. And all these economic difficulties were seen as having their origins in government, which represented an inadequate and narrow group of political interests, rather than the country as a whole. And this was seen as being especially harmful in a country so dependent on the international economy as the Netherlands.

The process of European integration was intimately linked to these other two processes. National re-assertion partly emanated from the search for a wider national consensus in democratic politics. The elements of the search for that consensus are not different in the Netherlands from elsewhere. They are, first, the attempt to sustain agricultural incomes after 1945, so that at the very least, the gap between agricultural incomes and industrial incomes would not continue to widen as it had done in the 1930s. They included what it would be accurate, I suppose, to call a high employment policy rather than a full employment policy. They included the attempts to industrialize the Netherlands so as to provide it with a more secure economic base. And they included the 'Welfare State', as it has been called in shorthand ever since, the piecemeal extension of welfare rights and welfare privileges to different sections of the population, beginning immediately in 1945 and continuing in every year from 1945 to 1953. In that search for consensus it is possible to see not merely the re-assertion of the nation state but the drive towards its completion. The model of the nation state and its re-assertion remained the model of the Jacobin nation state of 1793. When welfare was extended the phrase people came to use was 'welfare rights', rather than simply 'welfare concessions' – they were thought of as an extension of suffrage rights. In that sense consensus was a search for a deeper and a wider democracy and as part of that search for a deeper and a wider democracy national re-assertion became an attractive model. The programmes of political action which it proposed appealed to far more potential post-war voters than vague aspirations to European unity.

Where does the process of integration fit into these two processes? There are cases where integration was necessary to make these processes work. To give but one example, it seems fairly obvious that in a country, 40 per cent of whose export earnings came from agricultural exports to a west European area where every government was pursuing policies of agricultural protectionism for the same political reasons as the Netherlands, some kind of common policy would be the only way to guarantee the future of those export earnings. The first versions of the many Mansholt Plans with which the history of the European Community is embroidered are to be found in the Dutch cabinet in summer 1950, 16 years before they surface as operative models in the Community itself. This is but one example of the way that integration became the coping stone in the arch of national consensus and national re-assertion, one way of holding these processes together in the day-to-day world of real politics and the search for votes.

If we were to look at the people involved in Dutch politics after 1945 and try to search for the influence of the war and usually, of exile, on their views of the post-war world, we would come across a curious fact of contemporary history. Although so many Dutch politicians were intimately involved in the process of constructing an integrated Western Europe after 1945, not one of them ever really seems to have been since sanctified by the European Community. The corridors of the Berlaymont buildings are illuminated by overblown photographic icons of European saints – Monnet, Schuman, Adenauer, Hallstein – but we look in vain for those Dutchmen who are now seen by contemporary historians as having had so great an influence on the content and practice of the Treaty of Rome. This is partly to do with the fact that very few Dutch politicians in exile wrote so intimately of their mental processes during this experience as did the Belgians, the French or the Italians. The architect of the Common Agricultural Policy himself, Mansholt, who was in the Dutch resistance during the war, has never written a single word as to the way he came to his extreme federalist position immediately after 1945, a long way it would seem from plantation management in Java. His conviction that European federalism was the way forward was so strong that he seriously endangered his position in the Dutch cabinet three times between 1945 and 1950. No icon can be found in the Berlaymont of the Dutch Foreign Minister Jan-Willem Beyen, who more than any other European politician is responsible for the fact that the basic structure of the European Community became a common market.

This arbitrary election of the saints of Brussels and Luxembourg suggests that the history of European integration in the post-war world has been misinterpreted by the Community itself. It is true, of course, that many leading Dutch politicians after 1945, although playing a large part in the construction of some kind of over-arching integrationist framework in Western Europe, were no believers in ultimate political unification, much less European federalists. They saw national interest as the best basis for constructing a European Community. It was the support which integration gave to the re-assertion of this national interest that made integration necessary and thus acceptable, not an ideal with an easy romantic appeal, nor one that until recently could fit into the Community's prevailing ideology, where a different view of history had to be held.

If we look at the influence of the war and of exile on Dutch politicians the logical place to start would be to look at the socialists. This is partly because the Dutch socialist party really played an important part in Dutch political life only for the first time after 1945, when it was a member of virtually every coalition government for the next 12 years, but also because a small active group of socialists became by 1946 committed advocates of a federal government for Western Europe. Socialist federalists seem to me to have greatly weakened their cause in 1946 and 1947 in the Netherlands, by their conviction that a socialist Europe would be some kind of third force in the post-war world, a conviction which when the Marshall Plan came was seen as being largely irrelevant and possibly mischievous. After that Dutch socialist federalists were reduced to spending most of their time arguing for greater powers for the Council of Europe. Since this ran counter to the main thrust of Dutch foreign policy after the Marshall Plan, which was to pursue Dutch national interest more within the narrower framework of the ECSC, the federalist wing of the Dutch socialist party, vociferous though it was, was simply moved out to the sidelines both of socialist politics and of Dutch politics.

This may be illustrated from the attitudes of two leading lights of the party after 1945, Willem Drees, who became Prime Minister, and

Pieter Lieftinck, who became Minister of Finance. Both were deeply concerned that any entry by the Netherlands into a West European customs union, as had been proposed by France in 1944, in 1946, in 1948 and in 1949, should not carry with it the danger that the Netherlands might be forced into a European Political Community without adequate economic recompense. When this threat finally became specific and unavoidable after the 1950 proposals of the French Prime Minister Pleven for a European Defence Community they both became extremely antagonistic, speaking at length about the defence of 'socialist principles'. What they really meant by 'socialist principles' was the security of the domestic political consensus which they had tried to construct after 1945. They had no wish to gain short-term advantages in military security, if such there were for the Netherlands in the European Defence Community, and see at the same time the political consensus in the Netherlands destroyed. They had no wish to risk their policies of national economic development in the same cause and they had no wish to run the risk of a possible increase in unemployment imposed by following too closely the regime of the Bundesbank. It could be added that from a military aspect for at least a year and a half the proposed European Defence Community did not really provide for the physical defence of the Netherlands, since it provided only for the defence of the Rhine line and thus abandoned two-thirds of the actual geographical territory of the Netherlands to any potential invader from the start of an invasion.

These attitudes also underlay the objection of the socialists to rearmament in the face of strong American pressures at the end of 1950 and the start of 1951. Their argument was that a heavy commitment to rearmament would actually weaken the Netherlands by destroying the political consensus which had been created and so make the Netherlands more susceptible to hostile pressures and competition from the Soviet Union. Just as the balance of payments was beginning to swing into equilibrium after five years of deficits, the Netherlands was once again as the cost of rearmament rose in danger of having to run massive external deficits. These, they argued, would either detract from the gains of real income which would now accrue to the population after ten years of dire sacrifice, or alternatively rearmament would prove inflationary and destroy the competitive advantage which the Netherlands had in Western Europe as a result of the low wages which people had accepted for five years after the war in a mutual effort towards national re-assertion. And all this was to meet a military threat which neither Drees nor Lieftinck really believed was there. Their assumption was that there would be no real military threat from the

Soviet Union until 1955 at the earliest. If there was a threat to the Netherlands from the Soviet Union, that threat was the possibility of an internal collapse of Dutch society and government, a relapse into the conflictual politics of the 1930s. That was where the danger would come from, they thought, and this explains their vehement opposition to rearmament which was sustained throughout the political crisis of late 1951.

That political crisis marked the logical end of the reconstruction period in the Netherlands. It was obviously impossible to resist American demands for rearmament. There would be neither American aid nor American diplomatic support unless those demands were finally met. The resolution of the crisis, therefore, had to include rearmament, almost to the level that the Americans were insisting on in 1951. To achieve that there were two choices, to deflate by increasing the interest rates and allocating to rearmament all those sums of money which had been provisionally allocated to public expenditure, which was the advice of the Central Planning Bureau and most of the civil service, or alternatively to re-impose trade controls as the British and French had done in 1951 and abandon the programme of foreign trade liberalization which had been started in 1949 and 1950. Faced with these two choices, Drees, Lieftinck and the majority of the socialist party rejected both. They turned to the idea of deflecting the rearmament programme so that it would actually further national development in the Netherlands and pressed for specific guarantees that it would be used to develop the shipbuilding and electronics industries. This was the same resolution of a conflict ensuing from external pressures from greater powers that they would also turn to when faced with the European Political Community. They also found ways of deflecting this insistent demand from the Americans in order to strengthen the political consensus and the re-assertion of the nation which had been their great task since 1945.

When we examine their attitude to the second possibility of action in 1951 – the possibility that trade controls could be reimposed on the Dutch economy – we can see that they were in no way 'anti-European', as Drees was frequently accused of being, because their subsequent actions were based on a firm prior decision not to reimpose controls but actually to increase the level of openness of the Dutch economy of Western Europe and try to force the British and French to respond in the same way. To explain that prior decision a brief history of Dutch thinking about post-war economic relationships between the Netherlands and Western Europe from 1944 onwards is needed.

It was quite obvious by 1944 that very large credits would be needed for reconstruction. These were first arranged with the Belgian government through the Benelux agreements of September 1944. In that sense the Benelux agreement followed quite closely the pattern of the Franco-British monetary agreements of 1938 and 1940, by allowing wide swings on either side of the balance of payments, in this case credits by Belgium to the Netherlands specifically designed to allow the Netherlands to import Belgian steel and Belgian capital goods for reconstruction. Yet, as we know, these Benelux agreements carried an aura of meaning and of implication which went far beyond merely monetary matters. They set out to regulate specific long-standing historical disputes about transport and access to waterways, especially the matter of the construction of the Moerdijk Canal, a dispute which had seriously embittered pre-war Dutch–Belgian relationships. They were an attempt to remedy the lack of economic co-operation of the 1930s, beginning with Dutch–Belgian relationships, a course of action overwhelmingly influenced by the experience of exile in London where both governments learned that it was necessary to prove to the greater European powers that it was not, as they were beginning to think, actually the existence of small, inefficient, incapable and mutually hostile neutral states which had caused the chaos of the late 1930s. At the first meeting in the Savoy Grill Room, where the Benelux agreements were proposed in 1943, when these questions were broached by the Belgians, the Belgian idea was laid on the table that there should also be a customs union, leading eventually to a full economic union between Belgium and the Netherlands. The main cause of this suggestion on the Belgian side was fear that the future of Germany would be settled directly by the great powers without any Belgian or Dutch participation, unless there were some common Belgian–Dutch programme about what to do with Germany after the war. The justified fear was that the Allies would simply ignore Belgians and Dutch alike in the post-war regulation of Germany. As we know the Allies in fact did just that. They ignored Dutch and Belgian opinion almost entirely until the London Conference in late 1948.

The Dutch exiles, although divided by the Belgian proposals, mainly resisted them at first because it was felt that a customs union with Belgium, and even more an economic union with Belgium, would actually impede the process of national reconstruction and national re-assertion in the Netherlands after the war. It was felt that the Dutch were more in need of protection against Belgian industry and that a customs union with Belgium would actually impede the realization of post-war consensus and development. What was needed, it was argued, was simply a trade agreement to allow reconstruction on

Belgian funds and, of course, an agreement which would place Dutch agricultural exports on Belgian markets. These attitudes re-surfaced when the Dutch government went back to Holland and took office. It largely ignored for a year and a half what it had signed in the Benelux agreements. It was only in March 1947 that the Dutch finally made some political concessions to Belgian pressures for the customs union, but not very many.

Thinking about the international framework in which the Dutch national state would be re-asserted after the war was dominated, not by the Benelux agreements, but by Germany. That thinking passed through several stages. First, it passed through the stage of thinking about annexing a substantial area of Germany and peopling it with Dutch citizens. That was in lieu of reparations from Germany, for the assumption was that the Allies would not actually provide a sufficient volume of reparations from Germany to enable reconstruction in the Netherlands to take place. But the idea was also that if part of Germany were annexed the rest would be reinvigorated economically as quickly as possible, which, of course, the Allied occupiers of Germany were not in the business of doing in 1946 or 1947. Second, it passed through the stage of trying to bring pressure to bear on the Allied occupiers of Germany to facilitate Dutch trade with the occupation zones; to stop, that is, demanding dollars in payment for German exports and also to purchase Dutch agricultural exports to feed the occupying soldiers. Only Germany, it was rightly thought, could provide a satisfactory market on which the post-war economic development of the Netherlands could be based, and only Germany could substitute for the American capital goods which were needed for the reconstruction of the Dutch economy, the increasing imports of which were the underlying cause of the severe balance of payments crisis in summer 1947.

In both those first and second stages of thinking about Germany, Benelux actually proved quite useless to the Netherlands as a help. Belgian credits were running out by March 1946 and Belgium of course was as agriculturally protectionist as any other country in Western Europe. So at the time Belgian pressures to implement the customs union aspect of the Benelux agreements were simply seen as an impediment to the essential aims of Dutch policy at home and abroad. In April 1946 it was agreed to begin the customs union in one year's time, but it only began in January 1948 and as a customs union without any harmonization of taxes, without any removal of non-tariff barriers to trade, without any removal of quotas, and with only the most timid approximation of the two national tariffs to each other. It was not in any sense therefore a model for the future Treaty of Rome and could not fairly be described as a common market at all, indeed it was not even a tariff union. In June 1948 the further goal was agreed of an economic union between Belgium and the Netherlands, with a timetable for removal of economic controls in the Netherlands, and for stages of progress towards convertible currency for both Belgium and the Netherlands. But this too was never implemented in the Netherlands and the agreement had to be renounced under fierce domestic parliamentary political pressure.

Only the solution of the German problem, it became clear, could actually harmonize national re-assertion with the search for a political consensus, and only the solution of the German problem could bring about European integration. This was crucial to the Dutch attitude in April 1945 in the Tripartite Committee with France and Belgium, where the Dutch objected to all French proposals for a customs union between France and Benelux on the grounds that the Allies were busy dismantling the German economy and weakening it, whereas the future of the Netherlands depended on its economic links with a reconstructed Germany. The same attitude was crucial to the Dutch attitude to the proposals for the Franco-Italo-Benelux payments agreement and customs union in January 1946. French and Dutch policies towards Germany were still of an entirely different kind. It was also crucial to the Dutch reply to French proposals for the Fritalux/Finebel payments unions in 1949 and 1950. France would not include, even as late as 1949, a reconstructed and reinvigorated Federal Republic of Germany in any of these schemes. For any change in official French policy it was necessary to wait for the Schuman proposals in May 1950. Nevertheless, by then it had become evident to all Dutch politicians that the future of the Dutch nation in the post-war world depended on the commercial relationship with Western Europe, and above all on the commercial relationship with Germany, or with the Federal Republic after its creation.

From this originated a series of proposals to regulate the relationships. The first were foreign minister Dirk Stikker's proposals in 1950, the so-called Plan of Action for sectoral integration. The whole object of these proposals was the lowering and eventual removal of tariffs in Western Europe by the major economies. The Western European countries in OEEC were only removing quantitative restrictions on their trade. GATT was responsible for tariffs and it must be said that after 1948 GATT really did nothing very much until the early 1960s, much to the Dutch fury. The Stikker proposals called for the gradual sectoral integration of the sectors of the Dutch industrial economy with other economies through the equalization of prices and costs by foreign trade. They called forth at once vehement objections from agriculture minister Sicco Mansholt, on the grounds that it was impossible to proceed that way with agriculture without endangering political consensus. Agriculture needed something altogether more interventionist if the problem of agricultural incomes was to be resolved. It was in those circumstances that the first Mansholt Plan, remarkably like the future Mansholt Plans of the European Community, was actually drawn up. Stikker was forced to accept that if European integration came about through the Stikker Plan of Action, there would have to be 'special arrangements' for agriculture. And that too meant Germany, because Germany was the market to which Dutch agricultural exports must increase.

Beyen's proposals for a common market came in 1953. It is important to consider how Beyen actually progressed to this idea. He had considered long and hard in exile the failure of international economic arrangements in the 1930s. He was party to the Bretton Woods negotiations and the conclusion of his book on them, published at the end of the war, is a sympathetic defence of them. 'The world's outlook on the inevitability of social hardships', he wrote,

> has been fundamentally changed by the world war and by the consequence of the economic crisis of the thirties. The social hardships which the wars and the crisis of the thirties would have caused in the absence of government interference were humanly and politically unacceptable in any post-war settlement. To avoid social hardships by government interference in economic life will be the responsibility of all the national governments after the war. They cannot accept such responsibility and at the same time unconditionally subordinate their economic and financial policies to an international aim, like the stability of exchange rates. On the other hand, they cannot ignore that the social interests they have to protect are seriously threatened by the instability of exchange rates. Exchange stability, therefore, remains the common responsibility of all national governments. According to all modern conceptions, this common responsibility demands co-ordination and not subordination of national policies.

That was the starting point of Beyen's progress towards the idea of a European common market. This progress was further stimulated by the failure of the Stikker plan for sectoral integration and even more so by the Mansholt proposals, because it seemed evident to Beyen that if one was thinking about agriculture, one was thinking not simply

about tariff removal but about harmonizing the extremely complicated government intervention schemes which had developed in every
country's agricultural sector between 1945 and 1950. Beyen's cabinet
colleagues in 1953 were not so sure about the idea of a European
common market. They thought the common market might be a good
idea for the Dutch economy, but they were by no means sure that it
needed any kind of supranational European organization. So they
always imposed on him as a negotiator the strict condition that the
common market should be the first goal, supranationality only a second
goal. But Beyen never accepted this commitment in his heart, since he
had become intellectually convinced that there never would be a
common market unless there were some form of supranational government. The Netherlands was not an important enough country to
impose its own version of international commercial relationships on
other countries after the war. The experience of the inter-war period
had already shown that Dutch trade with Germany after 1933 had been
entirely at the whim of an autocratic government concerned only with
national German economic development and a government also which
had relegated the international sector of the German economy to the
least of its priorities. What Beyen sought, when he sought a supra-
national authority in Western Europe, was a guarantee of the irreversibility of post-war Dutch commercial relationships with the Federal
Republic, or a version as near irreversibility as it would be possible
to obtain in his imperfect world. The desire for a supranational
organization did not come from any belief in the virtues of supra-
national or international forms of government for Western Europe
in themselves, it came from the firm belief that without supranational
organization the Netherlands would not obtain the commercial
stability on which the post-war consensus depended and which alone
would permit the pursuit of the post-war national objectives.

The proposals were made in 1953 because the greater European
powers were then discussing the European defence community and
the European political community which was to be attached to it.
Beyen was simply not prepared to accept any over-arching political
structure in Western Europe unless it guaranteed the Netherlands'
own economic interests. For six months after the French National
Assembly voted down these arrangements nothing more was heard of
the common market proposals, but when Mendès-France fell from
office Beyen resurrected them and worked extremely hard to sell them
to Monnet and to Spaak. They were not in the least interested in the
common market at the time, but only in organizations like Euratom or a
common European transport policy, the sort of thing that Monnet felt

would build on the administrative structure of the Coal and Steel Community. As we know, the foreign ministers, in what is now seen as an historic meeting at Messina, though it seemed a small event at the time, accepted both the Spaak/Monnet proposals on the one hand and Beyen's proposals on the other, and allowed the Spaak *ad hoc* committee to study both. The Spaak committee was very pessimistic about the chances of any kind of common market, mainly because Spaak was not very interested in it, but also because of the agricultural problems involved. In any case, when the Treaty of Rome was first being actively discussed the French government had little or no intention of taking part in a Western European common market. Throughout that period Beyen had to maintain the Dutch position that a guarantee of West European commercial relationships, for which the political machinery was to be a common market, was a *sine qua non* of Dutch participation in an integrated Western European political framework. In this guaranteed system it was the guarantees given by all about the future of commercial relationships with Germany that were most important to the economic security at which Dutch national re-assertion aimed and on which it depended.

The post-war world made it clear that if there was to be a re-assertion and a re-creation of the Dutch national state, this could only be achieved through a Dutch–German reconciliation. From occupation, resistance and exile was born the political system which was to restore the Dutch national state and state apparatus in greater security than before the war. But the irony of history was that their ultimate restoration and security depended above all on a measure of surrender of national sovereignty to their enemy occupier, for only this could guarantee the economic success on which maintaining the post-war political consensus depended.

Albert Kersten

Alan Milward has not paid much attention to the British role in European integration or the Dutch view of the British role. That is an issue to which I want to give some attention, but before doing so I shall have to dispose of two other issues: first of all, the role of the Second World War as the point of departure for European integration, and in the second place, my doubts on the logical progression from the May 1940 defeat of the Dutch to European integration so far as the Dutch government-in-exile is concerned.

So, first of all, the Second World War as the starting point for European integration.

With great delight, our political leaders remind us of the reputation of military planners for preparing the unmaking of the failures of the previous war. It is their privilege that they are not aware that they behave in the same way. Most of the post-war planning during the Second World War was directed by the obsession of avoiding the mistakes made after the Great War, and the nationalistic policies of the thirties. Global and regional co-operation became favourite recipes for dealing with a variety of international problems in the fields of security, economic and military relations and the treatment of former enemy countries. Of course, this co-operation concept did not originate in Netherlands eyes in the dark period of the World War itself; it had been revived, for attempts to bring about regional co-operation had already been made in the inter-war years, especially in the field of economic relations.

The Dutch had made a substantial contribution to these efforts. In the late 1920s, the Economic Committee of the League of Nations, with the Dutch Prime Minister Dr Colijn in the chair, had tried to fight protectionist trade barriers and to design new systems for international economic relations, but the Committee's tariff schemes proved unachievable. Belgium, the Netherlands and Luxembourg built a new form of trade relationship in the Convention of Ouchy. This agreement of July 1932 provided a mutual reduction of tariffs of the free countries without granting a reduction to third states under the 'most favoured nation' clause, which was a regular article in trade agreements among nations at that time. This attempt to create a tariff zone which

213

other states could join was soon frustrated by a British veto. Any comparison with the preferential system of the British Commonwealth was rejected as inappropriate. The British reaction to this Convention as well as to the less dangerous Convention of Oslo of December 1930 was an all-out negative.

The Oslo co-operation – it was no more than an intentional declaration on advance information regarding tariff changes – got an overemphasized importance in British eyes. In the field of international trade, it remained ineffective in spite of many Oslo state meetings of the signatory states (Belgium, Denmark, Luxembourg, Netherlands, Norway and Sweden). However, it was more important that at an international level studies were made on new forms of international economic relations, studies which did not depart from the bilateral trade agreements but which focused on larger groupings of states with common interests.

It would be too categorical to say that Great Britain isolated itself in the Commonwealth system, for it participated in several commodity restriction agreements. However, a splendid isolation behind the protectionist barriers of the Commonwealth system and a high degree of lack of interest were characteristic of the British attitude. It continued thinking along the lines of the British Commonwealth as an empire independent from the rest of the world, while other European states made their first, however careful, exercises in new forms of economic co-operation. Of course, outside government offices more intensive discussion had taken off after the Great War on the necessity of creating larger economic units on the European continent. The mainstay of this was the anxiety about Europe's competitive power in the international markets, especially against the United States. A European Customs Union was propagated as a remedy in those days.

I come now to my second point, the logical progression from the defeat in May 1940 to European integration.

Developments before the war seem to confirm the thesis of logical progression. However, one should keep in mind that the tendency referred to concerns economic co-operation. The German aggression of May 1940 changed the attitude of the Dutch. In the pre-war years, trade relations had been predominant in Dutch foreign policy. The German invasion caused a psychological shock which, for the moment at least, concentrated the discussion of the post-war international position on security: security against future German aggression.

The Dutch Foreign Minister, van Kleffens, was the first to conclude that the Netherlands could not defend its territorial integrity independently. It needed stronger partners, outside the European continent. Although he admitted an inter-relationship between security and the international economic order he did not develop any plan which crystallized this general statement. His draft for a global system of regional security organizations reflected his obsession with security. Moreover, it emphasized his aim to achieve an influential position for his country in world affairs. But van Kleffens was too clever to claim a position equal to the great powers – the United States, Great Britain, France, China or the Soviet Union; because of her colonial possessions in South East Asia, he developed a concept of middle power for the Netherlands. According to this concept, the Netherlands could perform as an important power next to the great powers. The shock of May 1940 had made van Kleffens aware that security co-operation, preferably with the United States and Great Britain, was indispensable; but at the same time he did not want his country, be it in Europe, in the western hemisphere or in South East Asia, to be at the mercy of these powers. His efficient emphasis on the importance of the great powers seemed to constitute the logical consequence of the discontinuation of the pre-war policy of non-involvement. Instead of concentrating on the European scene, van Kleffens practised a global approach in his concepts for post-war planning. He had chosen regional sub-structure because he had lost faith in a globally connected security system like that of the League of Nations. So, European or, better, Western European security co-operation was regarded as a jewel for regaining considerable influence on international decision-making; the traditional non-involvement policy was no longer realistic. Van Kleffens' opinion was shared by many other cabinet members, senior officials and members of the business community in London.

In the centre of this combined regional and global co-operation approach was the main colonial possession: the Netherlands East Indies. It impeded the drafting of a clear-cut concentrated European post-war policy. Like the French, the Dutch were convinced of the uniqueness of their mission in the East Indies. In their view its execution had been interrupted by the Japanese occupation in March 1942, but nobody doubted its continuation after Victory Day in the Far East. The few individuals who predicted that the occupation would accelerate the process of decolonization were deliberately excluded from post-war planning. The premise that the post-war Empire would include the metropolitan country as well as the East Indies greatly influenced the post-war planning. The participation of any strong regional entity was out of the question because it was deemed to sever the essential life-line between the two main parts of the kingdom. This consisted of the Netherlands in Western Europe as well as the Indies in South East Asia. Thus the design for a global system based on regional groupings provided the imperial bond. Because the supposition of the restoration of the pre-war British Empire was almost general among the Dutch-in-exile, I have difficulty with a logical progression from the May 1940 defeat to European integration. As long as the concept of the Dutch Empire with its European and South East Asian balancing parts was regarded as vital, an integrated Western European structure was unthinkable. Only very loose concepts could be regarded as feasible. Only when, after the war, in 1947–48, the restoration of the Empire proved to be impossible due to the Indonesian revolution, the concept of an integrated Western Europe came to the centre of Dutch foreign policy as a feasible alternative.

To be clear, I do not say that the Dutch-in-exile did not think of Western European regional co-operation. On the contrary, it was an accepted view that economic units had become larger than national units, as Beyen had stated by the end of 1942. Also, a general preparedness for national co-operation was imminent but it was seen within the framework of a restored Dutch Empire.

I come now to my third point: Dutch views on the British role in European co-operation and integration.

By tradition, the Dutch felt a special relationship with the British. The Second World War emphasized the situation. The Dutch became aware that their security depended on British and American assistance. In December 1942, foreign minister van Kleffens indicated this relationship by calling the Netherlands the 'bridgehead' against Germany, Great Britain the 'base' and the United States the 'arsenal'. Despite the great American contribution to the Allied war effort, the Dutch and most Western European exiled governments regarded Great Britain as the leading nation. In every design for post-war European co-operation, Britain was the leading force. Every schedule for co-operation was discussed with the British and their adherence and participation was often sought. However, attempts to acquire British support for affiliation to the Benelux military co-operation met a cold shoulder. This disinterest in British attitudes did not discourage the Dutch and other small continental European governments during and after the war from lobbying for British support. The Dutch attitude contributed to the traditional distrust of France and its international policy. Since Germany had disappeared as a political power in Europe, Britain was the only remaining trustworthy and reliable great power. Gradually, however, Dutch opinion changed on the necessity of British involvement in post-war European co-operation. As to security, no doubts came to the fore on the crucial British role in Western Europe.

Regarding economic and military co-operation, a change came along. As early as 1946 the Dutch government realized that Dutch and European reconstruction was dependent on German reconstruction. The policies of the occupying powers in Germany, Britain included, impeded every step in this direction. The military curtain that the occupying powers had erected around their zones in Germany aggravated the situation. Gradually, a mixed attitude towards Britain was felt. On the one hand, close co-operation was striven for, and a British leading role was preferred, but at the same time the British policies frustrated this national drive for British leadership.

The Paris Conference of 1947 on the European recovery programme constituted a turning point. According to the Benelux main negotiator, Hans Luschfeldt, the British attitude became frustrating because Britain was keen for leadership only, not for effective co-operation in Western European reconstruction. British leadership in European co-operation became more and more unlikely because Whitehall gave preference to its Commonwealth roles and was not willing to transfer any of its power to an international authority. In fact, an ambiguous situation continued until the mounting of the Schuman Plan in May 1950. Until then, French policies towards Germany had rejected any treatment of Germany on an equal footing. To the Dutch, the French offer for entwining the new Federal Republic of Bonn in a supra-national Western European structure constituted a political breakthrough. They consented to participate in the negotiations on the Schuman Plan, although they had great doubts on the feasibility of the supra-national aspects of the plan. And like the British, they agreed to discussions on the French proposal because it opened a new perspective for Germany's role in Western Europe, an option which the Dutch government had promoted since 1946.

The Schuman Plan was a point of separation between the Dutch and the British regarding possible future economic co-operation in Western Europe. The Dutch would have preferred the larger structure of European economic co-operation but they opted for the smaller setting of the six nations of the Schuman Plan because in their view some degree of transfer of national sovereignty was necessary. Within a wider field this was unattainable.

I am aware that the process of European integration can be discussed more fully in a wider perspective than that of the bilateral Anglo-Dutch relationship. For the moment, I conclude by drawing your attention to three points:

(1) Security has been an essential issue in post-war Dutch foreign policy; any solution without British involvement was unthinkable.

(2) In evolving a policy of non-involvement and neutrality by signing the Treaty of Brussels in March 1948, the Dutch tried to gain influence in international decision-making by using the Benelux as a basis for collective action together with Belgium and Luxembourg.

(3) The traditional dependence on international trade, and the increased demand for foreign markets due to the post-war reconstruction programme, made the Dutch aware of the need for European co-operation and integration. This internationalist attitude, and the policy of Germany's equal position in Western Europe, were dictated by Dutch national interests. It was for these economic reasons that the Dutch took a more positive, less cynical stance towards the Schuman Plan than the British who for the time preferred to stick to the Commonwealth.

E. P. Wellenstein

Please allow me to make three preliminary remarks:

First, it might seem that this conference consists of two distinct parts, the wartime events and the post-war developments in the realm of Anglo-Dutch relations. For me personally, these two different parts are closely interlinked; my experience and activities after the Second World War follow from what I witnessed and did in the occupied Netherlands. European co-operation and integration cannot be understood properly without the drama of 1939–45.

My second preliminary remark concerns the scope of my contribution to this debate: I will leave out military aspects of European and Anglo-Dutch co-operation because our minister of defence, Dr Frits Bolkestein, has already dealt with that dimension previously.

My third introductory remark consists in asking your indulgence because I find myself under a triple handicap:

- I am the last speaker of no fewer than four on the theme of post-war co-operation in Western Europe;
- I am the very last speaker of the whole conference, which has asked so much of your attention for three days;
- and I am *not* a professional historian, like Professor Milward and Professor Kersten. I am simply a witness, to some extent an eye-witness, of the events and the developments we examine and analyse here. I am what the French call *un témoin de l'histoire*, somebody who has participated and who, for that sole reason, cannot be impartial and even less neutral. My archives consist of my memories, my files are what I remember and are therefore partial in the sense of incomplete.

Having stated my handicaps, let me start my story where Professor Kersten left us: in the first half of 1950, when the French had launched the Schuman plan and the British had declined to go along with this new approach. For the then Dutch government, the Schuman plan coincided more or less with an initiative of the minister of foreign affairs, Dirk Stikker, to provide the Organization for European Economic Co-operation with a new and ambitious programme of work. This 'Stikker plan' tried to tackle the vexed problem of tariff reductions as an extension of the liberalization programme which OEEC had dealt

219

with so successfully. But that liberalization was limited to the progressive elimination of quantitative restrictions (helped along by the European Payments Union, which paved the way for the convertibility of European currencies). Tariffs were another matter, much more sensitive economically as well as politically. Stikker's plan – which in a way was of the same inspiration as the abortive Convention of Ouchy, recalled a while ago by Professor Kersten – failed totally, not only because of British and French opposition, but also because of Scandinavian reservations (preference for Nordic arrangements, about which they had high hopes at the time, no doubt played a role here).

In a general way, efforts to move beyond the abolition of quantitative and currency restrictions within the framework of OEEC brought out very clearly the existence of countries with – and without – preferential tariff arrangements like the Commonwealth preferences and the analogous French arrangements. The only way for the Benelux countries to cut through this knot appeared to be the participation in more ambitious schemes than OEEC-like approaches. In the Coal and Steel Community, the 'common market' was a kind of by-product of a set of common rules and common policies. Moreover, the French plan had an overriding political objective, i.e. defining a place for the brand new Federal Republic of Germany that could satisfy the self-esteem of the new German political elite and at the same time lay at rest French and other misgivings.

These latter political objectives could be fully endorsed by the then Dutch government. More than that, the Schuman Plan implied that restrictions on German economic development imposed by the occupying Allies would in due course simply have to fall away, meaning a more dynamic hinterland for the economies of the Benelux countries and thus better economic perspectives for themselves. Similarly, equal access to German coal and steel was of vital interest for the Low Countries. All this was now in sight, without complicated discussions with the Allies and without delicate negotiations with the authorities in Bonn.

But whoever wanted the benefits of the common market for coal and steel had to swallow the common rules and common policies, plus the institutional machinery required to run the organization. With this institutional machinery, a high authority empowered to take majority decisions, the Dutch – and their Benelux colleagues – had some problems. As we know, they introduced the idea of a Council of Ministers in the negotiations and the French, after a thorough debate, accepted this major amendment to their plan. This has had far-reaching consequences, since the institutional model of the ECSC was later to become the blueprint for the institutional machinery of the EEC, with one significant change: the powers of the Council of Ministers were to be much greater in the EEC than in the ECSC.

It would be wrong to pretend that the Dutch introduced their institutional amendment in 1950 in order to facilitate a later accession of the British, but there is little doubt that the powerful position of the Council of Ministers as it has worked out in the Community is not to the dislike of the British. It decidedly facilitated British entry in 1973, as we shall see later.

How did the Dutch react to the fact that they were in the ECSC without the British? They were certainly somewhat *étonnés de se trouver ensemble*, it was not the club life they had dreamed of during and immediately after the war. But it was the only club offering them solutions to their economic problems in a war-devastated Western Europe – and it was useful for the 'German problem'. But in the Dutch view the formula should not and could not be extended to matters of security and strategy. Nevertheless, my country had come a long way, as I can illustrate by three quotations from Dutch Prime Ministers:

— The first is Prime Minister de Geer, our first Prime Minister in the Second World War period, totally at a loss after the German invasion and during his short period in exile in London. During the 'phoncy war' he once declared that the virtuous Netherlands were a beacon, a lighthouse, which would help the great powers steer a course to peaceful waters. Unfortunately, he did not know the Japanese saying that darkness reigns at the foot of the lighthouse.

— His successor, Prime Minister Gerbrandy, a man of undoubted courage and determination, found the idea of a Community of European nations so unpalatable that he called the proponents of such a crazy concept 'Merchants of folly' (*Kolderverkopers*): 'They do not understand each other, although they know each other's language.'

— And then our Prime Minister during the negotiations of the Treaties of Rome, the 'grand old man' Dr Willem Drees: looking back on the first ten years of the EEC in 1967 he declared himself to have been somewhat sceptical when the treaties were signed in Rome in 1957. He had feared a rather protectionist policy. And he considered the six as a group 'unsuitable for general political purposes'. General de Gaulle had made this even worse: what he wanted was a continental Europe, and thus the EEC had become even less apt to conduct a general policy.

This is, in a nutshell, the official Dutch attitude up to 1970. In economic matters, the Dutch had hoped up to 1958 to have the best of both worlds by supporting the Maudling negotiations for a large European free trade area encompassing the EEC as an inner circle, but when these failed the dynamism of the EEC flying-start soon made them forget, especially when the UK asked for membership shortly afterwards. But they resisted attempts to deal with political and strategic matters in the framework of the six. (Maybe these attempts contributed precisely to the British decision to join?)

Thus the ground was prepared for the show-down with the Fouchet plan, the finest hour of Minister Joseph Luns and no doubt useful in a general European sense. General de Gaulle's ideas about political co-operation and a kind of general economic overview of what was already being dealt with in NATO and in the European Community would certainly have led to endless quarrels and ambiguities. The fact that this Fouchet plan was launched after de Gaulle's rebuff to Britain's first attempt at entry certainly contributed much to the Dutch misgivings and final refusal.

In the meantime, the institutional system of the Community, which the Dutch government in 1950 had looked upon with some suspicion, had become very popular in the Netherlands. 'Supranationalism' was the watchword. Dutch and in general Benelux politicians had discovered that their voice was much louder and better heard in this new framework than in any other international forum.

Enlargement of the EC in 1973 to nine member states, and later to ten and twelve, had reduced the status of the Netherlands in Community affairs well below their level of influence when Minister Luns fought with General de Gaulle in the sixties. It is indeed the irony of history that the members of the Six most interested in 'supra-nationality' were the staunchest supporters of British entry, which – by no fault of the British – would not enhance their position in the Community at all. This is also illustrated by the 'empty chair' episode in 1965, when General de Gaulle withdrew his representatives from Brussels because he disliked certain Commission proposals. This ended with what is wrongly called the 'Luxembourg compromise'; it was not a compromise at all, but an agreement to disagree, five against one: de Gaulle. Curiously enough, this so-called compromise was later invoked by successive British governments to deny the possibility that they might be overruled by a majority voting procedure, precisely what the Dutch prize so much – and rightly so I think – in the EC decision-making process.

A lot of water has passed through the Rhine since the British entry. The first period especially has had a sobering effect on the Dutch, who had expected a happier start with their friends at last in. I must add that my compatriots have not always been helpful either, e.g. with the protracted negotiations about financial contributions.

At present, I would say, co-operation between the two countries is satisfactory; the two prime ministers have even worked together closely during the last three European summits.

But there remains a difference of perspective, the one that made them choose different paths in 1950: the British government believes that with the single market of 1992 everything useful will have been accomplished, the Dutch are convinced that more steps will be necessary to build a solid structure; and they hope the British will come around to that same conclusion later, as they did on previous occasions.

The differences boil down to two main issues: further monetary integration, and the so-called social dimension. Two years ago, I would have added the environment to the list, but I feel that is over. Then there is the debate about regulation in general, but my feeling is that that is like the philosopher discussing the sex of the angels.

As to the 'social dimension', there is already a lot of it in the present Community and there can certainly be some more without introducing German co-determination all over the place in the 12 countries, which would be crazy – and impossible.

As to monetary matters: nobody can deny, it seems to me, that the EMS has brought very useful stability, even for those remaining outside it. And I am convinced that the liberalization of capital movements – already decided! – will require even more monetary stability, if we want this liberalization of capital movements to be sustainable. So we had better do something about it. Monetary plans will be discussed this very month by the Ministers of Finance, and then in June in Spain by the Prime Ministers. I do hope on that occasion the British and Dutch Prime Ministers will again see eye to eye, as they did at all the previous European summits. I am hopeful, but I am, with regret, not totally sure this time.

And then, beyond all these economic and financial problems, there is *the* major political issue which has been with us ever since the end of the Second World War: how to ensure that the Germans remain solidly anchored to the West – especially now, with East–West relations in full flux and the East in effervescence. This, the most crucial of all issues confronting us, in this part of the world, requires a clear concept, solidarity and understanding, between the nations of Western Europe, and with the USA. It requires not only a market, but a Community; not only marketeers, but real partners. But now I risk starting to speculate about the future, where I am supposed to deal with history.

223

DISCUSSION

Mr Scholte

I can't resist putting a question I often ponder as I think about the European Community, about which I don't know very much myself, and that is the conflict between the view of the European Community seeing it in the light of settling long-standing inter-European problems on the one hand, and on the other hand seeing it as an attempt to reconstruct identity, prosperity, power and sense of purpose, in a sense, for Europe in a post-war, post-colonial, bi-polar, American-led world. If one looks at the Netherlands policy as an historical example, and tries to get at an answer to that question, do the panel feel anything more specific can be said?

Professor Milward

I am sure that the European Community came into existence to settle domestic political and economic problems first. Foreign policy reasons for foreign policy purposes; they were of very limited utility in the 1950s, partly for the reasons that Professor Kersten has given – I mean, they settled the German problem which was the main one. All three speakers were extremely ambivalent about the European-American relationship. It worsened relationships between Community members and the UK, just as it did Dutch–British relationships in the 1950s; not I think the fault of the Dutch or the British certainly, but it made them worse. And of course the Community didn't and doesn't do anything to cater for the *defence* of Western Europe. It really adds very little to the physical security of any Western European country, then as now. If the Community exists primarily for settling domestic political problems it's not surprising that it's in such difficulties now – the difficulties that Dr Wellenstein was so polite about – because in the 1950s the political consensus that I spoke of prevailed over virtually every Western European country, except possibly Spain, which had nothing to do with the matter. Now these political consensuses are so different, aren't they? I mean, they might be very similar in the Netherlands and the UK, but I was for part of the year in Italy where the political consensus is still largely what it was in the 1950s and the 1960s; it simply hasn't changed in the way that it has changed in Britain or the Netherlands. So I think the basic problems of the Community are the problems of political change at varying speeds inside Western European countries. As a foreign policy arrangement, it is of the same very limited value now as it was in the 1950s, which I think wouldn't take away one bit from the remarks that Dr Wellenstein made at the end and which I would most heartily concur with. I mean, Germany is *the* problem for Western Europe, and *the* problem for the Community; and it might be one foreign policy problem on which the Community could bring Western European countries into some common position, which is desperately needed, I think, at this moment.

Peter Calvocoressi

Chairman, we have embarked in this last session on very wide seas indeed, and in spite of the concluding remarks of the third speaker, I am going to try and prod any or all of the three speakers into widening them a bit. I entirely concur with the last speaker's statement that the two essential problems at the moment for the Community are the social dimension, which I think Dr Wellenstein thought was under control, and the monetary issue which I would have thought was rather more urgent, if only because I simply do not see how you can have a common agricultural policy, or at any rate get out of the troubles that the common agricultural policy has got us into, without a common monetary policy or indeed a common currency. I would like to invite comment on that.

But I do also see two other problems, which seem to me not all that distant. The first is the constitution of the Community. We have had references to the balance of power which was established within the Schuman Plan and then re-established in rather a different form in the Community as between the Commission or the higher authority on the one hand and the Council of Ministers on the other. But neither of these things is very satisfactory in terms of democratic theory, to which we are all supposed to be deeply committed. But you've got a balance of power that has got to be established between three things, that is to say the Commission, the Council of Ministers and the parliament so-called, because it's only a quasi-parliament, it is a debating house. It has very little power to refuse supply because when it does, it refuses everything, and it doesn't in fact operate as a normal democratic legislature. At some point, I should have thought, this problem has got to be tackled. Now I know that the argument for tackling problems of this kind is always that it is not a very good moment to do so, but at what point does it become even more dangerous *not* to do so?

That is the first of my questions, and it is the least urgent in my mind. The second, which is more urgent, is the size of the Community. Did anybody imagine, ten years ago, that there were going to be 12 members? Now I'm not against new members because they are somehow poorer; in fact one needs poorer members in order to have an economic hinterland in which to plant one's surplus capital. Nor am I against them because they come from different parts of Europe and don't know about industry and speak foreign languages – any of those sorts of things. It's the sheer numbers – was it really wise to put expansion before consolidation? Anyhow it has been done. But have we not got to the point where we've got to say that the front door to the Community is closed?

OK, you don't say that to the Norwegians because they made a mistake in 1972 and are going to change it, etc., but you can't make exceptions to one person after another and be left with what I would call a Community. Am I right or am I wrong? If you go on allowing people to think they can join, and then finding it too rude not to allow them to join, which is the situation we get into, do we not then end up with a Europe which is not a community, something new and modern and vigorous, but going back to the Europe that we had before the war, which was simply a collection of states, in those days, a collection of first-, second- and third-rate states, but in the future are going to be a collection of second-, third- and fourth-rate states?

Albert Kersten

Democracy in the European Community – of course, it's a strange question. I will not enter into the political riches of 'I want more democracy in the Community at the moment' – I will speak as an historian and not as a citizen. It's very peculiar if you look at the history of this European organization that at the very beginning of the Council of Europe there was a consultative assembly which also had no power to give instruction to the Council of Ministers of that organization, and I think it is typical of the whole movement of European integration, as far as governments are concerned, that they have a clear tendency to keep the development of the organization in their own hands. You see it on the one hand by the drive to limit the powers of the high authority of the Coal and Steel Community, it's European Commission control by the Council of Europe, and there are always governments who want to keep power in their hands or at least they want to be able to steer it. In the desire to have great influence on the process of decision-making, a democratic structure of a full-power parliament isn't very useful. Some countries, for instance France, have been pushing since the beginning of this European integration movement, the co-operation movement for a real parliament in the European structure, but especially the

Benelux countries have opposed it from the very beginning and it's only I think since the 1970s that the Dutch government has been supporting an enlargement of the powers of the European parliament. I think on the other hand, if you choose greater powers for the European parliament, you have also to choose greater powers for the European Commission, for only then can you reach a balance between the institutions within the Community to get the real constitutional structure of legislative and executive in the Community with, on the other hand, a controlling institution like the Court in Luxembourg which checks that the rules are followed as they are inscribed in the European Treaties. So I think it's part of the whole process of developing the European constitution the way it began in the early 1950s as a development initiated by governments and not, let me say, by the federalist movement which wanted to depart from a constitutional structure, then gradually filling in all the executive powers. We have started from practical things which governments are doing, and I think it will take a long time to bring that complete structure in the constitutional sense into existence.

Drs Wellenstein

May I add one word to Professor Kersten's very complete analysis of the situation? There is a very nice short cut to solve this dilemma, and it's a real dilemma, you are right – that is to make better use of a possibility which the Treaty of Rome provides: the possibility for implementation of decided policies to be given to the Commission. If more use were made of that possibility, the direct responsibility of the Commission to the parliament would come into play.

Then your remark about currency. I agree with you that in the order of priorities, in view of the market of 1993, the currency problem is more directly linked as a necessity to the creation of that single market than the social dimension. The social dimension is linked in a general political fashion since the Treaty of Rome has a social aspect; when you develop the economic aspect there is some logic in trying to improve also the social aspect. But for currency there is a direct link to the functioning of that single market, in the sense that if we were to have wild currency fluctuations in a market which is really single and in which capital moves without hindrance, we can get disagreeable surprises of quite a great size, and therefore I agree with you that it is urgent to do something.

Professor Milward

Now there is a serious point which follows on from that. Common

227

markets don't lead to political unification, although that was widely said in the 1950s – the Habsburg monarchy was a common market, and it went exactly the opposite way. Common currencies demand political unification; they are the real surrender of national sovereignty. Proposals for a common currency have been there since 1950, perhaps since 1949, from the first proposals for the European payments union, and they've always been refused by the Western European nation states, and always refused on the grounds that that is a different process from anything that we've been talking about this afternoon – that is the process at which, as it were, national re-assertion ends, is pushed backwards, and real integration begins as being, as it were, the goal of all of us. They are therefore proposals for a common currency, something much more important than anything we've talked about this afternoon, except of course, the future of Germany. And yet, it seems to me, absolutely true that the freedom of capital movements, if that really comes – and it has been agreed – will wreck the European monetary system just as it wrecked Bretton Woods. It will be even worse than Dr Wellenstein predicts. So I don't know what you should do, but it's certainly a matter about which people should make up their minds here and now and I hope all those national governments will make up their mind very clearly. It seems to me much the most crucial decision they are faced with for 1992. Just one other comment on Mr Calvocoressi's remarks. What are you saying? That we should refuse all further candidature? There's only one serious candidate on the table, and that's Norway. Those neutral countries aren't going to be allowed to join anyway, not without much more serious things happening in Eastern Europe than are happening now, and I'm prepared to bet a very large sum of money that I'll be dead before Turkey becomes a member of the Common Market, if ever. So are you actually saying that we shouldn't let the Norwegians in, or are you not? Let me ask you.

Sir John Barnes

I hesitate to intervene at all because I've only been the occasional victim of the circumstances which have been so expertly described this afternoon. But I do have a bit of a philosophical difficulty with all three speeches, although Dr Wellenstein redressed the balance a little. I wonder whether we aren't underestimating the human factor. Professor Milward spoke about historical processes, but historical processes don't throw up human operators in our affairs. History does not make men, men make history. I'd like just to quote three examples.

First of all, the European movement was started by three men: Robert Schuman, Konrad Adenauer and Alcide de Gasperi, and even though the consequences of their actions may have been mainly economic, their motive was essentially political and quasi military. They were determined to avoid another conflict between Gaul and Teuton. Second, although I think Douglas Dodds-Parker will not agree with me, I think it was a pity that when the Conservative party came back to power in 1951 in this country, its leaders were still Winston Churchill and Anthony Eden, who were still living in the past. The spirit of the combined chiefs of staff died hard and that spirit spread into other aspects of policy as well. The third example of human influence in our affairs: I cannot think of any international institution in the last 40 years which could possibly have survived if it hadn't had powerful Dutchmen helping, and in many cases organizing its operations. I won't quote names; some of them are sitting here now, others have been mentioned today.

But against that background of events, may I come to Anglo-Dutch relations within Europe? It fell to my lot to be sent to The Hague just as we were joining the Community at the end of 1972, and I certainly had the strong impression then that the Dutch were extremely keen that we should come into the Community, largely because they saw us as a factor for democratizing it, and this brings me back to Peter Calvocoressi's point. They wanted us to democratize it in two ways: first, they wanted us to enhance the role of the parliament within the Community, given our parliamentary traditions; second, they wanted us to come in and help the smaller members to redress the balance of the domination of French and German interests which had been extremely powerful in the Community up to that date. We were ready to meet those aspirations, but it was unfortunate that very soon afterwards came the Yom Kippur war, in which our interests and the Dutch interests were completely divergent. Indeed our interests at that time coincided much more with the interests of France than they did with the interests of the Netherlands. This, I am afraid, started our membership of the Community off on the wrong foot as far as Anglo-Dutch relations were concerned. Then, more and more, the Common Agricultural Policy came to dominate the policy of the Community, and here again, the Netherlands began to see that its interests in agriculture, in particular, were much closer to those of France and Germany than they were to ours. I can't think how many times Dutch officials have said to me, 'Haven't you got a farm lobby too?', and my answer was, 'Yes, of course we have, but we have an even stronger consumer lobby.' In that way our interests diverged, but I think they've come back again to a very large extent since then, as Dr Wellenstein said. Our two Prime Ministers look at things in very much the same way.

I won't go into all the details of the present problems, but I think we do have to remember that the British intellectual approach differs from that of most of our Common Market partners. This shows itself essentially in our legal system, where the British common law has been built up on case histories, whereas most Continental systems are based on Roman-Dutch law, which starts from the application of theories to facts, and the facts are then derived from the theories. I am sure that every lawyer in this room will tell me I'm talking absolute nonsense; but I think there is a point in this and it is why we are having differences at the moment over the so-called social dimension. We see people attempting to impose doctrines on us which we're not quite sure correspond with the facts.

Professor Milward

I think diplomats have to believe that men always make history, don't they, otherwise they wouldn't be diplomats!

I don't deny the importance of Adenauer, Schuman and de Gasperi as remarkable people – I'd simply say that if I had to choose three architects of national consensus policies after 1945, I might choose those three above all others, and I might think that their role in history was primarily their role in creating a consensus inside their own country, and only secondarily in creating the Community. Robert Schuman, you know, voted for every single welfare provision in the French Assembly, usually against the rest of the MRP, and he did that, of course, out of his Catholic persuasions of the 1920s, and it's those persuasions that actually make him a mass democratic politician, as opposed to those Catholic politicians of the 1920s who felt they should take orders from the Catholic hierarchy rather than from a separate political party functioning in the National Assembly. And what I say about Schuman's Catholic convictions would go word for word for Adenauer's Catholic convictions, which led him in the same direction. Adenauer, too, voted for every welfare provision, and supported them, usually against majorities within the Christian Democrats, quite often overriding majority opinion in his own party. As for de Gasperi, I think he was only interested in European integration for four years, although I agree he was very profoundly supportive of it then. And he was interested in it because it provided for what he thought of as security for the Italian Republic, and by that he actually meant, not merely military security, but just as much democratic and spiritual security, so that really he was just like Willem Drees; from opposite sides of the political spectrum, he had a lot more in common with Willem Drees than he ever thought.

The last remark – facts versus theories – well, one should be careful about this, and the British argument – when Britain was, as both my fellow speakers so accurately said, 'being of no use to the Netherlands' after 1947–48 – was that they alone had interpreted the facts correctly and the Dutch were basing their actions on theory. And since nobody would now believe that this British view was correct, or very few people would, even in Britain, I think one has to be careful about arguing that the British have a rather finer perception of the facts than other people who were blinded by theories; at the moment I would be rather cautious about that.

Chairman

De Gaulle's name has been mentioned. After his long experience in Paris, can I draw Sir Brooks Richards on de Gaulle and the Market and keeping the British out? Or does he think a decent veil best drawn?

Sir Brooks Richards

I was indeed present when de Gaulle said, *'L'Angleterre est une île'*. It was an important moment in that first negotiation, but I think one has got to see what de Gaulle did at that time against a background in which he had proposed to Washington and to London, in effect, a tripartite control of the Western alliance and had been rebuffed, and I think there's no doubt that his exclusion of us from the Common Market owes something to that rebuff. It revived, no doubt, the injuries that he had sustained in the Second World War as an exile in this country, and it was once again the British siding with the deep sea and with Washington, rather than with him.

Drs Wellenstein

I think since I mentioned General de Gaulle on several occasions, in a rather negative way, I might give you also another angle on the role that General de Gaulle played in the early years of the European Community. The Treaty of Rome had a transition period of 12 years, cut up into four sections of three years; and when you passed from one phase to the next, there were complicated control procedures, and at every point, somebody could raise his finger and say, 'I'm not yet ready. I want an additional delay before moving on.' Now with the governments of the French Republic, before General de Gaulle took office for the second time in 1958, it may well have been that their coalitions were pro-European, in the sense that they supported the Treaty of Rome. Whether they would have had the power to govern in such a way that they could lead their country over these four hurdles to arrive in 1970 at the end of the transitional period, is less certain. General de Gaulle really did revive French economic and monetary policy, introduced the new franc and opened up his country to the winds of competition. He wanted with the aid of M. Pinay, the Minister of Economic Affairs, to put the country in a position to go through all the moves of the Treaty of Rome without failing any hurdle, which I think we really owe to de Gaulle. Europe and by definition the Community, with a weak France, is something I really would not like to live in, because it is an essential element of our equilibrium.

Sir Douglas Dodds-Parker

In May 1941 I was on the aeroplane which did the first operation into Belgium, and it went wrong. I had to go and explain to M. Spaak who was then Foreign Minister living in London, and he very kindly asked me to dinner – it was a great honour – and I remember him saying, 'Now when we've won this war, we must unite Europe. We cannot afford any more civil wars to destroy the rest of our civilization.' This was a very brave thing to say in May 1941 before either the Russians or the Americans were in the war, and that's always been the beacon as far as I'm concerned, since nearly 48 years ago.

I went to the Council of Europe first as a minister in 1954 and found that half those present had a resistance background, which we had to be a bit careful about in view of the fact that the Italians and the Germans were coming there too. It was rather like Freemasonry where people didn't talk about it in public, but in private; one had a very good international European co-operation on that basis. What John Barnes said is right. I spent ten years at the European Parliament between 1964 and 1975. We had various ideas that we ran; that members of the European Parliament and the Community should be paid a bonus for speaking English and English should be the only language used, and that would save an enormous amount of money and trouble. That was not welcomed by many people. We also suggested that there should be *écu* notes; all expenses, including those of members of parliament, should be paid in this, and they should go home and exchange them for what they could get. These were the sort of practical ideas that always attracted me. But as time goes on to 1992, the use of the *écu* commercially is increasing all the time. The points which you have raised, one talked about 40 years ago; I think we are a bit nearer a solution, but I regret that in my own country, very few members of the present government if any, have done their time at a European Assembly. We took Alec Home with us after he had been Prime Minister to lead the delegation for a year, and he said to me at the end, 'I wish I'd done this before I became a politician or a cabinet minister' – I think that's the sort of training one's got to try and get carried out.

FOCUS

Gordon Marsden

It is customary on these occasions, and possibly even more customary for winding up speeches and speakers, to offer some self-deprecatory remarks about fitness and competence to comment on the proceedings. I will make those customary remarks, but I will make them even more conscious perhaps than usual, of my limitations for speaking on this subject. I am not a twentieth-century historian by training, although by interest I have increasingly become one; nor am I, I must confess, or was I, a great student of Dutch history before my involvement in the tercentenary celebrations last year. But I do have one particular personal reminiscence to make, which I think is highly germane to remarks this afternoon, and that is to say that my particular great passion and great interest in medieval and renaissance history was fired in my teens when I read a book by the great Dutch historian, Johan Huizinga, called *The Waning of the Middle Ages*. It's particularly appropriate that I should cite that here this afternoon, because of course Johan Huizinga was one of the sad individual casualties of that terrible hunger winter of 1944–45. And that brings very sharply into focus what we actually had to say here this afternoon, because what Huizinga said about individualism it seems to me is highly relevant to what we have heard over the last two and a half days. 'What sort of idea can we form of an age', he wrote, 'if we can see no people in it? If we may only give generalized accounts, we do but make a desert, and call it history.' And for me, at any rate, one of the most striking things about the last two and a half days has been the way in which those individual accounts have been welded and brought into the fabric of history which we have had presented to us. So I think it's right that the conference should have focused on those contributions and on those reminiscences. And I for one – this I know is not news to students of twentieth-century Dutch history – was particularly struck by the remarks on the opening day of Louis de Jong and Gerard van Blokland about the role of Queen Wilhelmina. It seemed to me that in what they said the House of Orange motto *Je maintiendrai* was amply demonstrated, in the account they gave of the particular role she played during the war years. One hesitates to draw historical parallels and historical conclusions, but perhaps it is not unreasonable to say that in the position she took in 1940 she was echoing the views and the comments of that great English Queen of the sixteenth century, Elizabeth, who said, 'I have the heart and stomach of a King of England, even though I have the body of a weak and feeble woman.' Now Elizabeth I of course (I have to introduce this discordant note) was not terribly keen on Dutch rebels, and this is one of the things that history's great pageant tends to gloss over, and in the same way, William III, as the Secretary of State for Defence reminded us this morning, was not massively keen on England. And so these elements of *Realpolitik* are I think essential in this sort of gathering, when the temptation is to succumb to nostalgia and reminiscence. But in those mentions of *Realpolitik*, I think it is very important that we don't forget the essential unity of purpose that the Netherlands and the UK face in this century, and have faced ever since the Dutch won their independence in the sixteenth century. Three times in European history, in the sixteenth, the seventeenth and twentieth centuries, England and Holland found themselves side by side in the common purpose of resisting a power which threatened to overwhelm and dominate Europe. That is I think a cyclical lesson of history that even in these days, when we perhaps tend to be more dismissive than we once were of the theories of Arnold Toynbee, is well worth remembering.

And I think it is also right that the conference has not been afraid to touch on difficult issues. I refer here first of all to the question of Dutch neutrality, which was touched on by the Secretary of State for Defence this morning, but also to the remarks that took place in the discussion on the first day about the episode in the Dutch East Indies at the end of the Second World War.

If I may be permitted a personal comment here, about 18 months ago, I had a letter from a reader of *History Today*, an Englishman, who said he had some Dutch friends who were always talking to him about the problems between the British and the Dutch in Java in 1945–46 and could I, through the columns of the magazine, invite readers to contribute any experiences or any views they had. I have to confess in my ignorance at the time (one gets a large number of letters of such requests to a magazine) that when we printed it, I said to my editorial assistant, 'Well, perhaps we'll get a couple of letters in on that, but I'm not sure we'll be able to help Mr Freeman a great deal.' Well, in fact, we got not a couple, but nearly 20 letters, most of them from people who had been intimately concerned in serving in that particular time. We had responses both from Dutch academics and from British academics, and the resulting piece which we carried in the magazine, small though it was, and the massive correspondence which I forwarded to an equally bemused Mr Freeman, testified to the amount of interest there was in that particular episode; and what was encouraging about the comments was their sense of proportion, a sense of being able to look at that episode 40 years on without rancour, and to understand the motives and the importance of the individuals concerned.

If one is looking at a legacy from the period we have been examining over these last two and a half days, then I think one of the most important legacies that can be transmitted to any future generations is the legacy of resistance. I've been billed here today as a statutory young historian. If I can get the 'young' bit out of the way, I think that a lot of what has actually been said about the resistance in the Second World War in Holland and in other countries, is highly relevant to the attitudes and the viewpoints of young people today. I venture to suggest it may not always be relevant in a way that some of the older generation find particularly comfortable. I'd like to read to you, if I may, some comments that one of our contributors, Michael Houlihan, made when we did a special issue of the magazine, some four or five years ago, on the whole question of D-Day and resistance. What he had to say about the effects of the resistance on political and social thinking in Europe are well worth quoting.

In the politics of western Europe, however, many former members of the resistance moved into positions of prominence in both local and national government. Yet these were men and women who, during the war, had opted, for reasons of conscience, to live outside the rule of law, albeit outside the law of Nazis and collaborators.

Thus in the post-war world, resistance, the freedom of the individual to fight against laws, policies and forms of government, which he or she regards as morally repugnant, achieved political recognition and social respectability. It was difficult for former resistants, now in government, as well as countries such as Britain and the US, which had harboured resistance movements, to deny freedom and peaceful protest and civil resistance to others ... Resistance got people thinking about their political responsibilities. It brought home to them that voting every four or five years was not the only way in which they could participate in shaping and defining their society. Above all it emphasized that

it was they who shouldered the ultimate responsibility for preserving and improving that society.

Now that, as I say, is a legacy the current generation is very conscious
of, and when one hears accounts from the Second World War period,
such as the very moving interview with Christabel Bielenberg which
was on television recently, one of the things I think that we are struck
by, if I dare take the mantle of the younger generation upon myself, is
the need for that vigilance, for the need to be concerned when liberties
become chipped away, when minorities are singled out. They may not
always be comfortable liberties, as we've seen in the case of the Salman
Rushdie affair, they may not always be minorities with which the
majority of people feel comfortable, but they are essential safeguards
for avoiding that slippery slope to totalitarianism which the peoples
of Europe experienced in the 1940s. Because again, if I can quote
Rousseau on the concentration camps, 'Normal men do not know that
everything is possible', and that I think is a very important point for us
to remember.

But I've talked about remembering. How long should one remember?
I could, if I were being the devil's advocate, say that these two and a half
days here have been a very useful exercise of memory, or perhaps in
some cases, an exorcize of memory for many of the people who have
been here. But *anno domini* moves on and presumably one of the things
that the organizers of this conference had in mind, and I hope the
participants have in mind as well, is that the values and the individual
remembrances from that period should be carried on and should be
transmitted. It was one of the worst curses of totalitarianism, Hannah
Arendt tells us, that it attempted, not only to destroy people, but
to obliterate their identity and memory. In her work on the origins
of totalitarianism, she makes this point I think very succinctly:
'How important to the total domination apparatus this complete
disappearance of its victims is, can be seen in those instances, where for
one reason or another, the regime was confronted with the memory of
survivors.'

During the war one SS Commandant made the terrible mistake of
informing a French woman of her husband's death in a German
concentration camp. This slip caused a small avalanche of orders and
instructions to the camp commandants, warning them that under no
circumstances was information ever to be given to the outside world.
The point is that as far as the French widow was concerned, her husband
had ceased to live at the moment of his arrest, or rather had ceased ever
to have lived. In totalitarian countries, all places of detention ruled by

the police are made to be veritable holes of oblivion, into which people stumble by accident and without leaving behind them such ordinary traces of former existence as a body and a grave. Compared with this newest invention for doing away with people, the old-fashioned method of murder, political or criminal, is inefficient indeed. The murderer leaves behind him a corpse, and although he tries to efface the traces of his own identity, he has no power to efface the identity of his victim from the memory of the surviving world. The operation of the Secret Police, on the contrary, miraculously sees to it that the victim never existed at all. And therefore it seems to me – shedding the 'young' and turning to the 'historian' part of my role here today – that one of the roles of the historian, without being over-pious about the subject, is to do justice to the dead, to see that those lives do not disappear. I think it's encouraging, again in the long term, that even the worst aspects of totalitarianism in Hitler's Germany or in Stalin's Russia could not stamp out, as recent events have seen, absolutely basic humanitarian and liberal instincts from those peoples, and that I think is a very important lesson that history can transmit and which history can hope to preserve.

Garrett Mattingly, who wrote what many still consider to be one of the classic accounts of the defeat of the Spanish armada, spent a lot of his time, as an offshoot of the work that he did on renaissance diplomacy, in trying to rehabilitate the reputation of one of the ambassadors at Henry VII's court, from Spain, in the same way that he tried in that book to rehabilitate or do justice to the reputation of Medina Sidonia. I venture to suggest that one of the reasons Mattingly did that was not because, in the historical assessment of things, it really mattered whether Medina Sidonia was an honest man or a knave, or whether you thought that that anonymous civil servant or ambassador was an honest man or a knave, but because it was one of the things as an historian that he could do.

Some three or four years ago, we carried in the magazine a series of articles which we called 'Everyday life in Nazi Germany'. These were a series of articles which historians, both German and English, wrote for us, about what experience of living in Nazi Germany had been like, and I was particularly struck by one article on the experience of young people in Nazi Germany – not just the tales of what it was like to be in the Hitler Youth Movement, but also the tales of those small groups of young people who had resisted. One particular group, known rather romantically as the Edelweiss Pirates, and another group, the White Rose group, did something that on the face of it was entirely and utterly insignificant and quixotic. This small group of Catholic young people produced, on a particular night, a bundle of leaflets denouncing the Nazi regime and the war as anti-Christian. The leaflets were distributed very sporadically in a couple of towns, as far as I remember, but four or five people were rounded up, and they were subsequently executed. On the face of history, in terms of the history of the war, their action was insignificant – they could have been forgotten, they probably were forgotten by the vast majority of people, but by that historian referring to their tale in this particular article, he brought their actions to a wider group of people, and I think that is something which is extremely important. Doing justice to the dead means showing that there were righteous Germans as well as righteous Gentiles.

Now I speak to you at a time when the teaching of history in our schools is going through a great change in Britain. Many of you may know the debate which the Secretary of State for Education has launched about the core curriculum and the role history should play within that syllabus. As I speak, there is in fact a working party trying to draw up guidelines for what should or should not be taught in British schools about history. One of the things that has exercised the debate and the controversy very strongly has been this whole question of empathy. To what extent, when you're trying teach history to young people, should you encourage them to try to understand, try to enter into the feelings and the attitudes of the people of the period they are studying? Obviously as an academic discipline, that is a process which is fraught with danger, and analogies can be oversimplified. But it seems to me that it is something extremely important; and one of the things that this conference has done, certainly for me personally, and I would hope for some of the other younger people here who have been able to attend, has been to increase that power of empathy when looking at this period. I know that the comments he made ruffled more than a few feathers, and enlivened the debate, but I was particularly struck by what Leo Marks had to say in this context, when he was talking about *Englandspiel*. The pathos of 22- or 23-year-olds being put under that sort of moral pressure is something which I will carry with me very strongly as a memory of this conference.

That is the sort of empathy which I would hope would enable future generations to try to understand something about that commonality of values, cultural, political and social which have been referred to by many of the speakers this afternoon as the basis of the post-war reconstruction of Europe in which the Netherlands has played such a key part. That is why, in my view, Professor Foot, Herman Friedhoff and the others responsible for bringing this conference together, have done something which is not just going to be appreciated by those who have attended, who lived through the period concerned, and which has given them the opportunity to re-live and to discuss it and to see it from a new perspective, but which will also assist in that process of transmitting the values which that generation shared, and which I trust my generation will wish to continue to transmit. It is only, it seems to me, through that process of empathy in history that the impetus to do this, as opposed to the study of a dry academic discipline, will be maintained. Last night as I was looking on my bookshelves for Hannah Arendt and the relevant quotation from *Totalitarianism* which I've just read, I stumbled across a book of poems which I must confess I haven't even looked at since I was in High School, and I looked through it just out of curiosity, to see what representation there was from this period. I came across this poem by a young man called Bertram Warr who, in fact, was one of those who did not come back from the bombing raids, and it seems to me that what he has to say offers as relevant a historical testimony as any of the more erudite comments we may have heard over the last two and a half days.

> Every morning from this home,
> I go to the aerodrome.
> And at evening I return
> Save when work is to be done.
> Then we share the separate night
> Half a continent apart.
> Many endure worse than we:
> Division means by years and seas.
> Home and lover are contained,
> Even cursed within their breast.
> Leaving you now, with this kiss
> May your sleep tonight be blest,
> Shielded from the heart's alarms
> Until morning I return.
> Pray tomorrow I may be
> Close, my love, within these arms,
> And not lie dead in Germany.

Chairman

Thank you very much. I am in private duty bound to be grateful to you for opening with a reference to Huizinga, whom my wife was allowed to call Uncle – he married a cousin of her father's. He cared a great deal about the free society, we all care a great deal about the free society, or we wouldn't be here, and I hope that in the course of these two and a half days' discussions, we have on the whole generated more light than heat in our discussions of the free society. I knew when I asked Leo Marks to come that arguments that have been raging between him and me for a dozen years past would continue to rage, and I am delighted that they did.

I'm particularly grateful to all the speakers who have addressed you *ex cathedra* and indeed to all of you from the floor, who have been so patient in your attendance and so free with your contributions to our debates. We have, I hope, advanced historical knowledge a little – not a lot – it's an extremely difficult, cumbrous and complicated business to advance it a lot, as a number of the historians present know only too well.

We all owe a strong debt to the treasurer, Colonel Smit, for having borne, with Mr Friedhoff, the donkeywork of all the organizational problems that attend getting a conference of this type ready, such as writing to far more people than were actually able to turn up, and we also owe a large debt to Colonel Smit's staff. I hope at least those who are present at the back will stand up so that we may thank them [applause]. If it hadn't been for their unremitting pertinacity and hard work, the microphones would not have worked, nor would we have had anything to eat. We are also deeply grateful to the authorities of University College for having let us come here. I trust that its cultural counsellor will pass on to Ambassador Jonkman at least my very warm personal thanks for the strong support that the Dutch Embassy has given us throughout. All the meetings of the executive committee that have tried to put it together have taken place on Dutch Embassy premises and have been sustained by Dutch Embassy coffee, and the Ambassador's support in the background, and his wife's, have been a great help to us all. Most of you I hope met both of them at their delightful house last night when they were kind enough to entertain us all [applause]. We are also, as I mentioned at the beginning, but will mention again now, under a strong financial obligation to Unilever, who bore a large slice of the costs of the conference. Unilever – alone among the great international companies that work between England

241

and Holland as well as elsewhere – wrote us a very handsome cheque. The William and Mary Trust has also provided us with a great deal of assistance. Both governments also put their hands into their pockets. You will have received a large and inaccurate list of those who were going to be present. We were in much doubt on one point about whom we ought to ask. We settled in the end to sticking to having it an Anglo-Dutch Conference. But we did make a couple of exceptions: we invited two Germans, knowing when we did so that a number of Dutch ex-resisters might be very much put out at finding themselves even in the same room as a German. One of them, however, wasn't born till 1945, which we hoped let him off. This was Dr Hirschfeld, not now present, who has written an interesting book on the Netherlands under German occupation. As the name of the other is Stauffenberg, he is entitled to be here [applause]. He retired last week from being German Military Attaché in London, is moving on to another job, and was kind enough to spend part of his week's leave in listening to us. I shall now ask Professor Bachrach if he would care to wind the conference up.

CONCLUSION

Fred Bachrach

As the Honorary President of the Dutch Tercentenary Committee, and also on behalf of Charles Tidbury, the Chairman of the English Tercentenary Committee, it is my privilege to address a few concluding words to the Chairman of this unique conference. I am filled with admiration and gratitude for the remarkable way in which it was planned, conducted and given 'send-off', if I may put it like that, by our youngest historian. I am old enough, I dare say, to have a right to underline age. You see, in my time we were always taught as young students that a presentation for a large audience should end where it began; we should come full circle because that sends the audience home with a sense of relief. It was a brilliant idea, therefore, to invite for the opening of the discussion my colleague Emeritus Professor Kenneth Haley and for the summing-up Gordon Marsden. Professor Haley pointed to the fact that, after all, William III and Queen Wilhelmina had something essential in common; Gordon Marsden, at the end of the discussion, returned us to this combination of Royal names. Queen Wilhelmina and William had indeed more in common than meets the eye.

Now, I am of course personally what is called in this country 'a literary bloke' and as such inclined to romantic musings. But even in our present realistic context, I think it is worthwhile to quote, as a coda to what the editor of *History Today* has offered us, a few verses I came across the other morning in the British Library. I was looking up something entirely different in the poems of the eighteenth-century poet Richard Savage, when I chanced on his 'The Genius of Liberty'. In his poem that 'Genius', presented as speaking in England, declares:

> Here was my station when over the ocean wide
> The great Third William stretched his naval pride.
> I with my sacred influence swelled his soul
> Th'enslaved to free, th'enslaver to control.
> In vain let waves disperse and winds detain

He came, he said, in this begins my reign.
How just, how great, the plan is so designed
To humble tyrants and secure mankind.

The point, at the present juncture, is that a little further down the poet concludes the passage with

Where Nassau's rays extensive growth displayed
Their freedom ever found a sheltering shade.

This, then, is the fundamental point where we come full circle. In fact, I think it is crucial to remember that the connection between the Dutch people and the House of Orange is not merely a sentimental one but has a very true and real source in that, to us, this House is the embodiment of any and every fight for liberty. That, I feel, is the spirit in which we have today been enabled to arrive at the end of this in many ways unforgettable event.

Happily, although it may have begun as a purely historical exercise, with the aim of bringing some enlightenment to a generation which had come to think that it was perhaps not so terribly important to know who William was and what the Glorious Revolution seemed to be about, the commemoration has culminated in a contradiction of this attitude through a fascinating view of past, present and future. This is the justification of our joint efforts. Once again, we have been reminded of the immense value of the First William of Orange's motto in leading the revolt against Spanish tyranny:

N' est besoin d' espérer pour entreprendre,
Ni de réussir pour persévérer.

And so, if I may refer to this conference as an 'operation', its code-name surely would have been 'Continuity' and its assessment ended with 'objective achieved'.

POSTSCRIPT

H. C. Jorissen

It was appropriate that the conference on Anglo-Dutch relations in time of war should conclude with a look at the future. A discussion on the past is only truly meaningful when past events have a bearing on the present and the future.

My hope was that all three speakers would, each drawing from study or personal experiences and convictions, present a credible view of the future of Europe. I trusted beforehand that my compatriots would not fail to do so.

The Dutch nation has, from 1940 onwards, been inspired by the iron will and determination of the British people under the leadership of Sir Winston Churchill, the embodiment of its fighting spirit. The Netherlands nation continued to exist as one nation because, however brutal the Occupation, it passionately believed that, with its Queen Wilhelmina and Winston Churchill together, victory and liberation were an absolute certainty and that suffering and deprivation were the price worth paying.

That faith in Britain was justified.

The Battle of Arnhem proved to the Dutch that the gallantry of Sir Philip Sidney, who was killed in action in October 1586 at Zutphen, a few miles north of Arnhem, lived on in the soldiers who filled the skies and fought on their fields and in their streets – and fought on until all hope to win that battle had gone. But in spite of this severe set-back the spirit of the Dutch nation was rekindled and it held out to the end.

When liberation came after five bitter years, the British ranked first and foremost in their estimation and they fully expected them to fulfil their hopes for a future, free of fear and of want, a true rebirth in a secure and prosperous Europe.

Then came the defeat of Churchill in the general election in 1945. It left the Dutch utterly at a loss why their hero, whose every word had carried them through their ordeal, was dismissed from political power. But it proved that not all was lost. He again rallied the liberated

European nations in his momentous speech in Zürich when he said: 'When the Nazi power was broken I asked myself what was the best advice I could give my fellow citizens in our ravaged and exhausted continent. My counsel to Europe can be given in a single word: Unite!'

That counsel was to become fundamental policy of the Dutch government, overriding all other considerations. The Dutch were for that reason greatly disappointed when the United Kingdom did not join the European Coal and Steel Community, which, contrary to views nowadays, expressed and echoed by Professor Milward, was not created for national or economic reasons, but for reasons of European security and the prevention of armed conflicts which had twice ravaged Europe this century.

Those who believe that Konrad Adenauer and Robert Schuman acted on economic motives severely misjudge those great European statesmen.

Even greater than with the conclusion of the ECSC were the Dutch regrets for the absence of Britain in Rome. Since then successive Dutch governments worked unceasingly to create conditions for a British entry, which was realized in 1973. But after a few years we have witnessed, particularly during the last decade, a gradual weakening of the European political commitment which the Dutch and many others with them had hoped for.

Anglo-Dutch co-operation, as it took hold and developed during the war years and after, can ultimately only truly come to full growth within the framework of a European concert. The policies, thoughts and beliefs that a Customs Union or perfected Free Trade Area will suffice for future European prosperity and strength are a blot on the landscape and the only threatening cloud on the otherwise clear horizon of Anglo-Dutch relations.

LIST OF PARTICIPANTS

Drs, a familiar abbreviation in the Netherlands, stands for Doctorandus; equivalent to the English M.A., it denotes someone who has taken a second degree but not proceeded to a doctorate. A similar degree in law brings the prefix Mr.

Martin Agnew. With Force 133, SOE, Greece, 1944–46; formerly Regional Vice-President, American Express

Mrs Martin Agnew (*née* Rosemary Wylde). Born in England, spent war in Holland; one of two English women awarded Dutch Resistance Cross

Dr Christopher Andrew, F.R.Hist. Soc. Senior Tutor, Corpus Christi College, Cambridge, since 1981; author of *Secret Service*, 1985; founder-editor of *Intelligence and National Security*; a speaker

Mr P. Louis Baron d'Aulnis de Bourouill, RMWO, DSO. Longest serving surviving member of Bureau Inlichtingen; holder of Dutch Resistance Cross; a speaker

Professor Dr F. G. H. Bachrach, CBE. Emeritus Professor, Leiden University; former chairman, executive committee, William and Mary Trust

K.D. (Tex) Banwell, BEM. Agent extraordinary, formerly Long Range Desert Group

Sir John Barnes, KCMG, MBE. Royal Artillery 1939–46; H. M. Ambassador to the Netherlands, 1972–77; a Patron

Lady Barnes

Jhr Mr Gerard Beelaerts van Blokland. ADC to Queen Wilhelmina during the war; retired ambassador; a speaker

P. M. H. Bell. Reader in history, Liverpool University; author of *The Origins of the Second World War in Europe*, 1986

HRH Prince Bernhard of the Netherlands. Commander-in-chief, Dutch internal and external land forces, 1944–45; a Patron

Fred Beukers. Treasurer, Dutch Escapers Association

Rear-Admiral Robert den Boeft, RNN. Chief of Allied Staff, Northwood, 1984–88; a speaker

Marius Boerma. Holder of Dutch Resistance Cross; adviser, BBC TV series on SOE

Mrs Boerma

Dr Frits Bolkestein. Secretary of State for Defence in the Dutch government; a speaker

Professor Brian Bond. Professor of war studies, King's College, London; author of *British Military Policy between the Two World Wars*, 1980, etc; member of the advisory board

Sir Robin Brook, CMG, OBE. Senior posts in SOE, 1942–45; director, Bank of England, 1946–49; a director, United City Merchants

Robbert de Bruin. Former captain in Dutch Air Force; historian of Second World War

Michael Butler. Member of the support group which has acted for the Tercentenary Trust and other campaigns, including the Queen's Silver Jubilee; member, executive committee

Peter Calvocoressi. At Bletchley Park, 1940–45; author, with Guy Wint and John Pritchard, of *Total War* (2nd ed. 1989)

Sir Roger Cary, Bt. Served in Grenadier Guards, 1943–47; chief assistant to director of programmes, BBC TV, 1983–86; thereafter consultant to director-general, BBC; member, executive committee

Brian Cathcart. Assistant Foreign Editor, *The Independent*

Jonathan Chadwick. Secretary, Imperial War Museum; secretary, British National Committee on the History of the Second World War

Lieutenant-Colonel Derek Cooper, OBE, MC. Served in Irish Guards, 1936–41; transferred to Life Guards; VIII Corps liaison officer, Aug.–Oct. 1944; fought at Nijmegen

Gervase Cowell. SOE adviser to Foreign and Commonwealth Office

Sebastian Cox. Member of Air Historical Branch, Ministry of Defence

Sir Douglas Dodds-Parker. In SOE; MP for Banbury, 1949–59, Cheltenham, 1964–74

Dominic Flessati. Producer of BBC TV series on SOE

Helmut van der Flier. Director, London office, Dutch railways; a Sponsor

Professor M. R. D. Foot. Professor of modern history, Manchester,

1967–73; author of *SOE in France*, 1966, *Resistance*, 1976, *SOE: an outline history*, 1984, etc; chairman of the executive committee and of the conference

Colonel John Francis. Regimental Secretary, The Queen's Regiment; Grand Cross of the Crown Order of the Netherlands, 1988

Herman Friedhoff. Holder of Dutch Resistance Cross; retired publisher; author of *Requiem for the Resistance*, 1988; conference secretary

Frans van de Gender. Member, Dutch resistance in Eindhoven, 1940–45

Luc van Gent. Active in resistance; actor and stage director; director, municipal theatre, 's Hertogenbosch

Janet Gilbert. Curator, Netherlands Section, British Library

Professor Dr Daniel Goedhuis. Escaper, holds Dutch Resistance Cross; emeritus professor, Leiden University; sometime lecturer, University College, London

Dr Tanix Guest. Lecturer, Dutch department, University College, London; specialist in mediaeval Dutch

General Sir John Hackett, GCB, CBE, DSO, MC, DL, FRSL. Commanded 4 Parachute Brigade, 1943–44, in Italy and at Arnhem; Commander-in-Chief, Rhine Army, 1966–68; Principal, King's College, London, 1968–75; member of the advisory board; a speaker

Lady Hackett

Professor K. H. D. Haley, FBA. Emeritus professor of modern history, Sheffield University; author of *William of Orange and the English Opposition 1672–1679*, 1953; *The First Earl of Shaftesbury*, 1968; *The British and the Dutch*, 1988; etc.

The Hon. Archibald Hamilton, MP. Minister of State, ministry of defence, since 1988; parliamentary secretary of state for defence procurement, 1986–87; PPS to Prime Minister, 1987–88

Anna Harvey-Simoni. Formerly assistant keeper, British Library; author of *Publish and be Free*, 1975; compiling catalogue of Dutch books in British Library printed 1600–21

Colonel Roderick Hill, DSO, JP. Commanded 5th Battalion, Coldstream Guards, in Guards Armoured Division, 1944–45; Lord Lieutenant of Monmouthshire, 1965–74; of Gwent, 1974–79.

Dr Gerhard Hirschfeld. Fellow, German Historical Institute, London; sometime lecturer in modern history, Düsseldorf; author of *Nazi Rule and Dutch Collaboration*, 1988

Jhr Mr J. L. Rein Huydecoper van Nigtevecht. Immediate past ambassador in London; a Patron

Professor Jonathan Israel. Professor of Dutch studies, University College, London

Professor Jac Janssen. Emeritus professor of Egyptology, Leiden; in resistance; now at University College, London

His Excellency (Sir) Michael R. H. Jenkins, (K) CMG. British Ambassador to the Netherlands since 1988; author of *Arakcheev, Grand Vizier of the Russian Empire*, 1969

Hieke Jippes. London correspondent of *NRC-Handelsblad*

Matthew Jones. Research student, St Antony's College, Oxford, specializing in Anglo-American relations, 1939–45

Professor Louis de Jong. Formerly director of the Dutch State Institute for War Documentation; author of *The Kingdom of the Netherlands during World War II* (13 volumes in 27 parts, in Dutch); a speaker

His Excellency Dr P. J. H. Jonkman. Netherlands Ambassador to the Court of St James; formerly Lord Chamberlain to the Queen of the Netherlands

Mr H. C. Jorissen, DSC. Former motor torpedo boat commander, RNN; retired ambassador

Wio Joustra. London Correspondent of *De Volkskrant*

Drs Piet Kamphuis. Deputy head of the Military History Section of the Dutch Army; a speaker

Professor Dr Albert Kersten. Professor of diplomatic relations, University of Leiden; director of the Dutch State Institute for National History; a speaker

Sue Lampert. Netherlands Desk Officer, Western European department, Foreign and Commonwealth Office

Roger Laughton. Head of daytime programmes, BBC TV, 1986–88; director, co-productions, BBC Enterprises, since 1988

Laurence Le Quesne. Teaches history at Shrewsbury School; sometime professor of modern history in the universities of Tasmania and Sydney

Jaap Ludolph. An escaper; former section head Directorate-General Credit and Investment, EEC Commission

Drs Karel Margry. A young Dutch historian; author of *September 1944: Operation Market Garden*, 1984; organizer of the Resistance Museum in Amsterdam

Leo Marks. SOE's chief cipher officer; film impresario; a speaker

Gordon Marsden. Editor since 1985 of *History Today*, which produced a special 1688 issue in 1988; a speaker

Nancy Maxwell. English history teacher at Aiglon College, Glézières, Switzerland

Major Lorna McGregor. Assistant Private Secretary to the Minister of State at the Ministry of Defence

Helen Mendl-Schrama. Editor of the Anglo-Netherlands Society Bulletin

Professor Alan S. Milward, FBA. Professor of economic history, London School of Economics, since 1986; professor of contemporary history at the European University Institute, Florence; author of *The Reconstruction of Western Europe 1945–51*, 1984 (2nd ed. 1987); a speaker

Anthony Mitchell

Olivia Mitchell-Stas. Worked for the Dutch Government in Exile, 1943–45; from 1945–49 employed by the Netherlands Consulate and the Netherlands Embassy

Dr Bob Moore. Lecturer in European and international history, Bristol Polytechnic; author of *Refugees from Nazi Germany in the Netherlands*, 1986

Drs Harry Paape. Director of the Dutch State Institute for War Documentation; a speaker

The Rev Michael Pavey. Chaplain in the Royal Air Force, 1963–83; rose to be a Wing Commander; incumbent at Mark in Somerset, since 1983

Sir John Peck, KCMG. Assistant private secretary to the Prime Minister, 1940–46; Head of Chancery in The Hague, 1947–50; Ambassador to the Republic of Ireland, 1970–73; a speaker

Leen Pot, MBE. The leader of Group Kees in the Dutch Resistance; later a staff officer at the Bureau Inlichtingen in London; a speaker

Colonel Geoffrey Powell, MC. Served with the 4th Parachute Brigade throughout the Arnhem battle; served: 19th of Foot (The Green Howards), 1939–42; Parachute Regiment, 1942–64; author of *Men at Arnhem*, with Tom Angus, and *The Devil's Birthday*, 1984

Barry Price, OBE. Secretary of William and Mary Tercentenary Trust, since 1986; served Indian Army, 1944–47; a retired member of the Diplomatic Corps, who was successively Consul-General in Rotterdam and Amsterdam; a member, executive committee

David Ray. An economics teacher at Rugby School

Major-General Michael Reynolds, CB. Colonel of the Queen's Regiment, 1989; commander of Allied Command, Europe Mobile Force (Land), 1980–83

Sir Brooks Richards, KCMG, DSC. In SOE, 1940–46; Her Majesty's Ambassador to Greece, 1974–78; Deputy Secretary, Cabinet Office, 1978–80

Sue Roach. Curator, Netherlands Section, West European Branch, British Library

Kay Saunders. Member, Research Department, Foreign and Commonwealth Office

Lieutenant-Colonel Sweder Schellens. Adjutant to HRH Prince Bernhard

(Dr) Jan Aart Scholte. Lecturer in international relations, Sussex University, researching on the decolonization of Indonesia; a speaker

Dr Cees Schulten. Head of the Military History Section of the Dutch Army; a member of the advisory board

Mark Seaman. Member of the Research and Information Office at the Imperial War Museum

Colonel D. O. (Charles) Seymour. Head of Dutch Section, MI6, 1943–46

Dolf Simonsz. Counsellor for Press and Cultural Affairs, Royal Netherlands Embassy in London; member of the executive committee

Brigadier J. J. H. Simpson, CBE. Joined Coldstream Guards, 1945; commissioned Gordon Highlanders, 1946; commanded the Sultan of Brunei's Forces, 1968–71; commanded the SAS, 1972–75; Director of Defence Policy, War Office, 1976

Robert Slager. Member, Anglo-Netherlands Society

Ellis, Baroness de Smeth (*née* Brandon). Holder of the Dutch Resistance

Cross; an escaper

Colonel Jan Baron de Smeth. Formerly Military Governor of Gelderland Province

Colonel Jaap Smit. Military Attaché, Royal Netherlands Embassy; conference treasurer

Ine Smit-Verbakel. A history teacher at a secondary school in Holland

David Snoxall. lawyer; Company Secretary of Unilever, 1983–86; a member of the Anglo-Netherlands Society

Contessa Flavia Stampa Gruss

Brigadier-General Count Berthold Stauffenberg. Formerly Defence and Military Attaché, German Embassy in London

Timothy Stunt. A history master at Stowe School

Haye Thomas. London Correspondent of NOS (Dutch television and regional newspapers)

(Sir) Charles Tidbury. Chairman, William and Mary Tercentenary Trust, since 1986. Served King's Royal Rifle Corps, 1943–48 (despatches). Chairman, Whitbread & Co Ltd., 1978–84; a member of the advisory board

Dan van der Vat. Correspondent of the *Guardian*

Louis Velleman. A freelance international journalist

Professor Anthony Verrier. Visiting professor of modern history at the University of Calgary, Canada; researching Anglo-Franco-American relations during the Second World War

Edward Vernède. Private Secretary to HRH Prince Bernhard

Epko Vleck. Formerly employed by Philips

Drs E.P. Wellenstein. Secretary-General of the European Coal and Steel Community; Director-General for External Relations for the European Economic Community Commission, until 1976; a speaker

Derek White. Member of the Cultural Relations Department, Foreign and Commonwealth Office; British Consul in Marseilles, 1986–89; a member of the executive committee since March 1989

Dr Ralph White. Senior lecturer in the Department of Politics and Contemporary History, University of Salford

Mrs Ralph White (Judith). A sociologist

Colonel Pat Winnington, MBE. Grenadier Guards; D.A.Q.M.G., Guards Armoured Division, 1944

Christopher Woods, CMG, MC. SOE Adviser, Foreign and Commonwealth Office, 1982–88; served King's Royal Rifle Corps and SOE, 1942–47

Index

The International School
of Amsterdam

A.J. Ernststraat 875
P.O. Box 7983
1008 AD Amsterdam
The Netherlands